RAYMOND CARVER

All of Us

Raymond Carver was born in Clatskanie, Oregon, in 1938. His first collection of stories, *Will You Please Be Quiet, Please?* (a National Book Award nominee in 1977), was followed by *What We Talk About When We Talk About Love, Cathedral* (nominated for the Pulitzer Prize in 1984), and *Where I'm Calling From* in 1988, when he was inducted into the American Academy of Arts and Letters. He died in August of that year, shortly after completing the poems of *A New Path to the Waterfall*.

ALSO BY RAYMOND CARVER

All of Us

The Collected Poems

RAYMOND CARVER

VINTAGE CONTEMPORARIES

Vintage Books

A Division of Random House, Inc.

New York

All of us, all of us, all of us
trying to save
our immortal souls, some ways
seemingly more round-
about and mysterious
than others.

    from "In Switzerland"

I dedicate this edition of Raymond Carver's poems
to four couples, dear sustaining friends to Ray
and me: Bill and Maureen, Harold and Lynne,
Alfredo and Susan, Dick and Dorothy.

T. G.

CONTENTS

WHERE WATER COMES TOGETHER WITH
OTHER WATER (1985)

I

II

III

APPENDIXES:

Editor's Preface

Raymond Carver's life and work were cut short by his death at age fifty in 1988. As he makes plain in his poem "Gravy", however, even in his final days Carver counted himself a lucky man, a writer who had packed two lives into the time of less than one.

During the last five years of his postalcoholic "second life" Carver saw through the press three major collections of his poetry: *Fires* (1983), *Where Water Comes Together with Other Water* (1985), and *Ultramarine* (1986). A fourth collection, *A New Path to the Waterfall*, completed in the last weeks of his life, was published posthumously in 1989.

The poems in these four books comprise the reading text of *All of Us*, and for the first time make available all of Raymond Carver's poems in the final forms he approved. To enhance the picture of his development as a poet, Carver's nineteen uncollected poems from *No Heroics, Please: Uncollected Writings* (1991) are printed in the first appendix. The second appendix contains Tess Gallagher's introduction to *A New Path to the Waterfall*. The third and fourth appendixes offer detailed information about Carver's small-press books and his English collection *In a Marine Light: Selected Poems* (1987) respectively. The fifth appendix contains bibliographical and textual notes on individual poems in *All of Us*. The sixth appendix provides a brief chronology of Carver's life and work and the seventh and final appendix gives details of posthumous publications.

For this edition every known printing of each of Raymond Carver's poems was collated against the editor's copy-text: the first editions of *Fires*, *Where Water Comes Together with Other Water*, *Ultramarine*, *A New Path to the Waterfall*, and *No Heroics, Please*. The collation included magazine appearances, small-press publications, British editions, and advance uncorrected proofs. No use was made of manuscript materials, although setting typescripts were consulted wherever possible.

The headnotes in Appendix 5 give the publication history of each of Carver's major books of poetry. Bibliographical notes on individual poems record any first magazine appearance or separate publication ("*1st*") that preceded the inclusion of the poem in the copy-text. All inclusions in other books by Raymond Carver are recorded, as are any subsequent appearances in the form of broadsides, greeting cards, or limited editions. No bibliographical notes are given on poems published solely in the copy-text.

Textual notes provide a line-by-line record of variants between the copy-text and other printings of the poem. The variants recorded are selective rather than exhaustive. All changes in lineation are indicated, as are all verbal changes, with the exception of the categories listed below. The following six types of variants are not recorded except when they seem to have critical significance:

1) changes in spelling;
2) changes in punctuation;
3) changes in line runovers;
4) changes in the positioning of lines;
5) changes in spacing within lines or stanzas;
6) changes in anthology printings with which Carver had no direct involvement.

In addition, obvious typographical errors have been silently corrected.

Where a stanza break occurs at the head or foot of a page it is indicated by a single asterisk (*). The absence of an asterisk indicates that the text runs on without a break.

Within the notes, variant readings are separated by a slash mark (/). To the left of the slash is the reading text of *All of Us*; to the right are variant readings from other printings. In a few instances where an early version of a poem differs extensively from a later one, the early version has been printed in full for comparison. Emendations – corrections of the copy-text based on Carver's subsequent revisions – are clearly indicated.

Editing *All of Us* has been the work of several years and many hands. The book owes its conception to Tess Gallagher. Its realization was made possible by Bill Swainson of The Harvill Press. For assistance with collating and proofreading, I thank my research associates Raymond Ouellette, Anna Maria Rainone, and Jennifer Hocko. For inspiration, insight, and encouragement I thank my wife, Maureen P. Carroll.

WILLIAM L. STULL
University of Hartford
Connecticut, February 1996

Introduction

"Without hope and without despair" – this quiet banner of determination from Isak Dinesen flew over the last ten years of Raymond Carver's life. Most of these poems were written during that time, some in a great lunge of reception, almost two hundred drafted between October 1983 and August 1985.

Ray had written poetry and fiction in tandem, beginning in 1957. This collection, which spans more than thirty years, allows us to see that his poetry was not something he wrote between stories. Rather, it was the spiritual current out of which he moved to write the short stories for which, after his death, he would be called by the *Guardian* newspaper (London), "America's Chekhov". Now that the entirety of his poetry has been collected, its full mass and density can at last be appreciated.

It is said of Lao-tzu, the great Chinese author of the *Tao Te Ching*, that people became attached to his style because it had a "gem-like lucidity", was "radiant with humour and grace and large-heartedness and deep wisdom" (Stephen Mitchell). In looking for a way to characterize what endears Ray's poems to me, these remarks seem appropriate.

With poetry we come to love, and with Ray's in particular, at some point we surrender, and the consciousness of the speaker in the poems is taken into the bloodstream to be recirculated through our lives. We are grateful when a poet gives us new ways of thinking and feeling on trampled ground, and for radiance itself as that new way. What we also find in these poems is an extraordinary sensibility that stays approachable, even companionable.

Ray's presence in the poems, as with the man himself in life, continually disarms through some paradoxical capacity both for knowing and innocence. His self-humor steadily redeems him, along with his amazement and curiosity about the complexities of human life and its connection to animal life. I think of a moment in "Prosser", when he wants to find out what geese like about green wheat. He writes: "I ate some of it once too, to see." As in his fiction, he demonstrates often that he knows how to pace himself and knows too, with Isaac Babel, that a period in the right place can stop the heart: "Geese love this shattered wheat also. / They will die for it."

I recall a commentary on the life and work of Emily Dickinson in which Dickinson's poems were described as having arrived so directly out of the necessities of the soul that they violated even the notion of poetry as a formed artifact of language. They were instead the soul incarnate in its most vital appearance. The meaning was perhaps that language and the poet's nature were so in accord that the interlocutor of voice was wholly absorbed by what it was saying. In a similar way, Ray's artlessness burned so fiercely it consumed all trace of process. Once in a while we get a writer like this, a comet without a tail, yet whose arrival and impact are undeniable.

Anyone who has ever felt befriended by a poem at a crucial moment will recognize the place from which I prefer to regard this lifetime in poetry. For ten years I was Ray's companion and literary collaborator, and finally his wife. I saw the poems in draft and, from *Fires* onward had the great pleasure of arranging them in books. Because of this, I experienced the poems as intimates. Sojourners. The sinew of a shared life. And this intimacy embraces even those poems written before we met in 1977. Often in revised versions, they form an integral part of the story. Since this book is essentially the tracing of a passage from one shore to another, inception is as important as arrival.

I am stricken to the core by an early poem, "Morning, Thinking of Empire", where a mundane act becomes the chilling image for a marriage's inevitable interior dissolution: "I coolly crack the egg of a fine Leghorn chicken." The moment seems unsurvivable, the collapse of a shared universe rendered unflinchingly. In the context of the entire poem we experience it action by action, as a series of spiritually irretrievable moments which cut the partners off from each other and obliterate all hope for the regeneration of the marriage:

> We press our lips to the enameled rim of the cups
> and know this grease that floats
> over the coffee will one day stop our hearts.
> . . . .
> I coolly crack the egg of a fine Leghorn chicken.
> Your eyes film. You turn from me and look across
> the rooftops at the sea. Even the flies are still.
> I crack the other egg.
> Surely we have diminished one another.

The word "surely" here is a cliff and an avalanche, accompanied by the steel-eyed gaze and barely containable assessment of the speaker.

The poems, throughout, are keenly attentive to life as it is being lived, but from 1979 on they also make retrospective safaris into the jungle of old harms, renegotiated from safer, saner ground. Ray had gradually absorbed some attitudes I held toward time in poetry – for one thing, that it was more than lived time, and might therefore enlarge one's spiritual reach. My feeling that all time – past, present and future – exists within reach at the moment the poem is being written was helpful to him. He allowed himself to re-enter older work with the present moment as definitive and regenerative.

From early to late, the poems *are* beautifully clear, and this clarity, like the sweet clang of spring water to the mouth, needs no apology. Time spent reading Ray's poems becomes quickly fruitful, for the poems give themselves as easily and unselfconsciously as breath. Who wouldn't be disarmed by poetry which requires so much less of us than it unstintingly gives?

I am aware of those honed minds that find Ray's transparency somehow an insult to intelligence. They would have applied an editor like a tourniquet. I might have served as such, had I thought it true to his gift. I didn't. If Ray hadn't given and published in the ample way he did, I believe we would not receive his guileless offering with the same credulity and gratitude. Certainly poems like "My Boat", "The Old Days", "Woolworth's, 1954", "My Car", "Earwigs", "You Don't Know What Love Is", "Happiness", and any number of poems I love might have been omitted. Overreach was natural and necessary to him, and to fault him for it would be like spanking a cat for swallowing the goldfish.

The narrative directness of his poems, as well as the precision of phrase and image, amplifies access until we push through into yet another chamber of astonishing, unadorned truth. Suddenly, like deer caught at night in headlights, blind mystery stares back at us with equal force. We are pinioned – "flimsy as / balsa wood" ("Balsa Wood") – or told "the mind can't sleep, can only lie awake and / gorge" ("Winter Insomnia"), or birds arrive as omens, "the clacking of their bills / like iron on iron" ("The News Carried to Macedonia"). We glimpse the extravagant yet matter-of-fact sensuality of the world around us: "lean haunches" of deer "flicker / under an assault of white butterflies" ("Rhodes"). Wonder in everyday forms appears in a shirt on a clothesline filling out to "near human shape" ("Louise") or a hand reaches through to touch the sleeve of a suit inside a garment bag, a burial suit, and this "reaching through" ("Another Mystery") becomes an entrance to another world which is also the same world.

Many of the later poems have the daybook quality of nature and life observed moment to moment. We feel befriended and accompanied by the spirit in these. Ray's often third-person fictionalized stance places him alongside the reader, watching with conflicting feelings as events unfold. He is a poet of great suppleness of being, and his ability to hold contraries in balance while sorting out their ramifications, not oversubscribing to either side, amounts to courage for us all.

We are often with the poems as we are with our neighbors and loved ones, taking them for granted, failing deeply to assess their comings and goings – we are that used to them. Then one day something happens. A father's wallet, an ordinary, familiar object, comes into our hands, suddenly luminous with the power of the dead. In the final moments of Ray's "My Dad's Wallet" – perhaps a working-class version of Rilke's "Washing the Corpse" – it is "our breath coming and going" which signals death's communal arrival. Readers of his fiction will recognize that this phrase overlaps the ending of his story "What We Talk about When We Talk about Love". Sometimes, without embarrassment, Ray used the same events or recognitions in both poems and stories. The poems often clarify emotional or biographical ground left obscure in the stories. "Use it up," he used to say. "Don't save anything for later."

In the last lines of "The Caucasus: A Romance" the speaker calls his effort to represent what took place "but a rough record of the actual and the passing". This line might be a talisman for what Ray aimed at throughout – the felicitous hazard of rough record. While we may locate his pulse with this phrase, we must also understand that he revised tirelessly and that "rough" indicates truth unbeguiled, not carelessness. Ray meant to graft language onto experience in all its tenacious vitality, its rawness. To that end he gave us "yellow jackets and near / frostbite" ("Trying to Sleep Late on a Saturday Morning in November"), the "large dark bullethole / through the slender, delicate-looking / right hand" ("Wes Hardin: From a Photograph"), a heart "on the table" that is "a parody of affection" ("Poem for Dr Pratt, a Lady Pathologist"), the young man "who keeps on drinking / and getting spit on for years" ("Reading"). His brilliant intuition for moments of consequence can wield a scythe across a lifetime – "The dying body is a clumsy partner" ("The Garden") – or discover "violets cut just an hour before lunch" ("The Pipe").

There is the feeling that all Ray's poems are in some sense escapes into the act of self-witness, as in "The Poem I Didn't Write". Each one bears the scarred patina of words gotten down on the page however the writer could, something wrestled from the torrent, using only that language which came readily, even haphazardly. Artifice gives way to velocity, to daring – "But the soul is also a smooth son of a bitch" ("Radio Waves") – to improvisation and exactitude of the moment: "At night, a moon broad and deep as a serving dish / sallies out" ("The Caucasus: A Romance").

Clichés go by like underbrush: "my hair stood on end" ("Wenas Ridge"). Then suddenly we are ambushed by memory "like a blow to the calf" (also "Wenas Ridge"). Clichés in Carver cajole the actual, until his attentiveness brings the next nuance of miracle into focus: "Suddenly as at a signal, the birds / pass silently back into pine trees" ("With a Telescope Rod on Cowiche Creek"). His diction and syntax are American and find their antecedents in William Carlos Williams and Allen Ginsberg, Emily Dickinson and Louise Bogan. He also absorbed poets I brought close, including Rainer Maria Rilke, Theodore Roethke, Paul Celan, William Heyen, Seamus Heaney, Federico García Lorca, Robert Lowell, Czeslaw Milosz, Marianne Moore, Derek Mahon, W. B. Yeats and Anna Akhmatova.

From the vantage of his poetry, Ray's life took on pattern and reason and gratitude – "my whole life, in switchbacks, ahead of me" ("Wenas Ridge"). Poetry, helicopter-like, gave him maneuverability over rugged, hostile terrain, a place where he could admit such things as ambivalence about Jesus while he continued to pray to "snake" ("Wenas Ridge"). Perhaps in the blunt-nosed zigzag of poems he could attain elevation without the sleek evasions of elegance, irony or even the easy exit of transcendence – all of which he would have chosen to forgo had they not, for the most part, been outside his nature and his aesthetic.

We don't love his poetry for its biographical peaks and valleys alone – though who wouldn't marvel at a man who walks away from near death by alcohol, and who keeps writing with a brain tumor and two-thirds of a lung gone to cancer? Rather, it's the intensity of down-to-earth searching that holds us throughout, the poet's willingness to revisit extremities, the sites of loss. We admire his ability to embody experience in fresh language and actions which occur not as biography, but in moments created for and by those very poems: "I bashed that beautiful window. / And stepped back in" ("Locking Yourself Out, Then Trying to Get Back In").

Many American poetic voices of the past thirty years have traveled far, too far, on sincerity. Still more have proffered the sad and ofttimes dire contents of their lives as their main currency. Their sincerity often involves a subtle kind of salesmanship, an attempt to convince by forthrightness, by emptying a kit bag at the listener's feet, hoping for the reward of attention at any cost. Such writers assume themselves to be somehow bold and courageous for having torn the door off the confessional.

Ray's poetry escapes the pitfalls of the merely sincere by forming another kind of relationship with the reader. It attempts not the bond of commerce, but the bond of mutuality. The voice in the poems is, in fact, self-mutual, doubled and self-companioned to such a high degree in tone and stance that, indeed, we feel much relief in not being called out like the Mounties or inveigled to commiserate falsely. Ray is profitably his own interlocutor. The neighborliness and amplitude of the poems compel by a circuitry of strong emotional moments in which we join the events at a place beyond invitation. To our surprise we find we have come both to ourselves and our differences in another form.

Ray's appetite for inventorying domestic havoc is often relentless. We want to run from the room, from blear-eyed wisdom yoked to pain, to bitter fate: "She's caught / in the flywheel of a new love" ("Energy") or "far away – / another man is raising my children, / bedding my wife bedding my wife" ("Deschutes River"). The writer of these poems has outlived the world of no-remedy, and his artistic fortitude with the impossible encourages us toward our own forbearance.

The ravages of alcoholism and sexual betrayal give way to a new ease and largesse in the poems of *Where Water Comes Together with Other Water* (1985) and *Ultramarine* (1986), the work British readers first met in the collection *In a Marine Light* (1987), published the year before his death at age fifty from lung cancer. These poems expressed, among other things, a thankfulness even for his trials, and for having been delivered into a life he considered happy. This amplitude carried him into the final poems of *A New Path to the Waterfall* (1989), written in the last six months of his life. Art and life were his focus. Death, mosquito-like, hovered and supped at the periphery.

I recall in those last days being aware that I was, for Ray, the only reader of those poems he would have. I laughed and cried with them, reading them as they came. His humor, lashed as it was to pain, positively unraveled me. In "What the Doctor Said" we don't expect eagerness and the turnabout of thankfulness from a man receiving news of his oncoming death. But that is what we get:

> he said I'm real sorry he said
> I wish I had some other kind of news to give you
> I said Amen and he said something else
> I didn't catch and not knowing what else to do
> and not wanting him to have to repeat it
> and me to have to fully digest it
> I just looked at him
> for a minute and he looked back it was then
> I jumped up and shook hands with this man who'd just
>   given me

something no one else on earth had ever given me
I may even have thanked him habit being so strong

*

It's steelhead season, early January 1996. I've been rereading Ray's poems here at Sky House where he wrote so many of them. Below in the valley, men are walking the banks of Morse Creek, the river which became the central metaphor of *Where Water Comes Together with Other Water*.

Just yesterday our neighbor, Art LaMore, recalled Ray's amazing luck. One morning Ray had dropped a hook baited with salmon roe off the footbridge and caught a ten-pound steelhead. He'd carried it to Art's door, hooked over his fingers by its gills, to show him. He had felt blessed beyond reason. By the time I came home, he'd cleaned the fish on the kitchen floor. There are still knife marks in the linoleum. Men fish for years on Morse Creek and never catch a steelhead. I don't think Ray knew this or cared. He simply accepted the gift.

We often walked along this river, sorting out the end of a story, as with "Errand", or discussing our plans for trips. Always we found release and comfort in noticing – that pair of herons, ducks breaking into flight upriver, the picked-over carcass of a bird near the footpath, snow on the mountains – the very kinds of attentiveness which bind his poems so effortlessly to our days.

When I think of the will that carried him through a lifetime in poetry, I recall particularly one afternoon in the summer of 1988. We had finished assembling and revising his last book of poems, *A New Path to the Waterfall*. We were preparing for a fishing trip to Alaska which we knew would, in all likelihood, be our last. Ray wanted to go to Morse Creek once more, so I drove as close as I could get and we climbed out of the jeep onto the bank. We just stood together a while, looking into the water. Then, without saying anything, we began to walk toward the mouth where this freshwater river joins the Strait of Juan de Fuca, some seventy miles east of the Pacific. It was hard going for him and we had to stop often, to sit down and pull up, twenty feet at a time.

It was important, that walk, hyphenated by rests – his breath gathered inside him, again and again. We would talk quietly in those moments sitting on the ground, and I recall saying like a mantra, "It isn't far now." He was traveling on his remaining right lung, but carrying himself well in the effort, as if this were the way to do it, the way he had always done it. When we made it to the river mouth, there was an intake of joy for us both, to have crossed that ground. It was one of those actions that is so right it makes you able in another dimension, all the way back to the start of your life. We savored it, the river's freshwater outrush into salt water, that quiet standing up to life together, for as long as it was going to last.

"When it hurts we return to the banks of certain rivers," Czeslaw Milosz writes.* For Ray, I think poems, like rivers, were places of recognition and healing:

> Once I lay on the bank with my eyes closed,
> listening to the sound the water made,
> and to the wind in the tops of the trees. The same wind
> that blows out on the Strait, but a different wind, too.
> For a while I even let myself imagine I had died –
> and that was all right, at least for a couple
> of minutes, until it really sank in: *Dead*.
> As I was lying there with my eyes closed,
> just after I'd imagined what it might be like
> if in fact I never got up again, I thought of you.
> I opened my eyes then and got right up
> and went back to being happy again.
> I'm grateful to you, you see. I wanted to tell you.
>
> ("For Tess")

Ray made the ecstatic seem ordinary, within reach of anyone. He also knew something essential which is too often sacrificed for lesser concerns – that poetry isn't simply reticence served up for what we meant to say. It's a place to be ample and grateful, to make room for those events and people closest to our hearts. "I wanted to tell you." And then he did.

TESS GALLAGHER
Sky House
Port Angeles, Washington
14 January 1996

---

* "A Magic Mountain" in *Czeslaw Milosz: Selected Poems*, rev. ed. (New York: Ecco Press, 1980) 93.

Fires

And isn't the past inevitable,
now that we call the little
we remember of it "the past"?

— WILLIAM MATTHEWS, from *Flood*

Drinking While Driving

It's August and I have not
read a book in six months
except something called *The Retreat From Moscow*
by Caulaincourt.
Nevertheless, I am happy
riding in a car with my brother
and drinking from a pint of Old Crow.
We do not have any place in mind to go,
we are just driving.
If I closed my eyes for a minute
I would be lost, yet
I could gladly lie down and sleep forever
beside this road.
My brother nudges me.
Any minute now, something will happen.

Luck

I was nine years old.
I had been around liquor
all my life. My friends
drank too, but they could handle it.
We'd take cigarettes, beer,
a couple of girls
and go out to the fort.
We'd act silly.
Sometimes you'd pretend
to pass out so the girls
could examine you.
They'd put their hands
down your pants while

you lay there trying
not to laugh, or else
they would lean back,
close their eyes, and
let you feel them all over.
Once at a party my dad
came to the back porch
to take a leak.
We could hear voices
over the record player,
see people standing around
laughing and drinking.
When my dad finished
he zipped up, stared a while
at the starry sky – it was
always starry then
on summer nights –
and went back inside.
The girls had to go home.
I slept all night in the fort
with my best friend.
We kissed on the lips
and touched each other.
I saw the stars fade
toward morning.
I saw a woman sleeping
on our lawn.
I looked up her dress,
then I had a beer
and a cigarette.
Friends, I thought this
was living.
Indoors, someone
had put out a cigarette
in a jar of mustard.
I had a straight shot

from the bottle, then
a drink of warm collins mix,
then another whisky.
And though I went from room
to room, no one was home.
What luck, I thought.
Years later,
I still wanted to give up
friends, love, starry skies,
for a house where no one
was home, no one coming back,
and all I could drink.

Distress Sale

Early one Sunday morning everything outside –
the child's canopy bed and vanity table,
the sofa, end tables and lamps, boxes
of assorted books and records. We carried out
kitchen items, a clock radio, hanging
clothes, a big easy chair
with them from the beginning
and which they called Uncle.
Lastly, we brought out the kitchen table itself
and they set up around that to do business.
The sky promises to hold fair.
I'm staying here with them, trying to dry out.
I slept on that canopy bed last night.
This business is hard on us all.
It's Sunday and they hope to catch the trade
from the Episcopal church next door.
What a situation here! What disgrace!
Everyone who sees this collection of junk
on the sidewalk is bound to be mortified.
The woman, a family member, a loved one,
a woman who once wanted to be an actress,

she chats with fellow parishioners who
smile awkwardly and finger items
of clothing before moving on.
The man, my friend, sits at the table
and tries to look interested in what
he's reading – Froissart's *Chronicles* it is,
I can see it from the window.
My friend is finished, done for, and he knows it.
What's going on here? Can no one help them?
Must everyone witness their downfall?
This reduces us all.
Someone must show up at once to save them,
to take everything off their hands right now,
every trace of this life before
this humiliation goes on any longer.
Someone must do something.
I reach for my wallet and that is how I understand it:
I can't help anyone.

Your Dog Dies

it gets run over by a van.
you find it at the side of the road
and bury it.
you feel bad about it.
you feel bad personally,
but you feel bad for your daughter
because it was her pet,
and she loved it so.
she used to croon to it
and let it sleep in her bed.
you write a poem about it.
you call it a poem for your daughter,
about the dog getting run over by a van
and how you looked after it,
took it out into the woods

and buried it deep, deep,
and that poem turns out so good
you're almost glad the little dog
was run over, or else you'd never
have written that good poem.
then you sit down to write
a poem about writing a poem
about the death of that dog,
but while you're writing you
hear a woman scream
your name, your first name,
both syllables,
and your heart stops.
after a minute, you continue writing.
she screams again.
you wonder how long this can go on.

Photograph of My Father in His Twenty-Second Year

October. Here in this dank, unfamiliar kitchen
I study my father's embarrassed young man's face.
Sheepish grin, he holds in one hand a string
of spiny yellow perch, in the other
a bottle of Carlsbad beer.

In jeans and denim shirt, he leans
against the front fender of a 1934 Ford.
He would like to pose bluff and hearty for his posterity,
wear his old hat cocked over his ear.
All his life my father wanted to be bold.

But the eyes give him away, and the hands
that limply offer the string of dead perch
and the bottle of beer. Father, I love you,
yet how can I say thank you, I who can't hold my liquor either,
and don't even know the places to fish?

Hamid Ramouz (1818–1906)

This morning I began a poem on Hamid Ramouz –
soldier, scholar, desert explorer –
who died by his own hand, gunshot, at eighty-eight.

I had tried to read the dictionary entry on that curious man
to my son – we were after something on Raleigh –
but he was impatient, and rightly so.

It happened months ago, the boy is with his mother now,
but I remembered the name: Ramouz –
and a poem began to take shape.

All morning I sat at the table,
hands moving back and forth over limitless waste,
as I tried to recall that strange life.

Bankruptcy

Twenty-eight, hairy belly hanging out
of my undershirt (exempt)
I lie here on my side
on the couch (exempt)
and listen to the strange sound
of my wife's pleasant voice (also exempt).

We are new arrivals
to these small pleasures.
Forgive me (I pray the Court)
that we have been improvident.
Today, my heart, like the front door,
stands open for the first time in months.

The Baker

Then Pancho Villa came to town,
hanged the mayor
and summoned the old and infirm
Count Vronsky to supper.
Pancho introduced his new girl friend,
along with her husband in his white apron,
showed Vronsky his pistol,
then asked the Count to tell him
about his unhappy exile in Mexico.
Later, the talk was of women and horses.
Both were experts.
The girl friend giggled
and fussed with the pearl buttons
on Pancho's shirt until,
promptly at midnight, Pancho went to sleep
with his head on the table.
The husband crossed himself
and left the house holding his boots
without so much as a sign
to his wife or Vronsky.
That anonymous husband, barefooted,
humiliated, trying to save his life, he
is the hero of this poem.

Iowa Summer

The paperboy shakes me awake. "I have been dreaming you'd
    come,"
I tell him, rising from the bed. He is accompanied
by a giant Negro from the university who seems
itching to get his hands on me. I stall for time.
Sweat runs off our faces; we stand waiting.
I do not offer them chairs and no one speaks.

*

9

It is only later, after they've gone,
I realize they have delivered a letter.
It's a letter from my wife. "What are you doing
there?" my wife asks. "Are you drinking?"
I study the postmark for hours. Then it, too, begins to fade.
I hope someday to forget all this.

Alcohol

That painting next to the brocaded drapery
is a Delacroix. This is called a divan
not a davenport; this item is a settee.
Notice the ornate legs.
Put on your tarboosh. Smell the burnt cork
under your eyes. Adjust your tunic, so.
Now the red cummerbund and Paris; April 1934.
A black Citröen waits at the curb.
The street lamps are lit.
Give the driver the address, but tell him
not to hurry, that you have all night.
When you get there, drink, make love,
do the shimmy and the beguine.
And when the sun comes up over the Quarter
next morning and that pretty woman
you've had and had all night
now wants to go home with you,
be tender with her, don't do anything
you'll be sorry for later. Bring her home
with you in the Citroën, let her sleep
in a proper bed. Let her
fall in love with you and you
with her and then . . . something: alcohol,
a problem with alcohol, always alcohol —
what you've really done
and to someone else, the one
you meant to love from the start.

*

It's afternoon, August, sun striking
the hood of a dusty Ford
parked on your driveway in San Jose.
In the front seat a woman
who is covering her eyes and listening
to an old song on the radio.
You stand in the doorway and watch.
You hear the song. And it is long ago.
You look for it with the sun in your face.
But you don't remember.
You honestly don't remember.

For Semra, with Martial Vigor

How much do writers make? she said
first off
she'd never met a writer
before
Not much I said
they have to do other things as well
Like what? she said
Like working in mills I said
sweeping floors teaching school
picking fruit
whatnot
all kinds of things I said
In my country she said
someone who has been to college
would never sweep floors
Well that's just when they're starting out I said
all writers make lots of money
Write me a poem she said
a love poem
All poems are love poems I said
I don't understand she said

It's hard to explain I said
Write it for me now she said
All right I said
a napkin/a pencil
for Semra I wrote
Not now silly she said
nibbling my shoulder
I just wanted to see
Later? I said
putting my hand on her thigh
Later she said

O Semra Semra
Next to Paris she said
Istanbul is the loveliest city
Have you read Omar Khayyam? she said
Yes yes I said
a loaf of bread a flask of wine
I know Omar backwards
& forwards
Kahlil Gibran? she said
Who? I said
Gibran she said
Not exactly I said
What do you think of the military? she said
have you been in the military?
No I said
I don't think much of the military
Why not? she said
goddamn don't you think men
should go in the military?
Well of course I said
they should
I lived with a man once she said
a real man a captain
in the army
but he was killed

Well hell I said
looking around for a saber
drunk as a post
damn their eyes retreat hell
I just got here
the teapot flying across the table
I'm sorry I said
to the teapot
Semra I mean
Hell she said
I don't know why the hell
I let you pick me up

Looking for Work [1]

I've always wanted brook trout
for breakfast.

Suddenly, I find a new path
to the waterfall.

I begin to hurry.
Wake up,

my wife says,
you're dreaming.

But when I try to rise,
the house tilts.

Who's dreaming?
It's noon, she says.

My new shoes wait by the door.
They are gleaming.

Cheers

Vodka chased with coffee. Each morning
I hang the sign on the door:

OUT TO LUNCH

but no one pays attention; my friends
look at the sign and
sometimes leave little notes,
or else they call – *Come out and play,
Ray-mond*.

Once my son, that bastard,
slipped in and left me a colored egg
and a walking stick.
I think he drank some of my vodka.
And last week my wife dropped by
with a can of beef soup
and a carton of tears.
She drank some of my vodka, too, I think,
then left hurriedly in a strange car
with a man I'd never seen before.
They don't understand; I'm fine,
just fine where I am, for any day now
I shall be, I shall be, I shall be . . .

I intend to take all the time in this world,
consider everything, even miracles,
yet remain on guard, ever
more careful, more watchful,
against those who would sin against me,
against those who would steal vodka,
against those who would do me harm.

Rogue River Jet-Boat Trip,
Gold Beach, Oregon, July 4, 1977

They promised an unforgettable trip,
deer, marten, osprey, the site
of the Mick Smith massacre –
a man who slaughtered his family,
who burnt his house down around his ears –
a fried chicken dinner.
I am not drinking. For this
you have put on your wedding ring and driven
500 miles to see for yourself.
This light dazzles. I fill my lungs
as if these last years
were nothing, a little overnight portage.
We sit in the bow of the jet-boat
and you make small talk with the guide.
He asks where we're from, but seeing
our confusion, becomes
confused himself and tells us
he has a glass eye and we
should try to guess which is which.
His good eye, the left, is brown, is
steady of purpose, and doesn't
miss a thing. Not long past
I would have snagged it out
just for its warmth, youth, and purpose,
and because it lingers on your breasts.
Now, I no longer know what's mine, what
isn't. I no longer know anything except
I am not drinking – though I'm still weak
and sick from it. The engine starts.
The guide attends the wheel.
Spray rises and falls on all sides
as we head upriver.

You Don't Know What Love Is
(an evening with Charles Bukowski)

You don't know what love is Bukowski said
I'm 51 years old look at me
I'm in love with this young broad
I got it bad but she's hung up too
so it's all right man that's the way it should be
I get in their blood and they can't get me out
They try everything to get away from me
but they all come back in the end
They all came back to me except
the one I planted
I cried over that one
but I cried easy in those days
Don't let me get onto the hard stuff man
I get mean then
I could sit here and drink beer
with you hippies all night
I could drink ten quarts of this beer
and nothing it's like water
But let me get onto the hard stuff
and I'll start throwing people out windows
I'll throw anybody out the window
I've done it
But you don't know what love is
You don't know because you've never
been in love it's that simple
I got this young broad see she's beautiful
She calls me Bukowski
Bukowski she says in this little voice
and I say What

But you don't know what love is
I'm telling you what it is
but you aren't listening
There isn't one of you in this room
would recognize love if it stepped up
and buggered you in the ass
I used to think poetry readings were a copout
Look I'm 51 years old and I've been around
I *know* they're a copout
but I said to myself Bukowski
starving is even more of a copout
So there you are and nothing is like it should be
That fellow what's his name Galway Kinnell
I saw his picture in a magazine
He has a handsome mug on him
but he's a *teacher*
Christ can you imagine
But then you're teachers too
here I am insulting you already
No I haven't heard of him
or him either
They're all termites
Maybe it's ego I don't read much anymore
but these people who build
reputations on five or six books
termites
Bukowski she says
Why do you listen to classical music all day
Can't you hear her saying that
Bukowski why do you listen to classical music all day
That surprises you doesn't it
You wouldn't think a crude bastard like me
could listen to classical music all day
Brahms Rachmaninoff Bartok Telemann
Shit I couldn't write up here
Too quiet up here too many trees
I like the city that's the place for me

I put on my classical music each morning
and sit down in front of my typewriter
I light a cigar and I smoke it like this see
and I say Bukowski you're a lucky man
Bukowski you've gone through it all
and you're a lucky man
and the blue smoke drifts across the table
and I look out the window onto Delongpre Avenue
and I see people walking up and down the sidewalk
and I puff on the cigar like this
and then I lay the cigar in the ashtray like this
and take a deep breath
and I begin to write
Bukowski this is the life I say
it's good to be poor it's good to have hemorrhoids
it's good to be in love
But you don't know what it's like
You don't know what it's like to be in love
If you could see her you'd know what I mean
She thought I'd come up here and get laid
She just knew it
She told me she knew it
Shit I'm 51 years old and she's 25
and we're in love and she's jealous
Jesus it's beautiful
she said she'd claw my eyes out if I came up here and
     got laid
Now that's love for you
What do any of you know about it
Let me tell you something
I've met men in jail who had more style
than the people who hang around colleges
and go to poetry readings
They're bloodsuckers who come to see
if the poet's socks are dirty
or if he smells under the arms

Believe me I won't disappoint em
But I want you to remember this
there's only one poet in this room tonight
only one poet in this town tonight
maybe only one real poet in this country tonight
and that's me
What do any of you know about life
What do any of you know about anything
Which of you here has been fired from a job
or else has beaten up your broad
or else has been beaten up by your broad
I was fired from Sears and Roebuck five times
They'd fire me then hire me back again
I was a stockboy for them when I was 35
and then got canned for stealing cookies
I know what's it like I've been there
I'm 51 years old now and I'm in love
This little broad she says
Bukowski
and I say What and she says
I think you're full of shit
and I say baby you understand me
She's the only broad in the world
man or woman
I'd take that from
But you don't know what love is
They all came back to me in the end too
every one of em came back
except that one I told you about
the one I planted
We were together seven years
We used to drink a lot
I see a couple of typers in this room but
I don't see any poets
I'm not surprised
You have to have been in love to write poetry

and you don't know what it is to be in love
that's your trouble
Give me some of that stuff
That's right no ice good
That's good that's just fine
So let's get this show on the road
I know what I said but I'll have just one
That tastes good
Okay then let's go let's get this over with
only afterwards don't anyone stand close
to an open window

III

Morning, Thinking of Empire

We press our lips to the enameled rim of the cups
and know this grease that floats
over the coffee will one day stop our hearts.
Eyes and fingers drop onto silverware
that is not silverware. Outside the window, waves
beat against the chipped walls of the old city.
Your hands rise from the rough tablecloth
as if to prophesy. Your lips tremble . . .
I want to say to hell with the future.
Our future lies deep in the afternoon.
It is a narrow street with a cart and driver,
a driver who looks at us and hesitates,
then shakes his head. Meanwhile,
I coolly crack the egg of a fine Leghorn chicken.
Your eyes film. You turn from me and look across
the rooftops at the sea. Even the flies are still.
I crack the other egg.
Surely we have diminished one another.

The Blue Stones

If I call stones blue it is because
blue is the precise word, believe me.
— FLAUBERT

You are writing a love scene
between Emma Bovary and Rodolphe Boulanger,
but love has nothing to do with it.
You are writing about sexual desire,

that longing of one person to possess another
whose ultimate aim is penetration.
Love has nothing to do with it.
You write and write that scene
until you arouse yourself,
masturbate into a handkerchief.
Still, you don't get up from the desk
for hours. You go on writing that scene,
writing about hunger, blind energy –
the very nature of sex –
a fiery leaning into consequence
and eventually, utter ruin
if unbridled. And sex,
what is sex if it is not unbridled?

You walk on the strand that night
with your magpie friend, Ed Goncourt.
You tell him when you write
love scenes these days you can jackoff
without leaving your desk.
"Love has nothing to do with it," you say.
You enjoy a cigar and a clear view of Jersey.
The tide is going out across the shingle,
and nothing on earth can stop it.
The smooth stones you pick up and examine
under the moon's light have been made blue
from the sea. Next morning when you pull them
from your trouser pocket, they are still blue.

                                        – *for my wife*

Tel Aviv and Life on the Mississippi

This afternoon the Mississippi –
high, roily under a broiling sun,
or low, rippling under starlight,
set with deadly snags come out to fish

for steamboats —
the Mississippi this afternoon
has never seemed so far away.

Plantations pass in the darkness;
there's Jones's landing appearing out
of nowhere, out of pine trees,
and here at 12-Mile Point, Gray's
overseer reaches out of fog and receives
a packet of letters, souvenirs and such
from New Orleans.

Bixby, that pilot you loved,
fumes and burns:
D—nation, boy! he storms at you time and again.
Vicksburg, Memphis, St Looey, Cincinnati,
the paddleblades flash and rush, rush
upriver, soughing and churning
the dark water.

Mark Twain you're all eyes and ears,
you're taking all this down to tell later,
everything,
even how you got your name,
quarter twain, mark twain,
something every schoolboy knew
save one.

I hang my legs further over the banister
and lean back in shade,
holding to the book like a wheel,
sweating, fooling my life away,
as some children haggle,
then fiercely slap each other
in the field below.

The News Carried to Macedonia

On the banks of the
      river they call Indus today
we observe a kind of
bean
      much like the Egyptian bean
      also
crocodiles are reported
upstream & hillsides grown over
      with myrrh & ivy
          He believes
we have located the headwaters
of the River Nile
      we offer
sacrifice
hold games
      for the occasion
There is much rejoicing &
        the men think
      we shall turn back
These elephants their
emissaries offer
      are giant
terrifying beasts yet
      with a grin he yesterday
ran up a ladder onto
      the very top of one
      beast
The men
        cheered him & he
waved & they cheered him
      again
He pointed across the river
      & the men grew silent

The builders
busy themselves with great rafts
      at the water's edge
         on the morrow
we again set our faces
     to the East
Tonight
        wind   birds
fill the air
    the clacking of their bills
like iron on iron
The wind
      is steady is fragrant
    with jasmine
trail of the country behind us
The wind moves
      through the camp
stirs the tents of
the Hetaeri
     touches each
of the sleeping soldiers
Euoi! Euoi!
    men cry out
in their sleep & the horses
      prick their ears & stand
   shivering
In a few hours
they all shall wake
   with the sun
shall follow the wind
    even further

The Mosque in Jaffa

I lean over the balcony of the minaret.
My head swims.
A few steps away the man who intends
to betray me begins by pointing out
key sights —
market church prison whorehouse.
Killed, he says.
Words lost in the wind but
drawing a finger across his throat
so I will get it.
He grins.
The key words fly out —
Turks Greeks Arabs Jews
trade worship love murder
a beautiful woman.
He grins again at such foolishness.
He knows I am watching him.
Still he whistles confidently `
as we start down the steps
bumping against each other going down
commingling breath and bodies in the narrow
spiralling dark.
Downstairs, his friends are waiting
with a car. We all of us light cigarettes
and think what to do next.
Time, like the light in his dark eyes,
is running out as we climb in.

Not Far from Here

Not far from here someone
is calling my name.
I jump to the floor.

*

Still, this could be a trap.
Careful, careful.
I look under the covers for my knife.

But even as I curse God
for the delay, the door is thrown open
and a long-haired brat enters

carrying a dog.
What is it, child? (We are both
trembling.) What do you want?

But the tongue only hops and flutters
in her open mouth
as a single sound rises in her throat.

I move closer, kneel
and place my ear against the tiny lips.
When I stand up – the dog grins.

Listen, I don't have time for games.
Here, I say, here – and I send her away
with a plum.

Sudden Rain

•

Rain hisses onto stones as old men and women
drive donkeys to cover.
We stand in rain, more foolish than donkeys,
and shout, walk up and down in rain and accuse.

•

When rain stops the old men and women
who have waited quietly in doorways, smoking,
lead their donkeys out once more and up the hill.

•

Behind, always behind, I climb through the narrow
    streets.
I roll my eyes. I clatter against stones.

Balzac

I think of Balzac in his nightcap after
thirty hours at his writing desk,
mist rising from his face,
the gown clinging
to his hairy thighs as
he scratches himself, lingers
at the open window.
Outside, on the boulevards,
the plump white hands of the creditors
stroke moustaches and cravats,
young ladies dream of Chateaubriand
and promenade with the young men, while
empty carriages rattle by, smelling
of axle-grease and leather.
Like a huge draught horse, Balzac
yawns, snorts, lumbers
to the watercloset
and, flinging open his gown,
trains a great stream of piss into the
early nineteenth century
chamberpot. The lace curtain catches
the breeze. Wait! One last scene
before sleep. His brain sizzles as
he goes back to his desk – the pen,
the pot of ink, the strewn pages.

Country Matters

A girl pushes a bicycle through tall grass,
through overturned garden furniture, water
rising to her ankles. Cups without handles
sail upon the murky water, saucers
with fine cracks in the porcelain.
At the upstairs window, behind damask curtains,

the steward's pale blue eyes follow.
He tries to call.
Shreds of yellow note paper
float out onto the wintry air, but the girl
does not turn her head.
Cook is away, no one hears.
Then two fists appear on the window sill.
He leans closer to hear the small
whisperings, the broken story, the excuses.

This Room

This room for instance:
is that an empty coach
that waits below?

       Promises, promises,
       tell them nothing
       for my sake.

I remember parasols,
an esplanade beside the sea,
yet these flowers . . .

       Must I ever remain behind –
       listening, smoking,
       scribbling down the next far thing?

I light a cigarette
and adjust the window shade.
There is a noise in the street
growing fainter, fainter.

Rhodes

I don't know the names of flowers
or one tree from another,
nevertheless I sit in the square
under a cloud of Papisostros smoke
and sip Hellas beer.
Somewhere nearby there is a Colossus
waiting for another artist,
another earthquake.
But I'm not ambitious.
I'd like to stay, it's true,
though I'd want to hang out
with the civic deer that surround
the Hospitaler castle on the hill.
They are beautiful deer
and their lean haunches flicker
under an assault of white butterflies.

High on the battlement a tall, stiff
figure of a man keeps watch on Turkey.
A warm rain begins to fall.
A peacock shakes drops of water
from its tail and heads for cover.
In the Moslem graveyard a cat sleeps
in a niche between two stones.
Just time for a look
into the casino, except
I'm not dressed.

Back on board, ready for bed,
I lie down and remember
I've been to Rhodes.
But there's something else —
I hear again the voice
of the croupier calling

thirty-two, thirty-two
as my body flies over water,
as my soul, poised like a cat, hovers —
then leaps into sleep.

Spring, 480 BC

Enraged by what he called
       the impertinence of the Hellespont
             in blowing up a storm
         which brought to a halt
             his army of 2 million,
                 Herodotus relates
          that Xerxes ordered 300
             lashes be given
       that unruly body of water besides
      throwing in a pair of fetters, followed
          by a branding with hot irons.
You can imagine
       how this news was received
              at Athens; I mean
       that the Persians were on the march.

IV

Near Klamath

We stand around the burning oil drum
and we warm ourselves, our hands
and faces, in its pure lapping heat.

We raise steaming cups of coffee
to our lips and we drink it
with both hands. But we are salmon

fishermen. And now we stamp our feet
on the snow and rocks and move upstream,
slowly, full of love, toward the still pools.

Autumn

This yardful of the landlord's used cars
does not intrude. The landlord
himself, does not intrude. He hunches
all day over a swage,
or else is enveloped in the blue flame
of the arc-welding device.
      He takes note of me though,
often stopping work to grin
and nod at me through the window. He even
apologizes for parking his logging gear
in my living room.
      But we remain friends.
Slowly the days thin, and we
move together towards spring,
towards high water, the jack-salmon,
the sea-run cutthroat.

Winter Insomnia

The mind can't sleep, can only lie awake and
gorge, listening to the snow gather as
for some final assault.

It wishes Chekhov were here to minister
something – three drops of valerian, a glass
of rose water – anything, it wouldn't matter.

The mind would like to get out of here
onto the snow. It would like to run
with a pack of shaggy animals, all teeth,

under the moon, across the snow, leaving
no prints or spoor, nothing behind.
The mind is sick tonight.

Prosser

In winter two kinds of fields on the hills
outside Prosser: fields of new green wheat, the slips
rising overnight out of the plowed ground,
and waiting,
and then rising again, and budding.
Geese love this green wheat.
I ate some of it once too, to see.

And wheat stubble-fields that reach to the river.
These are the fields that have lost everything.
At night they try to recall their youth,
but their breathing is slow and irregular as
their life sinks into dark furrows.
Geese love this shattered wheat also.
They will die for it.

*

But everything is forgotten, nearly everything,
and sooner rather than later, please God —
fathers, friends, they pass
into your life and out again, a few women stay
a while, then go, and the fields
turn their backs, disappear in rain.
Everything goes, but Prosser.

Those nights driving back through miles of wheat
    fields —
headlamps raking the fields on the curves —
Prosser, that town, shining as we break over hills,
heater rattling, tired through to bone,
the smell of gunpowder on our fingers still:
I can barely see him, my father, squinting
through the windshield of that cab, saying, Prosser.

At Night the Salmon Move

At night the salmon move
out from the river and into town.
They avoid places with names
like Foster's Freeze, A & W, Smiley's,
but swim close to the tract
homes on Wright Avenue where sometimes
in the early morning hours
you can hear them trying doorknobs
or bumping against Cable TV lines.
We wait up for them.
We leave our back windows open
and call out when we hear a splash.
Mornings are a disappointment.

With a Telescope Rod
on Cowiche Creek

Here my assurance drops away. I lose
all direction. Gray Lady
onto moving waters. My thoughts
stir like ruffed grouse
in the clearing across the creek.

Suddenly, as at a signal, the birds
pass silently back into pine trees.

Poem for Dr Pratt, a Lady Pathologist

·

Last night I dreamt a priest came to me
holding in his hands white bones,
white bones in his white hands.
He was gentle,
not like Father McCormick with his webbed fingers.
I was not frightened.

·

This afternoon the maids come with their mops
and disinfectant. They pretend I'm not
there, talk of menstrual cycles as they
push my bed this way and that. Before leaving,
they embrace. Gradually, the room
fills with leaves. I am afraid.

·

The window is open. Sunlight.
Across the room a bed creaks, creaks
under the weight of lovemaking.
The man clears his throat. Outside,
I hear sprinklers. I begin to void.
A green desk floats by the window.

·

My heart lies on the table, a parody
of affection, while her fingers rummage
the endless string of entrails.
These considerations aside,
after all those years of adventure in the Far East,
I am in love with these hands, but
I'm cold beyond imagining.

Wes Hardin: From a Photograph

Turning through a collection
        of old photographs
I come to a picture of the outlaw,
        Wes Hardin, dead.
He is a big, moustached man
        in a black suitcoat
on his back over a boardfloor
        in Amarillo, Texas.
His head is turned at the camera
        and his face
seems bruised, the hair
        jarred loose.
A bullet has entered his skull
        from behind
coming out a little hole
        over his right eye.

Nothing so funny about that
        but three shabby men
in overalls stand grinning
        a few feet away.
They are all holding rifles
        and that one
at the end has on what must be
        the outlaw's hat.

Several other bullets are dotted
       here and there
under the fancy white shirt
       the deceased is wearing
– in a manner of speaking –
       but what makes me stare
is this large dark bullethole
       through the slender, delicate-looking
                                        right hand.

Marriage

In our cabin we eat breaded oysters and fries
with lemon cookies for dessert, as the marriage
of Kitty and Levin unfolds on Public TV.
The man in the trailer up the hill, our neighbor,
has just gotten out of jail again.
This morning he drove into the yard with his wife
in a big yellow car, radio blaring.
His wife turned off the radio while he parked,
and together they walked slowly
to their trailer without saying anything.
It was early morning, birds were out.
Later, he propped open the door
with a chair to let in spring air and light.

It's Easter Sunday night,
and Kitty and Levin are married at last.
It's enough to bring tears to the eyes, that marriage
and all the lives it touched. We go on
eating oysters, watching television,
remarking on the fine clothes and amazing grace
of the people caught up in this story, some of them
straining under the pressures of adultery,

separation from loved ones, and the destruction
they must know lies in store just after
the next cruel turn of circumstance, and then the
    next.

A dog barks. I get up to check the door.
Behind the curtains are trailers and a muddy
parking area with cars. The moon sails west
as I watch, armed to the teeth, hunting
for my children. My neighbor,
liquored up now, starts his big car, races
the engine, and heads out again, filled
with confidence. The radio wails,
beats something out. When he has gone
there are only the little ponds of silver water
that shiver and can't understand their being here.

The Other Life

Now for the other life. The one
without mistakes.
— LOU LIPSITZ

My wife is in the other half of this mobile home
making a case against me.
I can hear her pen *scratch, scratch.*
Now and then she stops to weep,
then — *scratch, scratch.*

The frost is going out of the ground.
The man who owns this unit tells me,
Don't leave your car here.
My wife goes on writing and weeping,
weeping and writing in our new kitchen.

The Mailman as Cancer Patient

Hanging around the house each day
the mailman never smiles; he tires
easily, is losing weight,
that's all; they'll hold the job —
besides, he needed a rest.
He will not hear it discussed.

As he walks the empty rooms, he
thinks of crazy things
like Tommy and Jimmy Dorsey,
shaking hands with Franklin D. Roosevelt
at Grand Coulee Dam,
New Year's Eve parties he liked best;
enough things to fill a book
he tells his wife, who
also thinks crazy things
yet keeps on working.
But sometimes at night
the mailman dreams he rises from his bed
puts on his clothes and goes
out, trembling with joy . . .

He hates those dreams
for when he wakes
there's nothing left; it is
as if he'd never been
anywhere, never done anything;
there is just the room,
the early morning without sun,
the sound of a doorknob
turning slowly.

Poem for Hemingway
& W. C. Williams

3 fat trout hang
    in the still pool
below the new
    steel bridge.
two friends
    come slowly up
the track.
    one of them,
ex-heavyweight,
    wears an old
hunting cap.
    he wants to kill,
that is catch & eat,
    the fish.
the other,
    medical man,
he knows the chances
    of that.
he thinks it fine
    that they should
simply hang there
    always
in the clear water.
    the two keep going
but they
    discuss it as
they disappear
    into the fading trees
& fields & light,
    upstream.

Torture

FOR STEPHEN DOBYNS

You are falling in love again. This time
it is a South American general's daughter.
You want to be stretched on the rack again.
You want to hear awful things said to you
and to admit these things are true.
You want to have unspeakable acts
committed against your person, things
nice people don't talk about in classrooms.
You want to tell everything you know
on Simon Bolivar, on Jorge Luis Borges,
on yourself most of all.
You want to implicate everyone in this!
Even when it's four o'clock in the morning
and the lights are burning still –
those lights that have been burning night and day
in your eyes and brain for two weeks –
and you are dying for a smoke and a lemonade,
but she won't turn off the lights that woman
with the green eyes and little ways about her,
even then you want to be her gaucho.
Dance with me, you imagine hearing her say
as you reach for the empty beaker of water.
Dance with me, she says again and no mistake.
She picks this minute to ask you, hombre,
to get up and dance with her in the nude.
No, you don't have the strength of a fallen leaf,
not the strength of a little reed basket
battered by waves on Lake Titicaca.
But you bound out of bed
just the same, amigo, you dance
across wide open spaces.

Bobber

On the Columbia River near Vantage,
Washington, we fished for whitefish
in the winter months; my dad, Swede –
Mr Lindgren – and me. They used belly-reels,
pencil-length sinkers, red, yellow, or brown
flies baited with maggots.
They wanted distance and went clear out there
to the edge of the riffle.
I fished near shore with a quill bobber and a cane pole.

My dad kept his maggots alive and warm
under his lower lip. Mr Lindgren didn't drink.
I liked him better than my dad for a time.
He let me steer his car, teased me
about my name "Junior," and said
one day I'd grow into a fine man, remember
all this, and fish with my own son.
But my dad was right. I mean
he kept silent and looked into the river,
worked his tongue, like a thought, behind the bait.

Highway 99E from Chico

The mallard ducks are down
for the night. They chuckle
in their sleep and dream of Mexico
and Honduras. Watercress
nods in the irrigation ditch
and the tules slump forward, heavy
with blackbirds.

Rice fields float under the moon.
Even the wet maple leaves cling
to my windshield. I tell you Maryann,
I am happy.

The Cougar

FOR JOHN HAINES AND KEITH WILSON

I stalked a cougar once in a lost box-canyon
off the Columbia River gorge near the town and river
of Klickitat. We were loaded for grouse. October,
gray sky reaching over into Oregon, and beyond,
all the way to California. None of us had been there,
to California, but we knew about that place – they had
restaurants
that let you fill your plate as many times as you wanted.

I stalked a cougar that day,
if stalk is the right word, clumping and scraping along
upwind of the cougar, smoking cigarettes too,
one after the other, a nervous, fat, sweating kid
under the best of circumstances, but that day
I stalked a cougar . . .

And then I was weaving drunk there in the living room,
fumbling to put it into words, smacked and scattered
with the memory of it after you two had put *your* stories,
black bear stories, out on the table.
Suddenly I was back in that canyon, in that gone state.
Something I hadn't thought about for years:
how I stalked a cougar that day.

So I told it. Tried to anyway,
Haines and I pretty drunk now. Wilson listening, listening,
then saying, You sure it wasn't a bobcat?
Which I secretly took as a put-down, he from the Southwest,
poet who had read that night,
and any fool able to tell a bobcat from a cougar,
even a drunk writer like me,
years later, at the smorgasbord, in California.

*

Hell. And then the cougar smooth-loped out of the brush
right in front of me – God, how big and beautiful he was –
jumped onto a rock and turned his head
to look at me. To look at *me*! I looked back, forgetting to shoot.
Then he jumped again, ran clear out of my life.

The Current

These fish have no eyes
these silver fish that come to me in dreams,
scattering their roe and milt
in the pockets of my brain.

But there's one that comes –
heavy, scarred, silent like the rest,
that simply holds against the current,

closing its dark mouth against
the current, closing and opening
as it holds to the current.

Hunter

Half asleep on top of this bleak landscape,
surrounded by chukkers,
I crouch behind a pile of rocks and dream
I embrace my babysitter.
A few inches from my face
her cool and youthful eyes stare at me from two remaining
wildflowers. There's a question in those eyes
I can't answer. Who is to judge these things?
But deep under my winter underwear,
my blood stirs.

*

Suddenly, her hand rises in alarm —
the geese are streaming off their river island,
rising, rising up this gorge.
I move the safety. The body gathers, leans to its work.
Believe in the fingers.
Believe in the nerves.
Believe in THIS.

Trying to Sleep Late on a Saturday Morning in November

In the living room Walter Cronkite
prepares us for the moon shot.
We are approaching
the third and final phase, this
is the last exercise.
I settle down,
far down into the covers.

My son is wearing his space helmet.
I see him move down the long airless corridor,
his iron boots dragging.

My own feet grow cold.
I dream of yellow jackets and near
frostbite, two hazards
facing the whitefish fishermen
on Satus Creek.

But there is something moving
there in the frozen reeds,
something on its side that is
slowly filling with water.
I turn onto my back.
All of me is lifting at once,
as if it were impossible to drown.

Louise

In the trailer next to this one
a woman picks at a child named Louise.
Didn't I tell you, Dummy, to keep this door closed?
Jesus, it's winter!
You want to pay the electric bill?
Wipe your feet, for Christ's sake!
Louise, what am I going to do with you?
Oh, what am I going to do with you, Louise?
the woman sings from morning to night.
Today the woman and child are out
hanging up wash.
Say hello to this man, the woman says
to Louise. Louise!
This is Louise, the woman says
and gives Louise a jerk.
Cat's got her tongue, the woman says.
But Louise has pins in her mouth,
wet clothes in her arms. She pulls
the line down, holds the line
with her neck
as she slings the shirt
over the line and lets go –
the shirt filling out, flapping
over her head. She ducks
and jumps back – jumps back
from this near human shape.

Poem for Karl Wallenda,
Aerialist Supreme

When you were little, wind tailed you
all over Magdeburg. In Vienna wind looked for you
in first one courtyard then another.
It overturned fountains, it made your hair stand on end.

In Prague wind accompanied serious young couples
just starting families. But you made their breaths catch,
those ladies in long white dresses,
the men with their moustaches and high collars.
It waited in the cuffs of your sleeves
when you bowed to the Emperor Haile Selassie.
It was there when you shook hands
with the democratic King of the Belgians.
Wind rolled mangoes and garbage sacks down the streets of
    Nairobi.
You saw wind pursuing zebras across the Serengeti Plain.
Wind joined you as you stepped off the eaves of suburban houses
in Sarasota, Florida. It made little noises
in trees at every crossroads town, every circus stop.
You remarked on it all your life,
how it could come from nowhere,
how it stirred the puffy faces of the hydrangeas
below hotel room balconies while you
drew on your big Havana and watched
the smoke stream south, always south,
toward Puerto Rico and the Torrid Zone.
That morning, 74 years old and 10 stories up,
midway between hotel and hotel, a promotional stunt
on the first day of spring, that wind
which has been everywhere with you
comes in from the Caribbean to throw itself
once and for all into your arms, like a young lover!
Your hair stands on end.
You try to crouch, to reach for wire.
Later, men come along to clean up
and to take down the wire. They take down the wire
where you spent your life. Imagine that: wire.

Deschutes River

This sky, for instance:
closed, gray,
but it has stopped snowing
so that is something. I am
so cold I cannot bend
my fingers.
Walking down to the river this morning
we surprised a badger
tearing a rabbit.
Badger had a bloody nose,
blood on its snout up to its sharp eyes:
        prowess is not to be confused
        with grace.

Later, eight mallard ducks fly over
without looking down. On the river
Frank Sandmeyer trolls, trolls
for steelhead. He has fished
this river for years
but February is the best month
he says.
Snarled, mittenless,
I handle a maze of nylon.
Far away —
another man is raising my children,
bedding my wife bedding my wife.

Forever

Drifting outside in a pall of smoke,
I follow a snail's streaked path down
the garden to the garden's stone wall.
Alone at last I squat on my heels, see

*

what needs to be done, and suddenly
affix myself to the damp stone.
I begin to look around me slowly
and listen, employing

my entire body as the snail
employs its body, relaxed, but alert.
Amazing! Tonight is a milestone
in my life. After tonight

how can I ever go back to that
other life? I keep my eyes
on the stars, wave to them
with my feelers. I hold on

for hours, just resting.
Still later, grief begins to settle
around my heart in tiny drops.
I remember my father is dead,

and I am going away from this
town soon. Forever.
Goodbye, son, my father says.
Toward morning, I climb down

and wander back into the house.
They are still waiting,
fright splashed on their faces,
as they meet my new eyes for the first time.

Where Water Comes Together
with Other Water

I

Woolworth's, 1954

Where this floated up from, or why,
I don't know. But thinking about this
since just after Robert called
telling me he'd be here in a few
minutes to go clamming.

How on my first job I worked
under a man named Sol.
Fifty-some years old, but
a stockboy like I was.
Had worked his way
up to nothing. But grateful
for his job, same as me.
He knew everything there was
to know about that dime-store
merchandise and was willing
to show me. I was sixteen, working
for six bits an hour. Loving it
that I was. Sol taught me
what he knew. He was patient,
though it helped I learned fast.

Most important memory
of that whole time: opening
the cartons of women's lingerie.
Underpants, and soft, clingy things
like that. Taking it out
of cartons by the handful. Something
sweet and mysterious about those

things even then. Sol called it
"linger-ey." "Linger-ey?"
What did I know? I called it
that for a while, too. "Linger-ey."

Then I got older. Quit being
a stockboy. Started pronouncing
that frog word right.
I knew what I was talking about!
Went to taking girls out
in hopes of touching that softness,
slipping down those underpants.
And sometimes it happened. God,
they let me. And they *were*
linger-ey, those underpants.
They tended to linger a little
sometimes, as they slipped down
off the belly, clinging lightly
to the hot white skin.
Passing over the hips and buttocks
and beautiful thighs, traveling
faster now as they crossed the knees,
the calves! Reaching the ankles,
brought together for this
occasion. And kicked free
onto the floor of the car and
forgotten about. Until you had
to look for them.

"Linger-ey."

Those sweet girls!
"Linger a little, for thou art fair."
I know who said that. It fits,
and I'll use it. Robert and his
kids and I out there on the flats
with our buckets and shovels.
His kids, who won't eat clams, cutting

up the whole time, saying "Yuck"
or "Ugh" as clams turned
up in the shovels full of sand
and were tossed into the bucket.
Me thinking all the while
of those early days in Yakima.
And smooth-as-silk underpants.
The lingering kind that Jeanne wore,
and Rita, Muriel, Sue, and her sister,
Cora Mae. All those girls.
Grownup now. Or worse.
I'll say it: dead.

Radio Waves

FOR ANTONIO MACHADO

This rain has stopped, and the moon has come out.
I don't understand the first thing about radio
waves. But I think they travel better just after
a rain, when the air is damp. Anyway, I can reach out
now and pick up Ottawa, if I want to, or Toronto.
Lately, at night, I've found myself
becoming slightly interested in Canadian politics
and domestic affairs. It's true. But mostly it was their
music stations I was after. I could sit here in the chair
and listen, without having to do anything, or think.
I don't have a TV, and I'd quit reading
the papers. At night I turned on the radio.

When I came out here I was trying to get away
from everything. Especially literature.
What that entails, and what comes after.
There is in the soul a desire for not thinking.
For being still. Coupled with this
a desire to be strict, yes, and rigorous.
But the soul is also a smooth son of a bitch,

not always trustworthy. And I forgot that.
I listened when it said, Better to sing that which is gone
and will not return than that which is still
with us and will be with us tomorrow. Or not.
And if not, that's all right too.
It didn't much matter, it said, if a man sang at all.
That's the voice I listened to.
Can you imagine somebody thinking like this?
That it's really all one and the same?
What nonsense!
But I'd think these stupid thoughts at night
as I sat in the chair and listened to my radio.

Then, Machado, your poetry!
It was a little like a middle-aged man falling
in love again. A remarkable thing to witness,
and embarrassing, too.
Silly things like putting your picture up.
And I took your book to bed with me
and slept with it near at hand. A train went by
in my dreams one night and woke me up.
And the first thing I thought, heart racing
there in the dark bedroom, was this —
It's all right, Machado is here.
Then I could fall back to sleep again.

Today I took your book with me when I went
for my walk. "Pay attention!" you said,
when anyone asked what to do with their lives.
So I looked around and made note of everything.
Then sat down with it in the sun, in my place
beside the river where I could see the mountains.
And I closed my eyes and listened to the sound
of the water. Then I opened them and began to read
"Abel Martin's Last Lamentations."
This morning I thought about you hard, Machado.
And I hope, even in the face of what I know about death,

that you got the message I intended.
But it's okay even if you didn't. Sleep well. Rest.
Sooner or later I hope we'll meet.
And then I can tell you these things myself.

Movement

Driving lickety-split to make the ferry!
Snow Creek and then Dog Creek
fly by in the headlights.
But the hour's all wrong – no time to think
about the sea-run trout there.
In the lee of the mountains
something on the radio about an old woman
who travels around inside a kettle.
Indigence is at the root of our lives, yes,
but this is not right.
Cut that old woman some slack,
for God's sake.
She's somebody's mother.
You there! It's late. Imagine yourself
with the lid coming down.
The hymns and requiems. The sense of movement
as you're borne along to the next place.

Hominy and Rain

In a little patch of ground beside
the wall of the Earth Sciences building,
a man in a canvas hat was on
his knees doing something in the rain
with some plants. Piano music
came from an upstairs window
in the building next door. Then
the music stopped.
And the window was brought down.

You told me those white blossoms
on the cherry trees in the Quad
smelled like a can of just-opened
hominy. Hominy. They reminded you
of that. This may or may not
be true. I can't say.
I've lost my sense of smell,
along with any interest I may ever
have expressed in working
on my knees with plants, or
vegetables. There was a barefoot

madman with a ring in his ear
playing his guitar and singing
reggae. I remember that.
Rain puddling around his feet.
The place he'd picked to stand
had Welcome Fear
painted on the sidewalk in red letters.

At the time it seemed important
to recall the man on his knees
in front of his plants.
The blossoms. Music of one kind,
and another. Now I'm not so sure.
I can't say, for sure.

It's a little like some tiny cave-in,
in my brain. There's a sense
that I've lost — not everything,
not everything, but far too much.
A part of my life forever.
Like hominy.

Even though your arm stayed linked
in mine. Even though that. Even
though we stood quietly in the
doorway as the rain picked up.
And watched it without saying
anything. Stood quietly.
At peace, I think. Stood watching
the rain. While the one
with the guitar played on.

The Road

What a rough night! It's either no dreams at all,
or else a dream that may or may not be
a dream portending loss. Last night I was dropped off
without a word on a country road.
A house back in the hills showed a light
no bigger than a star.
But I was afraid to go there, and kept walking.

Then to wake up to rain striking the glass.
Flowers in a vase near the window.
The smell of coffee, and you touching your hair
with a gesture like someone who has been gone for years.
But there's a piece of bread under the table
near your feet. And a line of ants
moving back and forth from a crack in the floor.
You've stopped smiling.

*

Do me a favor this morning. Draw the curtain and come
   back to bed.
Forget the coffee. We'll pretend
we're in a foreign country, and in love.

Fear

Fear of seeing a police car pull into the drive.
Fear of falling asleep at night.
Fear of not falling asleep.
Fear of the past rising up.
Fear of the present taking flight.
Fear of the telephone that rings in the dead of night.
Fear of electrical storms.
Fear of the cleaning woman who has a spot on her cheek!
Fear of dogs I've been told won't bite.
Fear of anxiety!
Fear of having to identify the body of a dead friend.
Fear of running out of money.
Fear of having too much, though people will not believe this.
Fear of psychological profiles.
Fear of being late and fear of arriving before anyone else.
Fear of my children's handwriting on envelopes.
Fear they'll die before I do, and I'll feel guilty.
Fear of having to live with my mother in her old age, and mine.
Fear of confusion.
Fear this day will end on an unhappy note.
Fear of waking up to find you gone.
Fear of not loving and fear of not loving enough.
Fear that what I love will prove lethal to those I love.
Fear of death.
Fear of living too long.
Fear of death.
        I've said that.

Romanticism

(FOR LINDA GREGG,
AFTER READING "CLASSICISM")

The nights are very unclear here.
But if the moon is full, we know it.
We feel one thing one minute,
something else the next.

The Ashtray

*You could write a story about this
ashtray, for example, and a man and a
woman. But the man and woman are
always the two poles of your story.
The North Pole and the South. Every
story has these two poles — he and she.*

— A. P. CHEKHOV

They're alone at the kitchen table in her friend's
apartment. They'll be alone for another hour, and then
her friend will be back. Outside, it's raining —
the rain coming down like needles, melting last week's
snow. They're smoking and using the ashtray . . . Maybe
just one of them is smoking . . . *He's* smoking! Never
mind. Anyway, the ashtray is filling up with
cigarettes and ashes.

She's ready to break into tears at any minute.
To plead with him, in fact, though she's proud
and has never asked for anything in her life.
He sees what's coming, recognizes the signs —
a catch in her voice as she brings her fingers
to her locket, the one her mother left her.
He pushes back his chair, gets up, goes over to
the window . . . He wishes it were tomorrow and he
were at the races. He wishes he was out walking,

using his umbrella . . . He strokes his mustache
and wishes he were anywhere except here. But
he doesn't have any choice in the matter. He's got
to put a good face on this for everybody's sake.
God knows, he never meant for things to come
to this. But it's sink or swim now. A wrong
move and he stands to lose her friend, too.

Her breathing slows. She watches him but
doesn't say anything. She knows, or thinks she
knows, where this is leading. She passes a hand
over her eyes, leans forward and puts her head
in her hands. She's done this a few times
before, but has no idea it's something
that drives him wild. He looks away and grinds
his teeth. He lights a cigarette, shakes out
the match, stands a minute longer at the window.

Then walks back to the table and sits
down with a sigh. He drops the match in the ashtray.
She reaches for his hand, and he lets her
take it. Why not? Where's the harm?
Let her. His mind's made up. She covers his
fingers with kisses, tears fall onto his wrist.

He draws on his cigarette and looks at her
as a man would look indifferently on
a cloud, a tree, or a field of oats at sunset.
He narrows his eyes against the smoke. From time
to time he uses the ashtray as he waits
for her to finish weeping.

Still Looking Out for
Number One

Now that you've gone away for five days,
I'll smoke all the cigarettes I want,
where I want. Make biscuits and eat them
with jam and fat bacon. Loaf. Indulge
myself. Walk on the beach if I feel
like it. And I feel like it, alone and
thinking about when I was young. The people
then who loved me beyond reason.
And how I loved them above all others.
Except one. I'm saying I'll do everything
I want here while you're away!
But there's one thing I won't do.
I won't sleep in our bed without you.
No. It doesn't please me to do so.
I'll sleep where I damn well feel like it —
where I sleep best when you're away
and I can't hold you the way I do.
On the broken sofa in my study.

Where Water Comes Together
with Other Water

I love creeks and the music they make.
And rills, in glades and meadows, before
they have a chance to become creeks.
I may even love them best of all
for their secrecy. I almost forgot
to say something about the source!
Can anything be more wonderful than a spring?
But the big streams have my heart too.
And the places streams flow into rivers.
The open mouths of rivers where they join the sea.

The places where water comes together
with other water. Those places stand out
in my mind like holy places.
But these coastal rivers!
I love them the way some men love horses
or glamorous women. I have a thing
for this cold swift water.
Just looking at it makes my blood run
and my skin tingle. I could sit
and watch these rivers for hours.
Not one of them like any other.
I'm 45 years old today.
Would anyone believe it if I said
I was once 35?
My heart empty and sere at 35!
Five more years had to pass
before it began to flow again.
I'll take all the time I please this afternoon
before leaving my place alongside this river.
It pleases me, loving rivers.
Loving them all the way back
to their source.
Loving everything that increases me.

II

Happiness

So early it's still almost dark out.
I'm near the window with coffee,
and the usual early morning stuff
that passes for thought.
When I see the boy and his friend
walking up the road
to deliver the newspaper.
They wear caps and sweaters,
and one boy has a bag over his shoulder.
They are so happy
they aren't saying anything, these boys.
I think if they could, they would take
each other's arm.
It's early in the morning,
and they are doing this thing together.
They come on, slowly.
The sky is taking on light,
though the moon still hangs pale over the water.
Such beauty that for a minute
death and ambition, even love,
doesn't enter into this.
Happiness. It comes on
unexpectedly. And goes beyond, really,
any early morning talk about it.

The Old Days

You'd dozed in front of the TV
but you hadn't been to bed yet
when you called. I was asleep,
or nearly, when the phone rang.
You wanted to tell me you'd thrown
a party. And I was missed.
It was like the old days, you
said, and laughed.
Dinner was a disaster.
Everybody dead drunk by the time
food hit the table. People
were having a good time, a great
time, a hell of a time, until
somebody took somebody
else's fiancée upstairs. Then
somebody pulled a knife.

But you got in front of the guy
as he was going upstairs
and talked him down.
Disaster narrowly averted,
you said, and laughed again.
You didn't remember much else
of what happened after that.
People got into their coats
and began to leave. You
must have dropped off for a few
minutes in front of the TV
because it was screaming at you
to get it a drink when you woke up.
Anyway, you're in Pittsburgh,
and I'm in here in this
little town on the other side
of the country. Most everyone
has cleared out of our lives now.

You wanted to call me up and say hello.
To say you were thinking
about me, and of the old days.
To say you were missing me.

It was then I remembered
back to those days and how
telephones used to jump when they rang.
And the people who would come
in those early-morning hours
to pound on the door in alarm.
Never mind the alarm felt inside.
I remembered that, and gravy dinners.
Knives lying around, waiting
for trouble. Going to bed
and hoping I wouldn't wake up.

I love you, Bro, you said.
And then a sob passed
between us. I took hold
of the receiver as if
it were my buddy's arm.
And I wished for us both
I could put my arms
around you, old friend.
I love you too, Bro.
I said that, and then we hung up.

Our First House in Sacramento

This much is clear to me now – even then
our days were numbered. After our first week
in the house that came furnished
with somebody else's things, a man appeared
one night with a baseball bat. And raised it.
I was not the man he thought I was.

Finally, I got him to believe it.
He wept from frustration after his anger
left him. None of this had anything to do
with Beatlemania. The next week these friends
of ours from the bar where we all drank
brought friends of theirs to our house —
and we played poker. I lost the grocery money
to a stranger. Who went on to quarrel
with his wife. In his frustration
he drove his fist through the kitchen wall.
Then he, too, disappeared from my life forever.
When we left that house where nothing worked
any longer, we left at midnight
with a U-Haul trailer and a lantern.
Who knows what passed through the neighbors' minds
when they saw a family leaving their house
in the middle of the night?
The lantern moving behind the curtainless
windows. The shadows going from room to room,
gathering their things into boxes.
I saw firsthand
what frustration can do to a man.
Make him weep, make him throw his fist
through a wall. Set him to dreaming
of the house that's his
at the end of the long road. A house
filled with music, ease, and generosity.
A house that hasn't been lived in yet.

Next Year

That first week in Santa Barbara wasn't the worst thing
to happen. The second week he fell on his head
while drinking, just before he had to lecture.
In the lounge, that second week, she took the microphone
from the singer's hands and crooned her own

torch song. Then danced. And then passed out
on the table. That's not the worst, either. They
went to jail that second week. He wasn't driving
so they booked him, dressed him in pajamas
and stuck him in Detox. Told him to get some sleep.
Told him he could see about his wife in the morning.
But how could he sleep when they wouldn't let him
close the door to his room?
The corridor's green light entered,
and the sound of a man weeping.
His wife had been called upon to give the alphabet
beside the road, in the middle of the night.
This is strange enough. But the cops had her
stand on one leg, close her eyes,
and try to touch her nose with her index finger.
All of which she failed to do.
She went to jail for resisting arrest.
He bailed her out when he got out of Detox.
They drove home in ruins.
This is not the worst. Their daughter had picked that night
to run away from home. She left a note:
"You're both crazy. Give me a break, PLEASE.
Don't come after me."
That's still not the worst. They went on
thinking they were the people they said they were.
Answering to those names.
Making love to the people with those names.
Nights without beginning that had no end.
Talking about a past as if it'd really happened.
Telling themselves that this time next year,
this time next year
things were going to be different.

To My Daughter

Everything I see will outlive me.
— ANNA AKHMATOVA

It's too late now to put a curse on you — wish you
plain, say, as Yeats did his daughter. And when
we met her in Sligo, selling her paintings, it'd worked —
she *was* the plainest, oldest woman in Ireland.
But she was safe.
For the longest time, his reasoning
escaped me. Anyway, it's too late for you,
as I said. You're grownup now, and lovely.
You're a beautiful drunk, daughter.
But you're a drunk. I can't say you're breaking
my heart. I don't have a heart when it comes
to this booze thing. Sad, yes, Christ alone knows.
Your old man, the one they call Shiloh, is back
in town, and the drink has started to flow again.
You've been drunk for three days, you tell me,
when you know goddamn well drinking is like poison
to our family. Didn't your mother and I set you
example enough? Two people
who loved each other knocking each other around,
knocking back the love we felt, glass by empty glass,
curses and blows and betrayals?
You must be crazy! Wasn't all that enough for you?
You want to die? Maybe that's it. Maybe
I think I know you, and I don't.
I'm not kidding, kiddo. Who are you kidding?
Daughter, you can't drink.
The last few times I saw you, you were out of it.
A cast on your collarbone, or else
a splint on your finger, dark glasses to hide
your beautiful bruised eyes. A lip
that a man should kiss instead of split.
Oh, Jesus, Jesus, Jesus Christ!

You've got to take hold now.
Do you hear me? Wake up! You've got to knock it off
and get straight. Clean up your act. I'm asking you.
Okay, telling you. Sure, our family was made
to squander, not collect. But turn this around now.
You simply must – that's all!
Daughter, you can't drink.
It will kill you. Like it did your mother, and me.
Like it did.

Anathema

The entire household suffered.
My wife, myself, the two children, and the dog
whose puppies were born dead.
Our affairs, such as they were, withered.
My wife was dropped by her lover,
the one-armed teacher of music who was
her only contact with the outside world
and the things of the mind.
My own girlfriend said she couldn't stand it
anymore, and went back to her husband.
The water was shut off.
All that summer the house baked.
The peach trees were blasted.
Our little flower bed lay trampled.
The brakes went out on the car, and the battery
failed. The neighbors quit speaking
to us and closed their doors in our faces.
Checks flew back at us from merchants –
and then mail stopped being delivered
altogether. Only the sheriff got through
from time to time – with one or the other
of our children in the back seat,
pleading to be taken anywhere but here.
And then mice entered the house in droves.

Followed by a bull snake. My wife
found it sunning itself in the living room
next to the dead TV. How she dealt with it
is another matter. Chopped its head off
right there on the floor.
And then chopped it in two when it continued
to writhe. We saw we couldn't hold out
any longer. We were beaten.
We wanted to get down on our knees
and say forgive us our sins, forgive us
our lives. But it was too late.
Too late. No one around would listen.
We had to watch as the house was pulled down,
the ground plowed up, and then
we were dispersed in four directions.

Energy

Last night at my daughter's, near Blaine,
she did her best to tell me
what went wrong
between her mother and me.
"Energy. You two's energy was all wrong."
She looks like her mother
when her mother was young.
Laughs like her.
Moves the drift of hair
from her forehead, like her mother.
Can take a cigarette down
to the filter in three draws,
just like her mother. I thought
this visit would be easy. Wrong.
This is hard, brother. Those years
spilling over into my sleep when I try
to sleep. To wake to find a thousand
cigarettes in the ashtray and every

light in the house burning. I can't
pretend to understand anything:
today I'll be carried
three thousand miles away into
the loving arms of another woman, not
her mother. No. She's caught
in the flywheel of a new love.
I turn off the last light
and close the door.
Moving toward whatever ancient thing
it is that works the chains
and pulls us so relentlessly on.

Locking Yourself Out, Then Trying to Get Back In

You simply go out and shut the door
without thinking. And when you look back
at what you've done
it's too late. If this sounds
like the story of a life, okay.

It was raining. The neighbors who had
a key were away. I tried and tried
the lower windows. Stared
inside at the sofa, plants, the table
and chairs, the stereo set-up.
My coffee cup and ashtray waited for me
on the glass-topped table, and my heart
went out to them. I said, *Hello, friends,*
or something like that. After all,
this wasn't so bad.
Worse things had happened. This
was even a little funny. I found the ladder.
Took that and leaned it against the house.
Then climbed in the rain to the deck,

swung myself over the railing
and tried the door. Which was locked,
of course. But I looked in just the same
at my desk, some papers, and my chair.
This was the window on the other side
of the desk where I'd raise my eyes
and stare out when I sat at that desk.
This is not like downstairs, I thought.
This is something else.

And it was something to look in like that, unseen,
from the deck. To be there, inside, and not be there.
I don't even think I can talk about it.
I brought my face close to the glass
and imagined myself inside,
sitting at the desk. Looking up
from my work now and again.
Thinking about some other place
and some other time.
The people I had loved then.

I stood there for a minute in the rain.
Considering myself to be the luckiest of men.
Even though a wave of grief passed through me.
Even though I felt violently ashamed
of the injury I'd done back then.
I bashed that beautiful window.
And stepped back in.

Medicine

All I know about medicine I picked up
from my doctor friend in El Paso
who drank and took drugs. We were buddies
until I moved East. I'm saying
I was never sick a day in my life.
But something has appeared

on my shoulder and continues to grow.
A wen, I think, and love the word
but not the thing itself, whatever
it is. Late at night my teeth ache
and the phone rings. I'm ill,
unhappy and alone. Lord!
Give me your unsteady knife,
doc. Give me your hand, friend.

Wenas Ridge

The seasons turning. Memory flaring.
Three of us that fall. Young hoodlums —
shoplifters, stealers of hubcaps.
Bozos. Dick Miller, dead now.
Lyle Rousseau, son of the Ford dealer.
And I, who'd just made a girl pregnant.
Hunting late into that golden afternoon
for grouse. Following deer paths,
pushing through undergrowth, stepping over
blow-downs. Reaching out for something to hold onto.

At the top of Wenas Ridge
we walked out of pine trees and could see
down deep ravines, where the wind roared, to the river.
More alive then, I thought, than I'd ever be.
But my whole life, in switchbacks, ahead of me.

Hawks, deer, coons we looked at and let go.
Killed six grouse and should have stopped.
Didn't, though we had limits.

Lyle and I climbing fifty feet or so
above Dick Miller. Who screamed – "Yaaaah!"
Then swore and swore. Legs numbing as I saw what.
That fat, dark snake rising up. Beginning to sing.
And how it sang! A timber rattler thick as my wrist.

It'd struck at Miller, but missed. No other way
to say it — he was paralyzed. Could scream, and swear,
not shoot. Then the snake lowered itself from sight
and went in under rocks. We understood
we'd have to get down. In the same way we'd got up.
Blindly crawling through brush, stepping over blow-downs,
pushing into undergrowth. Shadows falling from trees now
onto flat rocks that held the day's heat. And snakes.
My heart stopped, and then started again.
My hair stood on end. This was the moment
my life had prepared me for. And I wasn't ready.

We started down anyway. Jesus, please help me
out of this, I prayed. I'll believe in you again
and honor you always. But Jesus was crowded out
of my head by the vision of that rearing snake.
That singing. Keep believing in me, snake said,
for I will return. I made an obscure, criminal pact
that day. Praying to Jesus in one breath.
To snake in the other. Snake finally more real
to me. The memory of that day
like a blow to the calf now.

I got out, didn't I? But something happened.
I married the girl I loved, yet poisoned her life.
Lies began to coil in my heart and call it home.
Got used to darkness and its crooked ways.
Since then I've always feared rattlesnakes.
Been ambivalent about Jesus.
But someone, something's responsible for this.
Now, as then.

Reading

Every man's life is a mystery, even as
yours is, and mine. Imagine
a château with a window opening
onto Lake Geneva. There in the window
on warm and sunny days is a man
so engrossed in reading he doesn't look
up. Or if he does he marks his place
with a finger, raises his eyes, and peers
across the water to Mont Blanc,
and beyond, to Selah, Washington,
where he is with a girl
and getting drunk *for the first time*.
The last thing he remembers, before
he passes out, is that she spit on him.
He keeps on drinking
and getting spit on for years.
But some people will tell you
that suffering is good for the character.
You're free to believe anything.
In any case, he goes
back to reading and will not
feel guilty about his mother
drifting in her boat of sadness,
or consider his children
and their troubles that go on and on.
Nor does he intend to think about
the clear-eyed woman he once loved
and her defeat at the hands of eastern religion.
Her grief has no beginning, and no end.
Let anyone in the château, or Selah,
come forward who might claim kin with the man
who sits all day in the window reading,

like a picture of a man reading.
Let the sun come forward.
Let the man himself come forward.
What in Hell can he be reading?

Rain

Woke up this morning with
a terrific urge to lie in bed all day
and read. Fought against it for a minute.

Then looked out the window at the rain.
And gave over. Put myself entirely
in the keep of this rainy morning.

Would I live my life over again?
Make the same unforgivable mistakes?
Yes, given half a chance. Yes.

Money

In order to be able to live
on the right side of the law.
To always use his own name
and phone number. To go bail
for a friend and not give
a damn if the friend skips town.
Hope, in fact, she does.
To give some money
to his mother. And to his
children and their mother.
Not save it. He wants
to use it up before it's gone.
Buy clothes with it.
Pay the rent and utilities.
Buy food, and then some.

Go out for dinner when he feels like it.
And it's okay
to order anything off the menu!
Buy drugs when he wants.
Buy a car. If it breaks
down, repair it. Or else
buy another. See that
boat? He might buy one
just like it. And sail it
around the Horn, looking
for company. He knows a girl
in Porto Alegre who'd love
to see him in
his own boat, sails full,
turn into the harbor for her.
A fellow who could afford
to come all this way
to see her. Just because
he liked the sound
of her laughter,
and the way she swings her hair.

Aspens

Imagine a young man, alone, without anyone.
The moment a few raindrops streaked his glass
he began to scribble.
He lived in a tenement with mice for company.
I loved his bravery.

Someone else a few doors down
played Segovia records all day.
He never left his room, and no one could blame him.
At night he could hear the other's
typewriter going, and feel comforted.

*

Literature and music.
Everyone dreaming of Spanish horsemen
and courtyards.
Processions. Ceremony, and
resplendence.

Aspen trees.
Days of rain and high water.
Leaves hammered into the ground finally.
In my heart, this plot of earth
that the storm lights.

III

At Least

I want to get up early one more morning,
before sunrise. Before the birds, even.
I want to throw cold water on my face
and be at my work table
when the sky lightens and smoke
begins to rise from the chimneys
of the other houses.
I want to see the waves break
on this rocky beach, not just hear them
break as I did all night in my sleep.
I want to see again the ships
that pass through the Strait from every
seafaring country in the world —
old, dirty freighters just barely moving along,
and the swift new cargo vessels
painted every color under the sun
that cut the water as they pass.
I want to keep an eye out for them.
And for the little boat that plies
the water between the ships
and the pilot station near the lighthouse.
I want to see them take a man off the ship
and put another up on board.
I want to spend the day watching this happen
and reach my own conclusions.
I hate to seem greedy — I have so much
to be thankful for already.
But I want to get up early one more morning, at least.
And go to my place with some coffee and wait.
Just wait, to see what's going to happen.

The Grant

It's either this or bobcat hunting
with my friend Morris.
Trying to write a poem at six this
morning, or else running
behind the hounds with
a rifle in my hands.
Heart jumping in its cage.
I'm 45 years old. No occupation.
Imagine the luxuriousness of this life.
Try and imagine.
May go with him if he goes
tomorrow. But may not.

My Boat

My boat is being made to order. Right now it's about to leave
the hands of its builders. I've reserved a special place
for it down at the marina. It's going to have plenty of room
on it for all my friends: Richard, Bill, Chuck, Toby, Jim, Hayden,
Gary, George, Harold, Don, Dick, Scott, Geoffrey, Jack,
Paul, Jay, Morris, and Alfredo. All my friends! They know who
    they are.
Tess, of course. I wouldn't go anyplace without her.
And Kristina, Merry, Catherine, Diane, Sally, Annick, Pat,
    Judith, Susie, Lynne, Annie, Jane, Mona.
Doug and Amy! They're family, but they're also my friends,
and they like a good time. There's room on my boat
for just about everyone. I'm serious about this!
There'll be a place on board for everyone's stories.
My own, but also the ones belonging to my friends.
Short stories, and the ones that go on and on. The true
and the made-up. The ones already finished, and the ones still
    being written.

Poems, too! Lyric poems, and the longer, darker narratives.
For my painter friends, paints and canvases will be on board
    my boat.
We'll have fried chicken, lunch meats, cheeses, rolls,
French bread. Every good thing that my friends and I like.
And a big basket of fruit, in case anyone wants fruit.
In case anyone wants to say he or she ate an apple,
or some grapes, on my boat. Whatever my friends want,
name it, and it'll be there. Soda pop of all kinds.
Beer and wine, sure. No one will be denied anything, on
    my boat.
We'll go out into the sunny harbor and have fun, that's the idea.
Just have a good time all around. Not thinking
about this or that or getting ahead or falling behind.
Fishing poles if anyone wants to fish. The fish are out there!
We may even go a little way down the coast, on my boat.
But nothing dangerous, nothing too serious.
The idea is simply to enjoy ourselves and not get scared.
We'll eat and drink and laugh a lot, on my boat.
I've always wanted to take at least one trip like this,
with my friends, on my boat. If we want to
we'll listen to Schumann on the CBC.
But if that doesn't work out, okay,
we'll switch to KRAB, The Who, and the Rolling Stones.
Whatever makes my friends happy! Maybe everyone
will have their own radio, on my boat. In any case,
we're going to have a big time. People are going to have fun,
and do what they want to do, on my boat.

The Poem I Didn't Write

Here is the poem I was going to write
earlier, but didn't
because I heard you stirring.
I was thinking again
about that first morning in Zurich.

How we woke up before sunrise.
Disoriented for a minute. But going
out onto the balcony that looked down
over the river, and the old part of the city.
And simply standing there, speechless.
Nude. Watching the sky lighten.
So thrilled and happy. As if
we'd been put there
just at that moment.

Work

FOR JOHN GARDNER, D. SEPTEMBER 14, 1982

Love of work. The blood singing
in that. The fine high rise
of it into the work. A man says,
I'm working. Or, I worked today.
Or, I'm trying to make it work.
Him working seven days a week.
And being awakened in the morning
by his young wife, his head on the typewriter.
The fullness before work.
The amazed understanding after.
Fastening his helmet.
Climbing onto his motorcycle
and thinking about home.
And work. Yes, work. The going
to what lasts.

In the Year 2020

Which of us will be left then –
old, dazed, unclear –
but willing to talk about our dead friends?

Talk and talk, like an old faucet leaking.
So that the young ones,
respectful, touchingly curious,
will find themselves stirred
by the recollections.
By the very mention of this name
or that name, and what we did together.
(As we were respectful, but curious
and excited, to hear someone tell
about the illustrious dead ahead of us.)
Of which of us will they say
to their friends,
he knew so and so! He was friends with _____
and they spent time together.
He was at that big party.
Everyone was there. They celebrated
and danced until dawn. They put their arms
around each other and danced
until the sun came up.
Now they're all gone.
Of which of us will it be said –
he knew them? Shook hands with them
and embraced them, stayed overnight
in their warm houses. Loved them!

Friends, I do love you, it's true.
And I hope I'm lucky enough, privileged enough,
to live on and bear witness.
Believe me, I'll say only the most
glorious things about you and our time here!
For the survivor there has to be something
to look forward to. Growing old,
losing everything and everybody.

The Juggler at Heaven's Gate

FOR MICHAEL CIMINO

Behind the dirty table where Kristofferson is having
breakfast, there's a window that looks onto a nineteenth-
century street in Sweetwater, Wyoming. A juggler
is at work out there, wearing a top hat and a frock coat,
a little reed of a fellow keeping three sticks
in the air. Think about this for a minute.
This juggler. This amazing act of the mind and hands.
A man who juggles for a living.
Everyone in his time has known a star,
or a gunfighter. Somebody, anyway, who pushes somebody
around. But a juggler! Blue smoke hangs inside
this awful café, and over that dirty table where two
grownup men talk about a woman's future. And something,
something about the Cattlemen's Association.
But the eye keeps going back to that juggler.
That tiny spectacle. At this minute, Ella's plight
or the fate of the emigrants
is not nearly so important as this juggler's exploits.
How'd *he* get into the act, anyway? What's his story?
That's the story I want to know. Anybody
can wear a gun and swagger around. Or fall in love
with somebody who loves somebody else. But to *juggle*
for God's sake! To give your life to that.
To go with that. Juggling.

My Daughter and Apple Pie

She serves me a piece of it a few minutes
out of the oven. A little steam rises
from the slits on top. Sugar and spice –
cinnamon – burned into the crust.
But she's wearing these dark glasses

in the kitchen at ten o'clock
in the morning – everything nice –
as she watches me break off
a piece, bring it to my mouth,
and blow on it. My daughter's kitchen,
in winter. I fork the pie in
and tell myself to stay out of it.
She says she loves him. No way
could it be worse.

Commerce

A swank dinner. Food truly wonderful
and plenty of it. It was the way I always dreamed
it would be. And it just kept coming
while we talked about the bottom line.
Even when we weren't talking about it,
it was there – in the oysters, the lamb,
the sauces, the fine white linen, the cutlery
and goblets. It said, Here is your life, enjoy.
This is the poem I wanted to live to write! Then
to come upon the spirit in a flaming dessert –
the streaks of fire shooting up, only to drop
back, as if exhausted.

Driving home afterwards, my head aswim
from overeating. What a swine! I deserve
everything that fellow's going to say about me.
Falling asleep in my pants on top of the covers.
But not before thinking about wolves,
a sultry day in the woods.
My life staked down in the clearing.
When I try to turn my head to reveal
the fleshy neck, I can't move.
I don't have the energy. Let them go

for the belly, those brother wolves
with the burning eyes.
To have come this far in a single night!
But then I never knew when to stop.

The Fishing Pole of
the Drowned Man

I didn't want to use it at first.
Then I thought, no, it would
give up secrets and bring me luck –
that's what I needed then.
Besides, he'd left it behind for me
to use when he went swimming that time.
Shortly afterwards, I met two women.
One of them loved opera and the other
was a drunk who'd done time
in jail. I took up with one
and began to drink and fight a lot.
The way this woman could sing and carry on!
We went straight to the bottom.

A Walk

I took a walk on the railroad track.
Followed that for a while
and got off at the country graveyard
where a man sleeps between
two wives. Emily van der Zee,
Loving Wife and Mother,
is at John van der Zee's right.
Mary, the second Mrs van der Zee,
also a Loving Wife, to his left.
First Emily went, then Mary.
After a few years, the old fellow himself.

Eleven children came from these unions.
And they, too, would all have to be dead now.
This is a quiet place. As good a place as any
to break my walk, sit, and provide against
my own death, which comes on.
But I don't understand, and I don't understand.
All I know about this fine, sweaty life,
my own or anyone else's,
is that in a little while I'll rise up
and leave this astonishing place
that gives shelter to dead people. This graveyard.
And go. Walking first on one rail
and then the other.

My Dad's Wallet

Long before he thought of his own death,
my dad said he wanted to lie close
to his parents. He missed them so
after they went away.
He said this enough that my mother remembered,
and I remembered. But when the breath
left his lungs and all signs of life
had faded, he found himself in a town
512 miles away from where he wanted most to be.

My dad, though. He was restless
even in death. Even in death
he had this one last trip to take.
All his life he liked to wander,
and now he had one more place to get to.

The undertaker said he'd arrange it,
not to worry. Some poor light
from the window fell on the dusty floor
where we waited that afternoon
until the man came out of the back room

and peeled off his rubber gloves.
He carried the smell of formaldehyde with him.
He was a big man, this undertaker said.
Then began to tell us why
he liked living in this small town.
This man who'd just opened my dad's veins.
How much is it going to cost? I said.

He took out his pad and pen and began
to write. First, the preparation charges.
Then he figured the transportation
of the remains at 22 cents a mile.
But this was a round-trip for the undertaker,
don't forget. Plus, say, six meals
and two nights in a motel. He figured
some more. Add a surcharge of
$210 for his time and trouble,
and there you have it.

He thought we might argue.
There was a spot of color on
each of his cheeks as he looked up
from his figures. The same poor light
fell in the same poor place on
the dusty floor. My mother nodded
as if she understood. But she
hadn't understood a word of it.
None of it had made any sense to her,
beginning with the time she left home
with my dad. She only knew
that whatever was happening
was going to take money.
She reached into her purse and brought up
my dad's wallet. The three of us
in that little room that afternoon.
Our breath coming and going.

*

We stared at the wallet for a minute.
Nobody said anything.
All the life had gone out of that wallet.
It was old and rent and soiled.
But it was my dad's wallet. And she opened
it and looked inside. Drew out
a handful of money that would go
toward this last, most astounding, trip.

IV

Ask Him

Reluctantly, my son goes with me
through the iron gates
of the cemetery in Montparnasse.
"What a way to spend a day in Paris!"
is what he'd like to say. Did, in fact, say.
He speaks French. Has started a conversation
with a white-haired guard who offers himself
as our informal guide. So we move slowly,
the three of us, along row upon row of graves.
Everyone, it seems, is here.

It's quiet, and hot, and the street sounds
of Paris can't reach. The guard wants to steer us
to the grave of the man who invented the submarine,
and Maurice Chevalier's grave. And the grave
of the 28-year-old singer, Nonnie,
covered with a mound of red roses.

I want to see the graves of the writers.
My son sighs. He doesn't want to see any of it.
Has seen enough. He's passed beyond boredom
into resignation. Guy de Maupassant; Sartre; Sainte-Beuve;
Gautier; the Goncourts; Paul Verlaine and his old comrade,
Charles Baudelaire. Where we linger.

None of these names, or graves, have anything to do
with the untroubled lives of my son and the guard.
Who can this morning talk and joke together
in the French language under a fine sun.
But there are several names chiseled on Baudelaire's stone,
and I can't understand why.

Charles Baudelaire's name is between that of his mother,
who loaned him money and worried all her life
about his health, and his stepfather, a martinet
he hated and who hated him and everything he stood for.
"Ask your friend," I say. So my son asks.
It's as if he and the guard are old friends now,
and I'm there to be humored.
The guard says something and then lays
one hand over the other. Like that. Does it
again. One hand over the other. Grinning. Shrugging.
My son translates. But I understand.
"Like a sandwich, Pop," my son says. "A Baudelaire sandwich."

At which the three of us walk on.
The guard would as soon be doing this as something else.
He lights his pipe. Looks at his watch. It's almost time
for his lunch, and a glass of wine.
"Ask him," I say, "if he wants to be buried
in this cemetery when he dies.
Ask him where he wants to be buried."
My son is capable of saying anything.
I recognize the words *tombeau* and *mort*
in his mouth. The guard stops.
It's clear his thoughts have been elsewhere.
Underwater warfare. The music hall, the cinema.
Something to eat and the glass of wine.
Not corruption, no, and the falling away.
Not annihilation. Not his death.

He looks from one to the other of us.
Who are we kidding? Are we making a bad joke?
He salutes and walks away.
Heading for a table at an outdoor café.
Where he can take off his cap, run his fingers
through his hair. Hear laughter and voices.
The heavy clink of silverware. The ringing

of glasses. Sun on the windows.
Sun on the sidewalk and in the leaves.
Sun finding its way onto his table. His glass. His hands.

Next Door

The woman asked us in for pie. Started
telling about her husband, the man who
used to live there. How he had to be carted
off to the nursing home. He wanted
to cover this fine oak ceiling
with cheap insulation, she said. That was the first
sign of anything being wrong. Then he had
a stroke. A vegetable now. Anyway,
next, the game warden stuck the barrel
of his pistol into her son's ear.
And cocked the hammer. But the kid
wasn't doing that much wrong, and the game
warden is the kid's uncle, don't you see?
So everybody's on the outs. Everybody's
nuts and nobody's speaking to anybody
these days. Here's a big bone the son
found at the mouth of the river.
Maybe it's a human bone? An arm bone
or something? She puts it back on the window-
sill next to a bowl of flowers.
The daughter stays in her room all day,
writing poems about her attempted suicide.
That's why we don't see her. Nobody sees
her anymore. She tears up the poems
and writes them over again. But one of these
days she'll get it right. Would you believe it —
the car threw a rod? That black car
that stands like a hearse
in the yard next door. The engine winched out,
swinging from a tree.

The Caucasus: A Romance

Each evening an eagle soars down from the snowy
crags and passes over camp. It wants to see
if it's true what they say back in Russia: the only
career open to young men these days
is the military. Young men of good family, and a few
others – older, silent men – men who've blotted their
copybooks, as they call it out here. Men like
the Colonel, who lost his ear in a duel.

Dense forests of pine, alder, and birch. Torrents
that fall from dizzying precipices. Mist. Clamorous
rivers. Mountains covered with snow even now, even
in August. Everywhere, as far as the eye can reach,
profusion. A sea of poppies. Wild buckwheat that
shimmers in the heat, that waves and rolls to the horizon.
Panthers. Bees as big as a boy's fist. Bears that won't
get out of a man's way, that will tear a body to
pieces and then go back to the business of rooting
and chuffing like hogs in the rich undergrowth. Clouds
of white butterflies that rise, then settle and
rise again on slopes thick with lilac and fern.

Now and then a real engagement with the enemy.
Much howling from their side, cries, the drum
of horses' hooves, rattle of musket fire, a Chechen's ball
smashing into a man's breast, a stain that blossoms
and spreads, that ripples over the white uniform like crimson
petals opening. Then the chase begins: hearts racing,
minds emptying out entirely as the Emperor's young
men, dandies all, gallop over plains, laughing,
yelling their lungs out. Or else they urge
their lathered horses along forest trails, pistols
ready. They burn Chechen crops, kill Chechen stock,
knock down the pitiful villages. They're soldiers,
after all, and these are not maneuvers. Shamil,
the bandit chieftain, he's the one they want most.

*

At night, a moon broad and deep as a serving dish
sallies out from behind the peaks. But this
moon is only for appearance's sake. Really, it's
armed to the teeth, like everything else out here.
When the Colonel sleeps, he dreams of a drawing room –
one drawing room in particular – oh, clean and elegant,
most comfortable drawing room! Where friends lounge
in plush chairs, or on divans, and drink from
little glasses of tea. In the dream, it is always
Thursday, 2–4. There is a piano next to the window
that looks out on Nevsky Prospect. A young woman
finishes playing, pauses, and turns to the polite
applause. But in the dream it is the Circassian
woman with a saber cut across her face. His friends
draw back in horror. They lower their eyes, bow,
and begin taking their leave. Goodbye, goodbye,
they mutter. In Petersburg they said that out here,
in the Caucasus, sunsets are everything.
But this is not true; sunsets are not enough.
In Petersburg they said the Caucasus is a country that gives
rise to legend, where heroes are born every day.
They said, long ago, in Petersburg, that reputations
were made, and lost, in the Caucasus. *A gravely
beautiful place*, as one of the Colonel's men put it.

The officers serving under him will return
home soon, and more young men will come to take
their places. After the new arrivals dismount
to pay their respects, the Colonel will keep them
waiting a time. Then fix them with a stern but
fatherly gaze, these slim young men with tiny
mustaches and boisterous high spirits, who look
at him and wonder, who ask themselves what it is
he's running from. But he's not running. He likes it
here, in the Caucasus, after a fashion. He's even
grown used to it – or nearly. There's plenty to do,

God knows. Plenty of grim work in the days, and months,
ahead. Shamil is out there in the mountains somewhere –
or maybe he's on the Steppes. The scenery is lovely,
you can be sure, and this but a rough record
of the actual and the passing.

A Forge, and a Scythe

One minute I had the windows open
and the sun was out. Warm breezes
blew through the room.
(I remarked on this in a letter.)
Then, while I watched, it grew dark.
The water began whitecapping.
All the sport-fishing boats turned
and headed in, a little fleet.
Those wind-chimes on the porch
blew down. The tops of our trees shook.
The stove pipe squeaked and rattled
around in its moorings.
I said, "A forge, and a scythe."
I talk to myself like this.
Saying the names of things –
capstan, hawser, loam, leaf, furnace.
Your face, your mouth, your shoulder
inconceivable to me now!
Where did they go? It's like
I dreamed them. The stones we brought
home from the beach lie face up
on the windowsill, cooling.
Come home. Do you hear?
My lungs are thick with the smoke
of your absence.

The Pipe

The next poem I write will have firewood
right in the middle of it, firewood so thick
with pitch my friend will leave behind
his gloves and tell me, "Wear these when you
handle that stuff." The next poem
will have night in it, too, and all the stars
in the Western Hemisphere; and an immense body
of water shining for miles under a new moon.
The next poem will have a bedroom
and living room for itself, skylights,
a sofa, a table and chairs by the window,
a vase of violets cut just an hour before lunch.
There'll be a lamp burning in the next poem;
and a fireplace where pitch-soaked
blocks of fir flame up, consuming one another.
Oh, the next poem will throw sparks!
But there won't be any cigarettes in that poem.
I'll take up smoking the pipe.

Listening

It was a night like all the others. Empty
of everything save memory. He thought
he'd got to the other side of things.
But he hadn't. He read a little
and listened to the radio. Looked out the window
for a while. Then went upstairs. In bed
realized he'd left the radio on.
But closed his eyes anyway. Inside the deep night,
as the house sailed west, he woke up
to hear voices murmuring. And froze.
Then understood it was only the radio.
He got up and went downstairs. He had
to pee anyway. A little rain

that hadn't been there before was
falling outside. The voices
on the radio faded and then came back
as if from a long way. It wasn't
the same station any longer. A man's voice
said something about Borodin,
and his opera *Prince Igor*. The woman
he said this to agreed, and laughed.
Began to tell a little of the story.
The man's hand drew back from the switch.
Once more he found himself in the presence
of mystery. Rain. Laughter. History.
Art. The hegemony of death.
He stood there, listening.

In Switzerland

First thing to do in Zurich
is take the No. 5 "Zoo" trolley
to the end of the track,
and get off. Been warned about
the lions. How their roars
carry over from the zoo compound
to the Flutern Cemetery.
Where I walk along
the very beautiful path
to James Joyce's grave.
Always the family man, he's here
with his wife, Nora, of course.
And his son, Giorgio,
who died a few years ago.
Lucia, his daughter, his sorrow,
still alive, still confined
in an institution for the insane.
When she was brought the news
of her father's death, she said:

What is he doing under the ground, that idiot?
When will he decide to come out?
He's watching us all the time.
I lingered a while. I think
I said something aloud to Mr Joyce.
I must have. I know I must have.
But I don't recall what,
now, and I'll have to leave it at that.

A week later to the day, we depart
Zurich by train for Lucerne.
But early that morning I take
the No. 5 trolley once more
to the end of the line.
The roar of the lions falls over
the cemetery, as before.
The grass has been cut.
I sit on it for a while and smoke.
Just feels good to be there,
close to the grave. I didn't
have to say anything this time.

That night we gambled at the tables
at the Grand Hotel–Casino
on the very shore of Lake Lucerne.
Took in a strip show later.
But what to do with the memory
of that grave that came to me
in the midst of the show,
under the muted, pink stage light?
Nothing to do about it.
Or about the desire that came later,
crowding everything else out,
like a wave.
Still later, we sat on a bench
under some linden trees, under stars.
Made love with each other.
Reaching into each other's clothes for it.

The lake a few steps away.
Afterwards, dipped our hands
into the cold water.
Then walked back to our hotel,
happy and tired, ready to sleep
for eight hours.

All of us, all of us, all of us
trying to save
our immortal souls, some ways
seemingly more round-
about and mysterious
than others. We're having
a good time here. But hope
all will be revealed soon.

V

A Squall

Shortly after three p.m. today a squall
hit the calm waters of the Strait.
A black cloud moving fast,
carrying rain, driven by high winds.

The water rose up and turned white.
Then, in five minutes, was as before –
blue and most remarkable, with just
a little chop. It occurs to me
it was this kind of squall
that came upon Shelley and his friend,
Williams, in the Gulf of Spezia, on
an otherwise fine day. There they were,
running ahead of a smart breeze,
wind-jamming, crying out to each other,
I want to think, in sheer exuberance.
In Shelley's jacket pockets, Keats's poems,
and a volume of Sophocles!
Then something like smoke on the water.
A black cloud moving fast,
carrying rain, driven by high winds.

Black cloud
hastening along the end
of the first romantic period
in English poetry.

My Crow

A crow flew into the tree outside my window.
It was not Ted Hughes's crow, or Galway's crow.
Or Frost's, Pasternak's, or Lorca's crow.
Or one of Homer's crows, stuffed with gore,
after the battle. This was just a crow.
That never fit in anywhere in its life,
or did anything worth mentioning.
It sat there on the branch for a few minutes.
Then picked up and flew beautifully
out of my life.

The Party

Last night, alone, 3000 miles away from the one
I love, I turned the radio on to some jazz
and made a huge bowl of popcorn
with lots of salt on it. Poured butter over it.
Turned out the lights and sat in a chair
in front of the window with the popcorn and
a can of Coke. Forgot everything important
in the world while I ate popcorn and looked out
at a heavy sea, and the lights of town.
The popcorn runny with butter, covered with
salt. I ate it up until there was nothing
left except a few Old Maids. Then
washed my hands. Smoked a couple more cigarettes
while I listened to the beat of the little
music that was left. Things had quieted way down,
though the sea was still running. Wind gave
the house a last shake when I rose
and took three steps, turned, took three more steps, turned.
Then I went to bed and slept wonderfully,
as always. My God, what a life!
But I thought I should explain, leave a note anyhow,

about this mess in the living room
and what went on here last night. Just in case
my lights went out, and I keeled over.
Yes, there was a party here last night.
And the radio's still on. Okay.
But if I die today, I die happy – thinking
of my sweetheart, and of that last popcorn.

After Rainy Days

After rainy days and the same serious doubts –
strange to walk past the golf course,
sun overhead, men putting, or teeing, whatever
they do on those green links. To the river that flows
past the clubhouse. Expensive houses on either side
of the river, a dog barking at this kid
who revs his motorcycle. To see a man fighting
a large salmon in the water just below
the footbridge. Where a couple of joggers have stopped
to watch. Never in my life have I seen anything
like this! Stay with him, I think, breaking
into a run. For Christ's sake, man, hold on!

Interview

Talking about myself all day
brought back
something I thought over and
done with. What I'd felt
for Maryann – Anna, she calls
herself now – all those years.

*

I went to draw a glass of water.
Stood at the window for a time.
When I came back
we passed easily to the next thing.
Went on with my life. But
that memory entering like a spike.

Blood

We were five at the craps table
not counting the croupier
and his assistant. The man
next to me had the dice
cupped in his hand.
He blew on his fingers, said
Come *on*, baby! And leaned
over the table to throw.
At that moment, bright blood rushed
from his nose, spattering
the green felt cloth. He dropped
the dice. Stepped back amazed.
And then terrified as blood
ran down his shirt. God,
what's happening to me?
he cried. Took hold of my arm.
I heard Death's engines turning.
But I was young at the time,
and drunk, and wanted to play.
I didn't have to listen.
So I walked away. Didn't turn back, ever,
or find this in my head, until today.

Tomorrow

Cigarette smoke hanging on
in the living room. The ship's lights
out on the water, dimming. The stars
burning holes in the sky. Becoming ash, yes.
But it's all right, they're supposed to do that.
Those lights we call stars.
Burn for a time and then die.
Me hell-bent. Wishing
it were tomorrow already.
I remember my mother, God love her,
saying, Don't wish for tomorrow.
You're wishing your life away.
Nevertheless, I wish
for tomorrow. In all its finery.
I want sleep to come and go, smoothly.
Like passing out of the door of one car
into another. And then to wake up!
Find tomorrow in my bedroom.
I'm more tired now than I can say.
My bowl is empty. But it's my bowl, you see,
and I love it.

Grief

Woke up early this morning and from my bed
looked far across the Strait to see
a small boat moving through the choppy water,
a single running light on. Remembered
my friend who used to shout
his dead wife's name from hilltops
around Perugia. Who set a plate
for her at his simple table long after
she was gone. And opened the windows

so she could have fresh air. Such display
I found embarrassing. So did his other
friends. I couldn't see it.
Not until this morning.

Harley's Swans

I'm trying again. A man has to begin
over and over — to try to think and feel
only in a very limited field, the house
on the street, the man at the corner drug store.
— SHERWOOD ANDERSON, FROM A LETTER

Anderson, I thought of you when I loitered
in front of the drug store this afternoon.
Held onto my hat in the wind and looked down
the street for my boyhood. Remembered my dad
taking me to get haircuts —

that rack of antlers mounted on a wall
next to the calendar picture of a rainbow
trout leaping clear of the water
with a hook in its jaw. My mother.
How she went with me to pick out
school clothes. That part embarrassing
because I needed to shop in men's wear
for man-sized pants and shirts.
Nobody, then, who could love me,
the fattest kid on the block, except my parents.

So I quit looking and went inside.
Had a Coke at the soda fountain
where I gave some thought to betrayal.
How that part always came easy.
It was what came after that was hard.
I didn't think about you anymore, Anderson.
You'd come and gone in an instant.

But I remembered, there at the fountain,
Harley's swans. How they got there
I don't know. But one morning he was taking
his school bus along a country road
when he came across 21 of them just down
from Canada. Out on this pond
in a farmer's field. He brought his school bus
to a stop, and then he and his grade-schoolers
just looked at them for a while and felt good.

I finished the Coke and drove home.
It was almost dark now. The house
quiet and empty. The way
I always thought I wanted it to be.
The wind blew hard all day.
Blew everything away, or nearly.
But still this feeling of shame and loss.
Even though the wind ought to lay now
and the moon come out soon, if this is
anything like the other nights.
I'm here in the house. And I want to try again.
You, of all people, Anderson, can understand.

VI

Elk Camp

Everyone else sleeping when I step
to the door of our tent. Overhead,
stars brighter than stars ever were
in my life. And farther away.
The November moon driving
a few dark clouds over the valley.
The Olympic Range beyond.

I believed I could smell the snow that was coming.
Our horses feeding inside
the little rope corral we'd thrown up.
From the side of the hill the sound
of spring water. Our spring water.
Wind passing in the tops of the fir trees.
I'd never smelled a forest before that
night, either. Remembered reading how
Henry Hudson and his sailors smelled
the forests of the New World
from miles out at sea. And then the next thought –
I could gladly live the rest of my life
and never pick up another book.
I looked at my hands in the moonlight
and understood there wasn't a man,
woman, or child I could lift a finger
for that night. I turned back and lay
down then in my sleeping bag.
But my eyes wouldn't close.

The next day I found cougar scat
and elk droppings. But though I rode
a horse all over that country,
up and down hills, through clouds

and along old logging roads,
I never saw an elk. Which was
fine by me. Still, I was ready.
Lost to everyone, a rifle strapped
to my shoulder. I think maybe
I could have killed one.
Would have shot at one, anyway.
Aimed just where I'd been told —
behind the shoulder at the heart
and lungs. "They might run,
but they won't run far.
Look at it this way," my friend said.
"How far would you run with a piece
of lead in your heart?" That depends,
my friend. That depends. But that day
I could have pulled the trigger
on anything. Or not.
Nothing mattered anymore
except getting back to camp
before dark. Wonderful
to live this way! Where nothing
mattered more than anything else.
I saw myself through and through.
And I understood something, too,
as my life flew back to me there in the woods.

And then we packed out. Where the first
thing I did was take a hot bath.
And then reach for this book.
Grow cold and unrelenting once more.
Heartless. Every nerve alert.
Ready to kill, or not.

The Windows of the Summer Vacation Houses

They withheld judgment, looking down at us
silently, in the rain, in our little boat –
as three lines went into the dark water
for salmon. I'm talking of the Hood Canal
in March, when the rain won't let up.
Which was fine by me. I was happy
to be on the water, trying out
new gear. I heard of the death,
by drowning, of a man I didn't know.
And the death in the woods of another,
hit by a snag. *They don't call them
widow-makers for nothing.*
Hunting stories of bear,
elk, deer, cougar – taken in and out
of season. More hunting stories.
Women, this time. And this time
I could join in. It used to be girls.
Girls of 15, 16, 17, 18 – and we
the same age. Now it was women. And married
women at that. No longer girls. Women.
Somebody or other's wife. The mayor
of this town, for instance. His wife.
Taken. The deputy sheriff's wife, the same.
But he's an asshole, anyway.
Even a brother's wife. *It's not anything
to be proud of, but somebody had to go
and do his homework for him.* We caught
two small ones, and talked a lot, and laughed.
But as we turned in to the landing
a light went on in one of those houses
where nobody was supposed to be.
Smoke drifted up from the chimney
of this place we'd looked at as empty.

And suddenly, like that – I remembered Maryann.
When we were both young.
The rare coin of those mint days!
It was there and gone
by the time we hooked the boat to the trailer.
But it was something to recall.
It turned dark as I watched the figure
move to stand at the window and look

down. And I knew then those things that happened
so long ago must have happened, but not
to us. No, I don't think people could go on living
if they had lived those things. It couldn't
have been us.

The people I'm talking about – I'm sure
I must have read about somewhere.
They were not the main characters, no,
as I'd thought at first and for a long
while after. But some others you
sympathized with, even loved, and cried for –
just before they were taken away
to be hanged, or put somewhere.

We drove off without looking back
at the houses. Last night
I cleaned fish in the kitchen.

This morning it was still dark
when I made coffee. And found blood
on the porcelain sides of the sink.
More blood on the counter. A trail
of it. Drops of blood on the bottom
of the refrigerator where the fish
lay wrapped and gutted.
Everywhere this blood. Mingling with thoughts
in my mind of the time we'd had –
that dear young wife, and I.

Memory [1]

Cutting the stems from a quart
basket of strawberries – the first
this spring – looking forward to how
I would eat them tonight, when I was
alone, for a treat (Tess being away),
I remembered I forgot to pass along
a message to her when we talked:
somebody whose name I forget
called to say Susan Powell's
grandmother had died, suddenly.
Went on working with the strawberries.
But remembered, too, driving back
from the store. A little girl
on roller skates being pulled along
the road by this big friendly-
looking dog. I waved to her.
She waved back. And called out
sharply to her dog, who kept
trying to nose around
in the sweet ditch grass.
    It's nearly dark outside now.
Strawberries are chilling.
A little later on, when I eat them,
I'll be reminded again – in no particular
order – of Tess, the little girl, a dog,
roller skates, memory, death, etc.

Away

I had forgotten about the quail that live
on the hillside over behind Art and Marilyn's
place. I opened up the house, made a fire,
and afterwards slept like a dead man.
The next morning there were quail in the drive

and in the bushes outside the front window.
I talked to you on the phone.
Tried to joke. Don't worry
about me, I said, I have the quail
for company. Well, they took flight
when I opened the door. A week later
and they still haven't come back. When I look
at the silent telephone I think of quail.
When I think of the quail and how they
went away, I remember talking to you that morning
and how the receiver lay in my hand. My heart —
the blurred things it was doing at the time.

Music

Franz Liszt eloped with Countess Marie d'Agoult,
who wrote novels. Polite society washed its hands
of him, and his novelist-countess-whore.
Liszt gave her three children, and music.
Then went off with Princess Wittgenstein.
Cosima, Liszt's daughter, married
the conductor, Hans von Bülow.
But Richard Wagner stole her. Took her away
to Bayreuth. Where Liszt showed up one morning.
Long white hair flouncing.
Shaking his fist. Music. Music!
Everybody grew more famous.

Plus

"Lately I've been eating a lot of pork.
Plus, I eat too many eggs and things,"
this guy said to me in the doc's office.
"I pour on the salt. I drink twenty cups
of coffee every day. I smoke.

I'm having trouble with my breathing."
Then lowered his eyes.
"Plus, I don't always clear off the table
when I'm through eating. I forget.
I just get up and walk away.
Goodbye until the next time, brother.
Mister, what do you think's happening to me?"
He was describing my own symptoms to a T.
I said, "What do you think's happening?
You're losing your marbles. And then
you're going to die. Or vice versa.
What about sweets? Are you partial
to cinnamon rolls and ice cream?"
"Plus, I crave all that," he said.
By this time we were at a place called Friendly's.
We looked at menus and went on talking.
Dinner music played from a radio
in the kitchen. It was our song, see.
It was our table.

All Her Life

I lay down for a nap. But every time I closed my eyes,
mares' tails passed slowly over the Strait
toward Canada. And the waves. They rolled up on the beach
and then back again. You know I don't dream.
But last night I dreamt we were watching
a burial at sea. At first I was astonished.
And then filled with regret. But you
touched my arm and said, "No, it's all right.
She was very old, and he'd loved her all her life."

The Hat

Walking around on our first day
in Mexico City, we come to a sidewalk café
on Reforma Avenue where a man in a hat
sits drinking a beer.
At first the man seems just like any
other man, wearing a hat, drinking a beer
in the middle of the day. But next to this man,
asleep on the broad sidewalk, is a bear
with its head on its paws. The bear's
eyes are closed, but not all the way. As if
it were there, and not there. Everyone

is giving the bear a wide berth.
But a crowd is gathering, too, bulging
out onto the Avenue. The man has
a chain around his waist. The chain
goes from his lap to the bear's collar,
a band of steel. On the table
in front of the man rests an iron bar
with a leather handle. And as if this
were not enough, the man drains the last
of his beer and picks up his bar.
Gets up from the table and hauls
on the chain. The bear stirs, opens its
mouth – old brown and yellow fangs.
But fangs. The man jerks on the chain,
hard. The bear rises to all fours now
and growls. The man slaps the bear on
its shoulder with the bar, bringing
a tiny cloud of dust. Growls something
himself. The bear waits while the man takes
another swing. Slowly, the bear rises
onto its hind legs, swings at air and at
that goddamned bar. Begins to shuffle

then, begins to snap its jaws as the man
slugs it again, and, yes, again

with that bar. There's a tamborine.
I nearly forgot that. The man shakes
it as he chants, as he strikes the bear
who weaves on its hind legs. Growls
and snaps and weaves in a poor dance.
This scene lasts forever. Whole seasons
come and go before it's over and the bear
drops to all fours. Sits down on its
haunches, gives a low, sad growl.
The man puts the tamborine on the table.
Puts the iron bar on the table, too.
Then he takes off his hat. No one
applauds. A few people see
what's coming and walk away. But not
before the hat appears at the edge
of the crowd and begins to make its
way from hand to hand
through the throng. The hat
comes to me and stops. I'm holding
the hat, and I can't believe it.
Everybody staring at it.
I stare right along with them.
You say my name, and in the same breath
hiss, "For God's sake, pass it along."
I toss in the money I have. Then
we leave and go on to the next thing.

Hours later, in bed, I touch you
and wait, and then touch you again.
Whereupon, you uncurl your fingers.
I put my hands all over you then —
your limbs, your long hair even, hair
that I touch and cover my face with,
and draw salt from. But later,

when I close my eyes, the hat
appears. Then the tamborine. The chain.

Late Night with Fog and Horses

They were in the living room. Saying their
goodbyes. Loss ringing in their ears.
They'd been through a lot together, but now
they couldn't go another step. Besides, for him
there was someone else. Tears were falling
when a horse stepped out of the fog
into the front yard. Then another, and
another. She went outside and said,
"Where did you come from, you sweet horses?"
and moved in amongst them, weeping,
touching their flanks. The horses began
to graze in the front yard.
He made two calls: one call went straight
to the sheriff — "someone's horses are out."
But there was that other call, too.
Then he joined his wife in the front
yard, where they talked and murmured
to the horses together. (Whatever was
happening now was happening in another time.)
Horses cropped the grass in the yard
that night. A red emergency light
flashed as a sedan crept in out of fog.
Voices carried out of the fog.
At the end of that long night,
when they finally put their arms around
each other, their embrace was full of
passion and memory. Each recalled
the other's youth. Now something had ended,
something else rushing in to take its place.
Came the moment of leave-taking itself.

"Goodbye, go on," she said.
And the pulling away.
Much later,
he remembered making a disastrous phone call.
One that had hung on and hung on,
a malediction. It's boiled down
to that. The rest of his life.
Malediction.

Venice

The gondolier handed you a rose.
Took us up one canal
and then another. We glided
past Casanova's palace, the palace of
the Rossi family, palaces belonging
to the Baglioni, the Pisani, and Sangallo.
Flooded. Stinking. What's left
left to rats. Blackness.
The silence total, or nearly.
The man's breath coming and going
behind my ear. The drip of the oar.
We gliding silently on, and on.
Who would blame me if I fall
to thinking about death?
A shutter opened above our heads.
A little light showed through
before the shutter was closed once
more. There is that, and the rose
in your hand. And history.

The Eve of Battle

There are five of us in the tent, not counting
the batman cleaning my rifle. There's
a lively argument going on amongst my brother
officers. In the cookpot, salt pork turns
alongside some macaroni. But these fine fellows
aren't hungry – and it's a good thing!
All they want is to harrumph about the likes
of Huss and Hegel, anything to pass the time.
Who cares? Tomorrow we fight. Tonight they want
to sit around and chatter about nothing, about
philosophy. Maybe the cookpot isn't there
for them? Nor the stove, or those folding
stools they're sitting on. Maybe there isn't
a battle waiting for them tomorrow morning?
We'd all like that best. Maybe
I'm not there for them, either. Ready
to dish up something to eat. *Un est autre*,
as someone said. I, or another, may as well be
in China. Time to eat, brothers,
I say, handing round the plates. But someone
has just ridden up and dismounted. My batman
moves to the door of the tent, then drops his plate
and steps back. Death walks in without saying
anything, dressed in coat-and-tails.
At first I think he must be looking for the Emperor,
who's old and ailing anyway. That would explain
it. Death's lost his way. What else could it be?
He has a slip of paper in his hand, looks us over
quickly, consults some names.
He raises his eyes. I turn to the stove.
When I turn back, everyone has gone. Everyone
except Death. He's still there, unmoving.
I give him his plate. He's come a long
way. He is hungry, I think, and will eat anything.

Extirpation

A little quietly outstanding uptown
piano music played in the background
as we sat at the bar in the lounge.

Discussing the fate of the last caribou herd in the US.
Thirty animals who roam a small corner
of the Idaho Panhandle. Thirty animals

just north of Bonner's Ferry,
this guy said. Then called for another round.
But I had to go. We never saw each other again.

Never spoke another word to each other,
or did anything worth getting excited about
the rest of our lives.

The Catch

Happy to have these fish!
In spite of the rain, they came
to the surface and took
the No. 14 Black Mosquito.
He had to concentrate,
close everything else out
for a change. His old life,
which he carried around
like a pack. And the new one,
that one too. Time and again
he made what he felt were the most
intimate of human movements.
Strained his heart to see
the difference between a raindrop
and a brook trout. Later,
walking across the wet field
to the car. Watching

the wind change the aspen trees.
He abandoned everyone
he once loved.

My Death

If I'm lucky, I'll be wired every whichway
in a hospital bed. Tubes running into
my nose. But try not to be scared of me, friends!
I'm telling you right now that this is okay.
It's little enough to ask for at the end.
Someone, I hope, will have phoned everyone
to say, "Come quick, he's failing!"
And they will come. And there will be time for me
to bid goodbye to each of my loved ones.
If I'm lucky, they'll step forward
and I'll be able to see them one last time
and take that memory with me.
Sure, they might lay eyes on me and want to run away
and howl. But instead, since they love me,
they'll lift my hand and say "Courage"
or "It's going to be all right."
And they're right. It is all right.
It's just fine. If you only knew how happy you've made me!
I just hope my luck holds, and I can make
some sign of recognition.
Open and close my eyes as if to say,
"Yes, I hear you. I understand you."
I may even manage something like this:
"I love you too. Be happy."
I hope so! But I don't want to ask for too much.
If I'm unlucky, as I deserve, well, I'll just
drop over, like that, without any chance
for farewell, or to press anyone's hand.
Or say how much I cared for you and enjoyed

your company all these years. In any case,
try not to mourn for me too much. I want you to know
I was happy when I was here.
And remember I told you this a while ago – April 1984.
But be glad for me if I can die in the presence
of friends and family. If this happens, believe me,
I came out ahead. I didn't lose this one.

To Begin With

He took a room in a port city with a fellow
called Sulieman A. Sulieman and his wife,
an American known only as Bonnie. One thing
he remembered about his stay there
was how every evening Sulieman rapped
at his own front door before entering.
Saying, "Right, hello. Sulieman here."
After that, Sulieman taking off his shoes.
Putting pita bread and hummus into his mouth
in the company of his silent wife.
Sometimes there was a piece of chicken
followed by cucumbers and tomatoes.
Then they all watched what passed for TV
in that country. Bonnie sitting in a chair
to herself, raving against the Jews.
At eleven o'clock she would say, "We have to sleep now."

But once they left their bedroom door open.
And he saw Sulieman make his bed on the floor
beside the big bed where Bonnie lay
and looked down at her husband.
They said something to each other in a foreign language.
Sulieman arranged his shoes by his head.
Bonnie turned off the light, and they slept.
But the man in the room at the back of the house

couldn't sleep at all. It was as if
he didn't believe in sleep any longer.
Sleep had been all right, once, in its time.
But it was different now.

Lying there at night, eyes open, arms at his sides,
his thoughts went out to his wife,
and his children, and everything that bore
on that leave-taking. Even the shoes
he'd been wearing when he left his house
and walked out. They were the real betrayers,
he decided. They'd brought him all this way
without once trying to do anything to stop him.
Finally, his thoughts came back to this room
and this house. Where they belonged.
Where he knew he was home.
Where a man slept on the floor of his own bedroom.
A man who knocked at the door of his own house,
announcing his meager arrival. Sulieman.
Who entered his house only after knocking
and then to eat pita bread and tomatoes
with his bitter wife. But in the course of those long nights
he began to envy Sulieman a little.
Not much, but a little. And so what if he did!
Sulieman sleeping on his bedroom floor.
But Sulieman sleeping in the same room,
at least, as his wife.

Maybe it was all right if she snored
and had blind prejudices. She wasn't so bad-
looking, that much was true, and if
Sulieman woke up he could at least
hear her from his place. Know she was there.
There might even be nights when he could reach
over and touch her through the blanket
without waking her. Bonnie. His wife.

*

124

Maybe in this life it was necessary to learn
to pretend to be a dog and sleep on the floor
in order to get along. Sometimes
this might be necessary. Who knows
anything these days?
At least it was a new idea and something,
he thought, he might have to try and understand.
Outside, the moon reached over the water
and disappeared finally. Footsteps

moved slowly down the street and came to a stop
outside his window. The streetlight
went out, and the steps passed on.
The house became still and, in one way at least,
like all the other houses – totally dark.
He held onto his blanket and stared at the ceiling.
He had to start over. To begin with –
the oily smell of the sea, the rotting tomatoes.

The Cranes

Cranes lifting up out of the marshland . . .
My brother brings his fingers to his temples
and then drops his hands.

Like that, he was dead.
The satin lining of autumn.
O my brother! I miss you now, and I'd like to have you back.

Hug you like a grown man
who knows the worth of things.
The mist of events drifts away.

Not in this life, I told you once.
I was given a different set of marching orders.
I planned to go mule-backing across the Isthmus.

*

Begone, though, if this is your idea of things!
But I'll think of you out there
when I look at those stars we saw as children.

The cranes wallop their wings.
In a moment, they'll find true north.
Then turn in the opposite direction.

VII

A Haircut

So many impossible things have already
happened in this life. He doesn't think
twice when she tells him to get ready:
He's about to get a haircut.

He sits in the chair in the upstairs room,
the room they sometimes joke and refer to
as the library. There's a window there
that gives light. Snow's coming
down outside as newspapers go down
around his feet. She drapes a big
towel over his shoulders. Then
gets out her scissors, comb, and brush.

This is the first time they've been
alone together in a while – with nobody
going anywhere, or needing to do
anything. Not counting the going
to bed with each other. That intimacy.
Or breakfasting together. Another
intimacy. They both grow quiet
and thoughtful as she cuts his hair,
and combs it, and cuts some more.
The snow keeps falling outside.
Soon, light begins to pull away from
the window. He stares down, lost and
musing, trying to read
something from the paper. She says,
"Raise your head." And he does.
And then she says, "See what you think

of it." He goes to look
in the mirror, and it's fine.
It's just the way he likes it,
and he tells her so.

It's later, when he turns on the
porchlight, and shakes out the towel
and sees the curls and swaths of
white and dark hair fly out onto
the snow and stay there,
that he understands something: He's
grownup now, a real, grownup,
middle-aged man. When he was a boy,
going with his dad to the barbershop,
or even later, a teenager, how
could he have imagined his life
would someday allow him the privilege of
a beautiful woman to travel with,
and sleep with, and take his breakfast with?
Not only that — a woman who would
quietly cut his hair in the afternoon
in a dark city that lay under snow
3000 miles away from where he'd started.
A woman who could look at him
across the table and say,
"It's time to put you in the barber's
chair. It's time somebody gave you
a haircut."

Happiness in Cornwall

His wife died, and he grew old
between the graveyard and his
front door. Walked with a gait.
Shoulders bent. He let his clothes
go, and his long hair turned white.

His children found him somebody.
A big middle-aged woman with
heavy shoes who knew how to
mop, wax, dust, shop, and carry in
firewood. Who could live
in a room at the back of the house.
Prepare meals. And slowly,
slowly bring the old man around
to listening to her read poetry
in the evenings in front of
the fire. Tennyson, Browning,
Shakespeare, Drinkwater. Men
whose names take up space
on the page. She was the butler,
cook, housekeeper. And after
a time, oh, no one knows or cares
when, they began to dress up
on Sundays and stroll through town.
She with her arm through his.
Smiling. He proud and happy
and with his hand on hers.
No one denied them
or tried to diminish this
in any way. Happiness is
a rare thing! Evenings he
listened to poetry, poetry, poetry
in front of the fire.
Couldn't get enough of that life.

Afghanistan

The sad music of roads lined with larches.
The forest in the distance resting under snow.

The Khyber Pass. Alexander the Great.
History, and lapis lazuli.

*

No books, no pictures, no knick-knacks please me.
But she pleases me. And lapis lazuli.

That blue stone she wears on her dear finger.
That pleases me exceedingly.

The bucket clatters into the well.
And brings up water with a sweet taste to it.

The towpath along the river. The footpath
Through the grove of almonds. My love

Goes everywhere in her sandals.
And wears lapis lazuli on her finger.

In a Marine Light near Sequim, Washington

The green fields were beginning. And the tall, white
farmhouses after the tidal flats and those little sand crabs
that were ready to run, or else turn and square off, if
we moved the rock they lived under. The languor
of that subdued afternoon. The beauty of driving
that country road. Talking of Paris, our Paris.
And then you finding that place in the book
and reading to me about Anna Akhmatova's stay there with
    Modigliani.
Them sitting on a bench in the Luxembourg Gardens
under his enormous old black umbrella
reciting Verlaine to each other. Both of them
"as yet untouched by their futures." When
out in the field we saw
a bare-chested young man with his trousers rolled up,
like an ancient oarsman. He looked at us without curiosity.
Stood there and gazed indifferently.
Then turned his back to us and went on with his work.
As we passed like a beautiful black scythe
through that perfect landscape.

Eagles

It was a sixteen-inch ling cod that the eagle
dropped near our feet
at the top of Bagley Creek canyon,
at the edge of the green woods.
Puncture marks in the sides of the fish
where the bird gripped with its talons!
That and a piece torn out of the fish's back.
Like an old painting recalled,
or an ancient memory coming back,
that eagle flew with the fish from the Strait
of Juan de Fuca up the canyon to where
the woods begin, and we stood watching.
It lost the fish above our heads,
dropped for it, missed it, and soared on
over the valley where wind beats all day.
We watched it keep going until it was
a speck, then gone. I picked up
the fish. That miraculous ling cod.
Came home from the walk and –
why the hell not? – cooked it
lightly in oil and ate it
with boiled potatoes and peas and biscuits.
Over dinner, talking about eagles
and an older, fiercer order of things.

Yesterday, Snow

Yesterday, snow was falling and all was chaos.
I don't dream, but in the night I dreamed
a man offered me some of his whiskey.
I wiped the mouth of the bottle
and raised it to my lips.
It was like one of those dreams of falling
where, they say, if you don't wake up

before you hit the ground,
you'll die. I woke up! Sweating.
Outside, the snow had quit.
But, my God, it looked cold. Fearsome.
The windows were ice to the touch
when I touched them. I got back
in bed and lay there the rest of the night,
afraid I'd sleep again. And find
myself back in that dream . . .
The bottle rising to my lips.
The indifferent man
waiting for me to drink and pass it on again.
A skewed moon hangs on until morning,
and a brilliant sun.
Before now, I never knew what it meant
to "spring out of bed."
    All day snow flopping off roofs.
The crunch of tires and footsteps.
Next door, there's an old fellow shoveling.
Every so often he stops and leans
on his shovel, and rests, letting
his thoughts go where they may.
Staying his heart.
Then he nods and grips his shovel.
Goes on, yes. Goes on.

Reading Something in the Restaurant

This morning I remembered the young man
with his book, reading at a table
by the window last night. Reading
amidst the coming and going of dishes
and voices. Now and then he looked
up and passed his finger across
his lips, as if pondering something,

or quieting the thoughts inside
his mind, the going
and coming inside his mind. Then
he lowered his head and went back
to reading. That memory
gets into my head this morning
with the memory of
the girl who entered the restaurant
that time long ago and stood shaking her hair.
Then sat down across from me
without taking her coat off.
I put down whatever book it was
I was reading, and she at once
started to tell me there was
not a snowball's chance in hell
this thing was going to fly.
She knew it. Then I came around
to knowing it. But it was
hard. This morning, my sweet,
you ask me what's new
in the world. But my concentration
is shot. At the table next
to ours a man laughs and laughs
and shakes his head at what
another fellow is telling him.
But what was that young man reading?
Where did that woman go?
I've lost my place. Tell me what it is
you wanted to know.

A Poem Not against Songbirds

Lighten up, songbirds. Give me a break.
No need to carry on this way,
even if it is morning. I need more sleep.

*

Where were you keeping yourselves when I was thirty?
When the house stayed dark and quiet all day,
as if somebody had died?

And this same somebody, or somebody else,
cooked a huge, morose meal for the survivors.
A meal that lasted ten years.

Go on, sweethearts. Come back in an hour,
my friends. Then I'll be wide awake.
You'll see. This time I can promise.

Late Afternoon, April 8, 1984

A little sport-fishing boat
    wallowing
in the rough waters of the Strait.
I put the glasses on him.
Old guy in a canvas hat,
looking grim. Worried,
as he should be.
The other boats have come in
long ago, counting
their blessings.
This fisherman
had to be clear out to Green Point
where giant halibut school.
When the wind struck!
Such force it bent the trees
and caused the water
to stand up.
As it's standing now.

But he'll make it!
If he keeps the bow into
the wind, and if he's lucky.
Even so I look up

the Coast Guard emergency number.
But I don't use it.
I keep watching – an hour, maybe less –
who knows what passes
through his mind, and mine,
in that time?
Then he turns in to the harbor,
where at once it grows calmer.
Takes off his hat then and waves it
like mad – like an old-time cowboy!
Something he won't ever forget.
You betcha.
    Me neither.

My Work

I look up and see them starting
down the beach. The young man
is wearing a packboard to carry the baby.
This leaves his hands free
so that he can take one of his wife's hands
in his, and swing his other. Anyone can see
how happy they are. And intimate. How steady.
They are happier than anyone else, and they know it.
Are gladdened by it, and humbled.
They walk to the end of the beach
and out of sight. That's it, I think,
and return to this thing governing
my life. But in a few minutes

they come walking back along the beach.
The only thing different
is that they have changed sides.
He is on the other side of her now,
the ocean side. She is on this side.
But they are still holding hands. Even more

in love, if that's possible. And it is.
Having been there for a long time myself.
Theirs has been a modest walk, fifteen minutes
down the beach, fifteen minutes back.
They've had to pick their way
over some rocks and around huge logs,
tossed up from when the sea ran wild.

They walk quietly, slowly, holding hands.
They know the water is out there
but they're so happy that they ignore it.
The love in their young faces. The surround of it.
Maybe it *will* last forever. If they are lucky,
and good, and forebearing. And careful. If they
go on loving each other without stint.
Are true to each other — that most of all.
As they will be, of course, as they will be,
as they know they will be.
I go back to my work. My work goes back to me.
A wind picks up out over the water.

The Trestle

I've wasted my time this morning, and I'm deeply ashamed.
I went to bed last night thinking about my dad.
About that little river we used to fish — Butte Creek —
near Lake Almanor. Water lulled me to sleep.
In my dream, it was all I could do not to get up
and move around. But when I woke early this morning
I went to the telephone instead. Even though
the river was flowing down there in the valley,
in the meadows, moving through ditch clover.
Fir trees stood on both sides of the meadows. And I was there.
A kid sitting on a timber trestle, looking down.
Watching my dad drink from his cupped hands.
Then he said, "This water's so good.

I wish I could give my mother some of this water."
My dad still loved her, though she was dead
and he'd been away from her for a long time.
He had to wait some more years
until he could go where she was. But he loved
this country where he found himself. The West.
For thirty years it had him around the heart,
and then it let him go. He went to sleep one night
in a town in northern California
and didn't wake up. What could be simpler?

I wish my own life, and death, could be so simple.
So that when I woke on a fine morning like this,
after being somewhere I wanted to be all night,
somewhere important, I could move most naturally
and without thinking about it, to my desk.

Say I did that, in the simple way I've described.
From bed to desk back to childhood.
From there it's not so far to the trestle.
And from the trestle I could look down
and see my dad when I needed to see him.
My dad drinking that cold water. My sweet father.
The river, its meadows, and firs, and the trestle.
That. Where I once stood.

I wish I could do that
without having to plead with myself for it.
And feel sick of myself
for getting involved in lesser things.
I know it's time I changed my life.
This life – the one with its complications
and phone calls – is unbecoming,
and a waste of time.
I want to plunge my hands in clear water. The way
he did. Again and then again.

For Tess

Out on the Strait the water is whitecapping,
as they say here. It's rough, and I'm glad
I'm not out. Glad I fished all day
on Morse Creek, casting a red Daredevil back
and forth. I didn't catch anything. No bites
even, not one. But it was okay. It was fine!
I carried your dad's pocketknife and was followed
for a while by a dog its owner called Dixie.
At times I felt so happy I had to quit
fishing. Once I lay on the bank with my eyes closed,
listening to the sound the water made,
and to the wind in the tops of the trees. The same wind
that blows out on the Strait, but a different wind, too.
For a while I even let myself imagine I had died –
and that was all right, at least for a couple
of minutes, until it really sank in: *Dead*.
As I was lying there with my eyes closed,
just after I'd imagined what it might be like
if in fact I never got up again, I thought of you.
I opened my eyes then and got right up
and went back to being happy again.
I'm grateful to you, you see. I wanted to tell you.

Ultramarine

> ... *sick*
> *With exile, they yearn homeward now, their eyes*
> *Tuned to the ultramarine, first-star-pierced dark*
> *Reflected on the dark, incoming waves* ...

— DEREK MAHON
from "Mt Gabriel" in *Antarctica* (1985)

I

This Morning

This morning was something. A little snow
lay on the ground. The sun floated in a clear
blue sky. The sea was blue, and blue-green,
as far as the eye could see.
Scarcely a ripple. Calm. I dressed and went
for a walk – determined not to return
until I took in what Nature had to offer.
I passed close to some old, bent-over trees.
Crossed a field strewn with rocks
where snow had drifted. Kept going
until I reached the bluff.
Where I gazed at the sea, and the sky, and
the gulls wheeling over the white beach
far below. All lovely. All bathed in a pure
cold light. But, as usual, my thoughts
began to wander. I had to will
myself to see what I was seeing
and nothing else. I had to tell myself *this* is what
mattered, not the other. (And I did see it,
for a minute or two!) For a minute or two
it crowded out the usual musings on
what was right, and what was wrong – duty,
tender memories, thoughts of death, how I should treat
with my former wife. All the things
I hoped would go away this morning.
The stuff I live with every day. What
I've trampled on in order to stay alive.
But for a minute or two I did forget
myself and everything else. I know I did.

For when I turned back I didn't know
where I was. Until some birds rose up
from the gnarled trees. And flew
in the direction I needed to be going.

What You Need for Painting

from a letter by Renoir

THE PALETTE:

Flake white	Rose madder
Chrome yellow	Cobalt blue
Naples yellow	Ultramarine blue
Yellow ocher	Emerald green
Raw umber	Ivory black
Venetian red	Raw sienna
French vermilion	Viridian green
Madder lake	White lead

DON'T FORGET:
Palette knife
Scraping knife
Essence of turpentine

BRUSHES?
Pointed marten-hair brushes
Flat hog-hair brushes

Indifference to everything except your canvas.
The ability to work like a locomotive.
An iron will.

An Afternoon

As he writes, without looking at the sea,
he feels the tip of his pen begin to tremble.
The tide is going out across the shingle.
But it isn't that. No,
it's because at that moment she chooses
to walk into the room without any clothes on.
Drowsy, not even sure where she is
for a moment. She waves the hair from her forehead.
Sits on the toilet with her eyes closed,
head down. Legs sprawled. He sees her
through the doorway. Maybe
she's remembering what happened that morning.
For after a time, she opens one eye and looks at him.
And sweetly smiles.

Circulation

And all at length are gathered in.
— LOUISE BOGAN

By the time I came around to feeling pain
and woke up, moonlight
flooded the room. My arm lay paralyzed,
propped like an old anchor under
your back. You were in a dream,
you said later, where you'd arrived
early for the dance. But after
a moment's anxiety you were okay
because it was really a sidewalk
sale, and the shoes you were wearing,
or not wearing, were fine for that.

*

"Help me," I said. And tried to hoist
my arm. But it just lay there, aching,
unable to rise on its own. Even after
you said "What is it? What's wrong?"
it stayed put — deaf, unmoved
by any expression of fear or amazement.
We shouted at it, and grew afraid
when it didn't answer. "It's gone to sleep,"
I said, and hearing those words
knew how absurd this was. But
I couldn't laugh. Somehow,
between the two of us, we managed
to raise it. *This can't be my arm*
is what I kept thinking as
we thumped it, squeezed it, and
prodded it back to life. Shook it
until that stinging went away.

We said a few words to each other.
I don't remember what. Whatever
reassuring things people
who love each other say to each other
given the hour and such odd
circumstance. I do remember
you remarked how it was light
enough in the room that you could see
circles under my eyes.
You said I needed more regular sleep,
and I agreed. Each of us went
to the bathroom, and climbed back in bed
on our respective sides.
Pulled the covers up. "Good night,"
you said, for the second time that night.
And fell asleep. Maybe
into that same dream, or else another.

*

I lay until daybreak, holding
both arms fast across my chest.
Working my fingers now and then.
While my thoughts kept circling
around and around, but always going back
where they'd started from.
That one inescapable fact: even while
we undertake this trip,
there's another, far more bizarre,
we still have to make.

The Cobweb

A few minutes ago, I stepped onto the deck
of the house. From there I could see and hear the water,
and everything that's happened to me all these years.
It was hot and still. The tide was out.
No birds sang. As I leaned against the railing
a cobweb touched my forehead.
It caught in my hair. No one can blame me that I turned
and went inside. There was no wind. The sea
was dead calm. I hung the cobweb from the lampshade.
Where I watch it shudder now and then when my breath
touches it. A fine thread. Intricate.
Before long, before anyone realizes,
I'll be gone from here.

Balsa Wood

My dad is at the stove in front of a pan with brains
and eggs. But who has any appetite
this morning? I feel flimsy as
balsa wood. Something has just been said.
My mom said it. What was it? Something,
I'll bet, that bears on money. I'll do my part

if I don't eat. Dad turns his back on the stove.
"I'm in a hole. Don't dig me deeper."
Light leaks in from the window. Someone's crying.
The last thing I recall is the smell
of burned brains and eggs. The whole morning
is shoveled into the garbage and mixed
with other things. Sometime later
he and I drive to the dump, ten miles out.
We don't talk. We throw our bags and cartons
onto a dark mound. Rats screech.
They whistle as they crawl out of rotten sacks
dragging their bellies. We get back in the car
to watch the smoke and fire. The motor's running.
I smell the airplane glue on my fingers.
He looks at me as I bring my fingers to my nose.
Then looks away again, toward town.
He wants to say something but can't.
He's a million miles away. We're both far away
from there, and still someone's crying. Even then
I was beginning to understand how it's possible
to be in one place. And someplace else, too.

The Projectile

FOR HARUKI MURAKAMI

We sipped tea. Politely musing
on possible reasons for the success
of my books in your country. Slipped
into talk of pain and humiliation
you find occurring, and reoccurring,
in my stories. And that element
of sheer chance. How all this translates
in terms of sales.
I looked into a corner of the room.
And for a minute I was 16 again,
careening around in the snow

in a '50 Dodge sedan with five or six
bozos. Giving the finger
to some other bozos, who yelled and pelted
our car with snowballs, gravel, old
tree branches. We spun away, shouting.
And we were going to leave it at that.
But my window was down three inches.
Only three inches. I hollered out
one last obscenity. And saw this guy
wind up to throw. From this vantage,
now, I imagine I see it coming. See it
speeding through the air while I watch,
like those soldiers in the first part
of the last century watched canisters
of shot fly in their direction
while they stood, unable to move
for the dread fascination of it.
But I *didn't* see it. I'd already turned
my head to laugh with my pals.
When something slammed into the side
of my head so hard it broke my eardrum and fell
in my lap, intact. A ball of packed ice
and snow. The pain was stupendous.
And the humiliation.
It was awful when I began to weep
in front of those tough guys while they
cried, *Dumb luck. Freak accident.*
A chance in a million!
The guy who threw it, he had to be amazed
and proud of himself while he took
the shouts and backslaps of the others.
He must have wiped his hands on his pants.
And messed around a little more
before going home to supper. He grew up
to have his share of setbacks and got lost
in his life, same as I got lost in mine.

He never gave that afternoon
another thought. And why should he?
So much else to think about always.
Why remember that stupid car sliding
down the road, then turning the corner
and disappearing?
We politely raise our teacups in the room.
A room that for a minute something else entered.

The Mail

On my desk, a picture postcard from my son
in southern France. The Midi,
he calls it. Blue skies. Beautiful houses
loaded with begonias. Nevertheless
he's going under, needs money fast.

Next to his card, a letter
from my daughter telling me her old man,
the speed-freak, is tearing down
a motorcycle in the living room.
They're existing on oatmeal,
she and her children. For God's sake,
she could use some help.

And there's the letter from my mother
who is sick and losing her mind.
She tells me she won't be here
much longer. Won't I help her make
this one last move? Can't I pay
for her to have a home of her own?

I go outside. Thinking to walk
to the graveyard for some comfort.
But the sky is in turmoil.
The clouds, huge and swollen with darkness,
about to spew open.

It's then the postman turns into
the drive. His face
is a reptile's, glistening and working.
His hand goes back – as if to strike!
It's the mail.

The Autopsy Room

Then I was young and had the strength of ten.
For anything, I thought. Though part of my job
at night was to clean the autopsy room
once the coroner's work was done. But now
and then they knocked off early, or too late.
For, so help me, they left things out
on their specially built table. A little baby,
still as a stone and snow cold. Another time,
a huge black man with white hair whose chest
had been laid open. All his vital organs
lay in a pan beside his head. The hose
was running, the overhead lights blazed.
And one time there was a leg, a woman's leg,
on the table. A pale and shapely leg.
I knew it for what it was. I'd seen them before.
Still, it took my breath away.

When I went home at night my wife would say,
"Sugar, it's going to be all right. We'll trade
this life in for another." But it wasn't
that easy. She'd take my hand between her hands
and hold it tight, while I leaned back on the sofa
and closed my eyes. Thinking of . . . something.
I don't know what. But I'd let her bring
my hand to her breast. At which point
I'd open my eyes and stare at the ceiling, or else
the floor. Then my fingers strayed to her leg.
Which was warm and shapely, ready to tremble

and raise slightly, at the slightest touch.
But my mind was unclear and shaky. Nothing
was happening. Everything was happening. Life
was a stone, grinding and sharpening.

Where They'd Lived

Everywhere he went that day he walked
in his own past. Kicked through piles
of memories. Looked through windows
that no longer belonged to him.
Work and poverty and short change.
In those days they'd lived by their wills,
determined to be invincible.
Nothing could stop them. Not
for the longest while.

                     In the motel room
that night, in the early morning hours,
he opened a curtain. Saw clouds
banked against the moon. He leaned
closer to the glass. Cold air passed
through and put its hand over his heart.
I loved you, he thought.
Loved you well.
Before loving you no longer.

Memory [2]

She lays her hand on his shoulder
at the checkout stand. But he won't
go with her, and shakes his head.

                *

She insists! He pays. She walks out
with him to his big car, takes one look,
laughs at it. Touches his cheek.

Leaves him with his groceries
in the parking lot. Feeling foolish.
Feeling diminished. Still paying.

The Car

The car with a cracked windshield.
The car that threw a rod.
The car without brakes.
The car with a faulty U-joint.
The car with a hole in its radiator.
The car I picked peaches for.
The car with a cracked block.
The car with no reverse gear.
The car I traded for a bicycle.
The car with steering problems.
The car with generator trouble.
The car with no back seat.
The car with the torn front seat.
The car that burned oil.
The car with rotten hoses.
The car that left the restaurant without paying.
The car with bald tires.
The car with no heater or defroster.
The car with its front end out of alignment.
The car the child threw up in.
The car *I* threw up in.
The car with the broken water pump.
The car whose timing gear was shot.
The car with a blown head-gasket.
The car I left on the side of the road.
The car that leaked carbon monoxide.

The car with a sticky carburetor.
The car that hit the dog and kept going.
The car with a hole in its muffler.
The car with no muffler.
The car my daughter wrecked.
The car with the twice-rebuilt engine.
The car with corroded battery cables.
The car bought with a bad check.
Car of my sleepless nights.
The car with a stuck thermostat.
The car whose engine caught fire.
The car with no headlights.
The car with a broken fan belt.
The car with wipers that wouldn't work.
The car I gave away.
The car with transmission trouble.
The car I washed my hands of.
The car I struck with a hammer.
The car with payments that couldn't be met.
The repossessed car.
The car whose clutch-pin broke.
The car waiting on the back lot.
Car of my dreams.
My car.

Stupid

It's what the kids nowadays call weed. And it drifts
like clouds from his lips. He hopes no one
comes along tonight, or calls to ask for help.
Help is what he's most short on tonight.
A storm thrashes outside. Heavy seas
with gale winds from the west. The table he sits at
is, say, two cubits long and one wide.
The darkness in the room teems with insight.
Could be he'll write an adventure novel. Or else

a children's story. A play for two female characters,
one of whom is blind. Cutthroat should be coming
into the river. One thing he'll do is learn
to tie his own flies. Maybe he should give
more money to each of his surviving
family members. The ones who already expect a little
something in the mail first of each month.
Every time they write they tell him
they're coming up short. He counts heads on his fingers
and finds they're all surviving. So what
if he'd rather be remembered in the dreams of strangers?
He raises his eyes to the skylights where rain
hammers on. After a while –
who knows how long? – his eyes ask
that they be closed. And he closes them.
But the rain keeps hammering. Is this a cloudburst?
Should he do something? Secure the house
in some way? Uncle Bo stayed married to Aunt Ruby
for 47 years. Then hanged himself.
He opens his eyes again. Nothing adds up.
It all adds up. How long will this storm go on?

Union Street: San Francisco, Summer 1975

In those days we were going places. But that Sunday
afternoon we were becalmed. Sitting around a table,
drinking and swapping stories. A party that'd been
going on, and off, since Friday a year ago.
Then Guy's wife was dropped off in front of the apartment
by her boyfriend, and came upstairs.
It's Guy's birthday, after all, give or take a day.
They haven't seen each other for a week,
more or less. She's all dressed up. He embraces her,
sort of, makes her a drink. Finds a place
for her at the table. Everyone wants to know
how she is, etc. But she ignores them all.

All those alcoholics. Clearly, she's pissed off
and as usual in the wrong company.
Where the hell has Guy been keeping himself?
she wants to know. She sips her drink and looks at him
as if he's brain-damaged. She spots a pimple
on his chin; it's an ingrown hair but it's filled
with pus, frightful, looks like hell. In front
of everyone she says, "Who have *you* been eating out
lately?" Staring hard at his pimple.
Being drunk myself, I don't recall how he answered.
Maybe he said, "I don't remember who it was;
I didn't get her name." Something smart.
Anyway, his wife has this kind of blistery rash,
maybe it's cold sores, at the edge of her mouth,
so she shouldn't be talking. Pretty soon,
it's like always: they're holding hands and laughing
like the rest of us, at little or nothing.

              Later, in the living room,
thinking everyone had gone out for hamburgers,
she blew him in front of the TV. Then said,
"Happy birthday, you son of a bitch!" And slapped his
glasses off. The glasses he'd been wearing
while she made love to him. I walked into the room
and said, "Friends, don't do this to each other."
She didn't flinch a muscle or wonder aloud
which rock I'd come out from under. All she said was
"Who asked you, hobo-urine?" Guy put his glasses on.
Pulled his trousers up. We all went out
to the kitchen and had a drink. Then another. Like that,
the world had gone from afternoon to night.

Bonnard's Nudes

His wife. Forty years he painted her.
Again and again. The nude in the last painting
the same young nude as the first. His wife.

As he remembered her young. As she was young.
His wife in her bath. At her dressing table
in front of the mirror. Undressed.

His wife with her hands under her breasts
looking out on the garden.
The sun bestowing warmth and color.

Every living thing in bloom there.
She young and tremulous and most desirable.
When she died, he painted a while longer.

A few landscapes. Then died.
And was put down next to her.
His young wife.

Jean's TV

My life's on an even keel
these days. Though who's to say
it'll never waver again?
This morning I recalled
a girlfriend I had just after
my marriage broke up.
A sweet girl named Jean.
In the beginning, she had no idea
how bad things were. It took
a while. But she loved me
a bunch anyway, she said.

                    *

And I know that's true.
She let me stay at her place
where I conducted
the shabby business of my life
over her phone. She bought
my booze, but told me
I wasn't a drunk
like those others said.
Signed checks for me
and left them on her pillow
when she went off to work.
Gave me a Pendleton jacket
that Christmas, one I still wear.

For my part, I taught her to drink.
And how to fall asleep
with her clothes on.
How to wake up
weeping in the middle of the night.
When I left, she paid two months'
rent for me. And gave me
her black and white TV.

We talked on the phone once,
months later. She was drunk.
And, sure, I was drunk too.
The last thing she said to me was,
Will I ever see my TV again?
I looked around the room
as if the TV might suddenly
appear in its place
on the kitchen chair. Or else
come out of a cupboard
and declare itself. But that TV
had gone down the road
weeks before. The TV Jean gave me.

*

I didn't tell her that.
I lied, of course. Soon, I said,
very soon now.
And put down the phone
after, or before, she hung up.
But those sleep-sounding words
of mine making me feel
I'd come to the end of a story.
And now, this one last falsehood
behind me,

                        I could rest.

Mesopotamia

Waking before sunrise, in a house not my own,
I hear a radio playing in the kitchen.
Mist drifts outside the window while
a woman's voice gives the news, and then the weather.
I hear that, and the sound of meat
as it connects with hot grease in the pan.
I listen some more, half asleep. It's like,
but not like, when I was a child and lay in bed,
in the dark, listening to a woman crying,
and a man's voice raised in anger, or despair,
the radio playing all the while. Instead,
what I hear this morning is the man of the house
saying "How many summers do I have left?
Answer me that." There's no answer from the woman
that I can hear. But what *could* she answer,
given such a question? In a minute,
I hear his voice speaking of someone who I think
must be long gone: "That man could say,
     'O, Mesopotamia!'
and move his audience to tears."
I get out of bed at once and draw on my pants.
Enough light in the room that I can see

where I am, finally. I'm a grown man, after all,
and these people are my friends. Things
are not going well for them just now. Or else
they're going better than ever
because they're up early and talking
about such things of consequence
as death and Mesopotamia. In any case,
I feel myself being drawn to the kitchen.
So much that is mysterious and important
is happening out there this morning.

The Jungle

"I only have two hands,"
the beautiful flight attendant
says. She continues
up the aisle with her tray and
out of his life forever,
he thinks. Off to his left,
far below, some lights
from a village high
on a hill in the jungle.

So many impossible things
have happened,
he isn't surprised when she
returns to sit in the
empty seat across from his.
"Are you getting off
in Rio, or going on to Buenos Aires?"

Once more she exposes
her beautiful hands.
The heavy silver rings that hold
her fingers, the gold bracelet
encircling her wrist.

*

They are somewhere in the air
over the steaming Mato Grosso.
It is very late.
He goes on considering her hands.
Looking at her clasped fingers.
It's months afterwards, and
hard to talk about.

Hope

*"My wife," said Pinnegar, "expects to see me go to the dogs
when she leaves me. It is her last hope."*
— D. H. LAWRENCE,
"JIMMY AND THE DESPERATE WOMAN"

She gave me the car and two
hundred dollars. Said, So long, baby.
Take it easy, hear? So much
for twenty years of marriage.
She knows, or thinks she knows,
I'll go through the dough
in a day or two, and eventually
wreck the car — which was
in my name and needed work anyway.
When I drove off, she and her boy-
friend were changing the lock
on the front door. They waved.
I waved back to let them know
I didn't think any the less
of them. Then sped toward
the state line. I *was* hell-bent.
She was right to think so.

*

I went to the dogs, and we
became good friends.
But I kept going. Went
a long way without stopping.
Left the dogs, my friends, behind.
Nevertheless, when I did show
my face at that house again,
months, or years, later, driving
a different car, she wept
when she saw me at the door.
Sober. Dressed in a clean shirt,
pants, and boots. Her last hope
blasted.
She didn't have a thing
to hope for anymore.

The House behind This One

The afternoon was already dark and unnatural.
When this old woman appeared in the field,
in the rain, carrying a bridle.
She came up the road to the house.
The house behind this one. Somehow
she knew Antonio Ríos had entered
the hour of his final combat.
Somehow, don't ask me how, she knew.

The doctor and some other people were with him.
But nothing more could be done. And so
the old woman carried the bridle into the room,
and hung it across the foot of his bed.
The bed where he writhed and lay dying.
She went away without a word.
This woman who'd once been young and beautiful.
When Antonio was young and beautiful.

Limits

All that day we banged at geese
from a blind at the top
of the bluff. Busted one flock
after the other, until our gun barrels
grew hot to the touch. Geese
filled the cold, grey air. But we still
didn't kill our limits.
The wind driving our shot
every whichway. Late afternoon,
and we had four. Two shy
of our limits. Thirst drove us
off the bluff and down a dirt road
alongside the river.

To an evil-looking farm
surrounded by dead fields of
barley. Where, almost evening,
a man with patches of skin
gone from his hands let us dip water
from a bucket on his porch.
Then asked if we wanted to see
something — a Canada goose he kept
alive in a barrel beside
the barn. The barrel covered over
with screen wire, rigged inside
like a little cell. He'd broken
the bird's wing with a long shot,
he said, then chased it down
and stuffed it in the barrel.
He'd had a brainstorm!
He'd use that goose as a live decoy.

In time it turned out to be
the damnedest thing he'd ever seen.
It would bring other geese
right down on your head.

So close you could almost touch them
before you killed them.
This man, he never wanted for geese.
And for this his goose was given
all the corn and barley
it could eat, and a barrel
to live in, and shit in.

I took a good long look and,
unmoving, the goose looked back.
Only its eyes telling me
it was alive. Then we left,
my friend and I. Still
willing to kill anything
that moved, anything that rose
over our sights. I don't
recall if we got anything else
that day. I doubt it.
It was almost dark anyhow.
No matter, now. But for years
and years afterwards, living
on a staple of bitterness, I
didn't forget that goose.
I set it apart from all the others,
living and dead. Came to understand
one can get used to anything,
and become a stranger to nothing.
Saw that betrayal is just another word
for loss, for hunger.

The Sensitive Girl

This is the fourth day I've been here.
But, no joke, there's a spider
on this pane of glass
that's been around even longer. It doesn't
move, but I know it's alive.

Fine with me that lights are coming on
in the valleys. It's pretty here,
and quiet. Cattle are being driven home.
If I listen, I can hear cowbells
and then the *slap-slap* of the driver's
stick. There's haze
over these lumpy Swiss hills. Below the house,
a race of water through the alders.
Jets of water tossed up,
sweet and hopeful.

There was a time
I would've died for love.
No more. That center wouldn't hold.
It collapsed. It gives off
no light. Its orbit
an orbit of weariness. But I worry
that time and wish I knew why.
Who wants to remember
when poverty and disgrace pushed
through the door, followed by a cop
to invest the scene
with horrible authority?
The latch was fastened, but
that never stopped anybody back then.
Hey, no one breathed in those days.
Ask her, if you don't believe me!
Assuming you could find her and

make her talk. That girl who dreamed
and sang. Who sometimes hummed
when she made love. The sensitive girl.
The one who cracked.

I'm a grown man now, and then some.
So how much longer do I have?
How much longer for that spider?
Where will he go, two days into fall,
the leaves dropping?

The cattle have entered their pen.
The man with the stick raises his arm.
Then closes and fastens the gate.

I find myself, at last, in perfect silence.
Knowing the little that is left.
Knowing I have to love it.
Wanting to love it. For both our sake.

II

The Minuet

Bright mornings.
Days when I want so much I want nothing.
Just this life, and no more. Still,
I hope no one comes along.
But if someone does, I hope it's her.
The one with the little diamond stars
at the toes of her shoes.
The girl I saw dance the minuet.
That antique dance.
The minuet. She danced that
the way it should be danced.
And the way she wanted.

Egress

I opened the old spiral notebook to see what I'd been
thinking in those days. There was one entry,
in a hand I didn't recognize as mine, but was mine.
All that paper I'd let go to waste back then!

Removing the door for Dr Kurbitz.

What on earth could that possibly mean to me,
or anyone, today? Then I went back
to that time. To just after being married. How I earned
our daily bread delivering for Al Kurbitz,
the pharmacist. Whose brother Ken – Dr Kurbitz
to me, the ear-nose-and-throat man – fell dead
one night after dinner, after
talking over some business deal. He died in the bathroom,
his body wedged between the door and toilet stool.

Blocking the way. First the *whump*
of a body hitting the floor, and then Mr Kurbitz
and his snazzy sister-in-law shouting "Ken! Ken!"
and pushing on the bathroom door.

Mr Kurbitz had to take the door off its hinges
with a screwdriver. It saved the ambulance drivers
a minute, maybe. He said his brother never knew
what hit him. Dead before he hit the floor.

Since then, I've seen doors removed from their hinges
many times, with and without the aid of screwdrivers.
But I'd forgotten about Dr Kurbitz, and so much else
from that time. Never, until today, did I connect
this act with dying.

                              In those days, death,
if it happened, happened to others. Old people
belonging to my parents. Or else people of consequence.
People in a different income bracket, whose death
and removal had nothing to do with me, or mine.

We were living in Dr Coglon's basement
apartment, and I was in love for the first time
ever. My wife was pregnant. We were thrilled
beyond measure or accounting for, given our mean
surroundings. And that, I'm saying, may be why
I never wrote more about Dr Kurbitz,
his brother Al, or doors that had to be taken off
their hinges for the sake of dead people.

What the hell! Who needed death and notebooks? We
were young and happy. Death was coming, sure.
But for the old and worn-out. Or else people in books.
And, once in a while, the well-heeled professionals
I trembled before and said "Yes, Sir" to.

Spell

Between five and seven this evening,
I lay in the channel of sleep. Attached
to this world by nothing more than hope,
I turned in a current of dark dreams.
It was during this time the weather
underwent a metamorphosis.
Became deranged. What before had been
vile and shabby, but comprehensible,
became swollen and
unrecognizable. Something utterly vicious.

In my despairing mood, I didn't
need it. It was the last thing on earth
I wanted. So with all the power I could muster,
I sent it packing. Sent it down the coast
to a big river I know about. A river
able to deal with foul weather
like this. So what if the river has to flee
to higher ground? Give it a few days.
It'll find its way.

Then all will be as before. I swear
this won't be more than a bad memory, if that.
Why, this time next week I won't remember
what I was feeling when I wrote this.
I'll have forgotten I slept badly
and dreamed for a time this evening . . .
to wake at seven o'clock, look out
at the storm and, after that first shock —
take heart. Think long and hard
about what I want, what I could let go
or send away. And then do it!
Like that. With words, and signs.

From the East, Light

The house rocked and shouted all night.
Toward morning, grew quiet. The children,
looking for something to eat, make
their way through the crazy living room
in order to get to the crazy kitchen.
There's Father, asleep on the couch.
Sure they stop to look. Who wouldn't?
They listen to his violent snores
and understand that the old way of life
has begun once more. So what else is new?
But the real shocker, what makes them stare,
is that their Christmas tree has been turned over.
It lies on its side in front of the fireplace.
The tree they helped decorate.
It's wrecked now, icicles and candy canes
litter the rug. How'd a thing like this happen, anyway?
And they see Father has opened
his present from Mother. It's a length of rope
half-in, half-out of its pretty box.
Let them both go hang
themselves, is what they'd like to say.
To hell with it, and
them, is what they're thinking. Meanwhile,
there's cereal in the cupboard, milk
in the fridge. They take their bowls
in where the TV is, find their show,
try to forget about the mess everywhere.
Up goes the volume. Louder, and then louder.
Father turns over and groans. The children laugh.
They turn it up some more so he'll for sure know
he's alive. He raises his head. Morning begins.

A Tall Order

This old woman who kept house for them,
she'd seen and heard the most amazing things.
Sights like plates and bottles flying.
An ashtray traveling like a missile
that hit the dog in the head.
Once she let herself in and found a huge
salad in the middle of the dining-room table.
It was sprinkled with moldy croutons.
The table was set for six, but nobody
had eaten. Dust filmed the cups and silver.
Upstairs a man pleaded
not to have his hair pulled by the roots again.
Please, please, please he cried.

Her job was to set the house in order.
At least make it like she'd left it last time.
That was all. Nobody asked her opinion,
and she didn't give it. She put on her apron.
Turned the hot water on full, drowning out
that other sound. Her arms went into the suds
to her elbows. She leaned on the counter.
And stared into the backyard where they kept
the rusty swing and jungle-gym set.
If she kept watching, she was sure to see
the elephant step out of the trees and trumpet
as it did every Monday at this house, at this hour.

The Author of Her Misfortune

For the world is the world . . .
And it writes no histories
That end in love.
— STEPHEN SPENDER

I'm not the man she claims. But
this much is true: the past is
distant, a receding coastline,
and we're all in the same boat,
a scrim of rain over the sea-lanes.
Still, I wish she wouldn't keep on
saying those things about me!
Over the long course
everything but hope lets you go, then
even that loosens its grip.
There isn't enough of anything
as long as we live. But at intervals
a sweetness appears and, given a chance,
prevails. It's true I'm happy now.
And it'd be nice if she
could hold her tongue. Stop
hating me for being happy.
Blaming me for her life. I'm afraid
I'm mixed up in her mind
with someone else. A young man
of no character, living on dreams,
who swore he'd love her forever.
One who gave her a ring, and a bracelet.
Who said, *Come with me. You can trust me.*
Things to that effect. I'm not that man.
She has me confused, as I said,
with someone else.

Powder-Monkey

When my friend John Dugan, the carpenter,
left this world for the next, he seemed
in a terrible hurry. He wasn't, of course.
Almost no one is. But he barely took time
to say goodbye. "I'll just put these tools away,"
he said. Then, "So long." And hurried
down the hill to his pickup. He waved, and
I waved. But between here and Dungeness,
where he used to live, he drifted
over the center line, onto Death's side.
And was destroyed by a logging truck.

                    He is working
under the sun with his shirt off, a blue
bandanna around his forehead to keep sweat from his eyes.
Driving nails. Drilling and planing lumber.
Joining wood together with other wood.
In every way taking the measure of this house.
Stopping to tell a story now and then,
about when he was a young squirt, working
as a powder-monkey. The close calls he'd had
laying fuses. His white teeth flashing when he laughs.
The blond handlebar mustache he loved to
pull on while musing. "So long," he said.

I want to imagine him riding unharmed
toward Death. Even though the fuse is burning.
Nothing to do there in the cab
of his pickup but listen to Ricky Skaggs,
pull on his mustache, and plan Saturday night.
This man with all Death before him.
Riding unharmed, and untouched,
toward Death.

Earwigs

FOR MONA SIMPSON

Your delicious-looking rum cake, covered with
almonds, was hand-carried to my door
this morning. The driver parked at the foot
of the hill, and climbed the steep path.
Nothing else moved in that frozen landscape.
It was cold inside and out. I signed
for it, thanked him, went back in.
Where I stripped off the heavy tape, tore
the staples from the bag, and inside
found the canister you'd filled with cake.
I scratched adhesive from the lid.
Prized it open. Folded back the aluminum foil.
To catch the first whiff of that sweetness!

It was then the earwig appeared
from the moist depths. An earwig
stuffed on your cake. Drunk
from it. He went over the side of the can.
Scurried wildly across the table to take
refuge in the fruit bowl. I didn't kill it.
Not then. Filled as I was with conflicting
feelings. Disgust, of course. But
amazement. Even admiration. This creature
that'd just made a 3,000-mile, overnight trip
by air, surrounded by cake, shaved almonds,
and the overpowering odor of rum. Carried
then in a truck over a mountain road and
packed uphill in freezing weather to a house
overlooking the Pacific Ocean. An earwig.
I'll let him live, I thought. What's one more,
or less, in the world? This one's special,
maybe. Blessings on its strange head.

*

I lifted the cake from its foil wrapping
and three more earwigs went over the side
of the can! For a minute I was so taken
aback I didn't know if I should kill them,
or what. Then rage seized me, and
I plastered them. Crushed the life from them
before any could get away. It was a massacre.
While I was at it, I found and destroyed
the other one utterly.
I was just beginning when it was all over.
I'm saying I could have gone on and on,
rending them. If it's true
that man is wolf to man, what can mere earwigs
expect when bloodlust is up?

I sat down, trying to quieten my heart.
Breath rushing from my nose. I looked
around the table, slowly. Ready
for anything. Mona, I'm sorry to say this,
but I couldn't eat any of your cake.
I've put it away for later, maybe.
Anyway, thanks. You're sweet to remember
me out here alone this winter.
Living alone.
Like an animal, I think.

NyQuil

Call it iron discipline. But for months
I never took my first drink
before eleven p.m. Not so bad,
considering. This was in the beginning
phase of things. I knew a man
whose drink of choice was Listerine.
He was coming down off Scotch.
He bought Listerine by the case,

and drank it by the case. The back seat
of his car was piled high with dead soldiers.
Those empty bottles of Listerine
gleaming in his scalding back seat!
The sight of it sent me home soul-searching.
I did that once or twice. Everybody does.
Go way down inside and look around.
I spent hours there, but
didn't meet anyone, or see anything
of interest. I came back to the here and now,
and put on my slippers. Fixed
myself a nice glass of NyQuil.
Dragged a chair over to the window.
Where I watched a pale moon struggle to rise
over Cupertino, California.
I waited through hours of darkness with NyQuil.
And then, sweet Jesus! the first sliver
of light.

The Possible

I spent years, on and off, in academe.
Taught at places I couldn't get near
as a student. But never wrote a line
about that time. Never. Nothing stayed
with me in those days. I was a stranger,
and an impostor, even to myself. Except
at that one school. That distinguished
institution in the midwest. Where
my only friend, and my colleague,
the Chaucerian, was arrested for beating his wife.
And threatening her life over the phone,
a misdemeanor. He wanted to put her eyes out.
Set her on fire for cheating.
The guy she was seeing, he was going to hammer him
into the ground like a fence post.

He lost his mind for a time, while she moved away
to a new life. Thereafter, he taught
his classes weeping drunk. More than once
wore his lunch on his shirt front.
I was no help. I was fading fast myself.
But seeing the way he was living, so to speak,
I understood I hadn't strayed so far from home
after all. My scholar-friend. My old pal.
At long last I'm out of all that.
And you. I pray your hands are steady,
and that you're happy tonight. I hope some woman
has just put her hand under your clean collar
a minute ago, and told you she loves you.
Believe her, if you can, for it's possible she means it.
Is someone who will be true, and kind to you.
All your remaining days.

Shiftless

The people who were better than us were *comfortable*.
They lived in painted houses with flush toilets.
Drove cars whose year and make were recognizable.
The ones worse off were *sorry* and didn't work.
Their strange cars sat on blocks in dusty yards.
The years go by and everything and everyone
gets replaced. But this much is still true –
I never liked work. My goal was always
to be shiftless. I saw the merit in that.
I liked the idea of sitting in a chair
in front of your house for hours, doing nothing
but wearing a hat and drinking cola.
What's wrong with that?
Drawing on a cigarette from time to time.
Spitting. Making things out of wood with a knife.

Where's the harm there? Now and then calling
the dogs to hunt rabbits. Try it sometime.
Once in a while hailing a fat, blond kid like me
and saying, "Don't I know you?"
Not, "What are you going to be when you grow up?"

The Young Fire Eaters of Mexico City

They fill their mouths with alcohol
and blow it over a lighted candle
at traffic signs. Anyplace, really,
where cars line up and the drivers
are angry and frustrated and looking
for distraction – there you'll find
the young fire eaters. Doing what they do
for a few pesos. If they're lucky.
But in a year their lips
are scorched and their throats raw.
They have no voice within a year.
They can't talk or cry out –
these silent children who hunt
through the streets with a candle
and a beer can filled with alcohol.
They are called *milusos*. Which translates
into "a thousand uses."

Where the Groceries Went

When his mother called for the second time
that day, she said:
"I don't have any strength left. I want
to lay down all the time."

"Did you take your iron?" he wanted to know.
He sincerely wanted to know. Praying daily,

hopelessly, that iron might make a difference.
"Yes, but it just makes me hungry. And I don't
have anything to eat."

He pointed out to her they'd shopped
for hours that morning. Brought home
eighty dollars' worth of food to stack
in her cupboards and the fridge.
"There's nothing to eat in this goddamn house
but baloney and cheese," she said.
Her voice shook with anger. "Nothing!"
"And how's your cat? How's Kitty doing?"
His own voice shook. He needed
to get off this subject of food; it never
brought them anything but grief.

"Kitty," his mother said. "Here, Kitty.
Kitty, Kitty. She won't answer me, honey.
I don't know this for sure, but I think
she jumped into the washing machine
when I was about to do a load. And before I forget,
that machine's making
a banging noise. I think there's something
the matter with it. Kitty! She won't
answer me. Honey, I'm afraid.
I'm afraid of everything. Help me, please.
Then you can go back to whatever it was
you were doing. Whatever
it was that was so important
I had to take the trouble
to bring you into this world."

What I Can Do

All I want today is to keep an eye on these birds
outside my window. The phone is unplugged
so my loved ones can't reach out and put the arm

on me. I've told them the well has run dry.
They won't hear of it. They keep trying
to get through anyway. Just now I can't bear to know
about the car that blew another gasket.
Or the trailer I thought I'd paid for long ago,
now foreclosed on. Or the son in Italy
who threatens to end his life there
unless I keep paying the bills. My mother wants
to talk to me too. Wants to remind me again how it was
back then. All the milk I drank, cradled in her arms.
That ought to be worth something now. She needs
me to pay for this new move of hers. She'd like
to loop back to Sacramento for the twentieth time.
Everybody's luck has gone south. All I ask
is to be allowed to sit for a moment longer.
Nursing a bite the shelty dog Keeper gave me last night.
And watching these birds. Who don't ask for a thing
except sunny weather. In a minute
I'll have to plug in the phone and try to separate
what's right from wrong. Until then
a dozen tiny birds, no bigger than teacups,
perch in the branches outside the window.
Suddenly they stop singing and turn their heads.
It's clear they've felt something.
They dive into flight.

The Little Room

There was a great reckoning.
Words flew like stones through windows.
She yelled and yelled, like the Angel of Judgment.

Then the sun shot up, and a contrail
appeared in the morning sky.
In the sudden silence, the little room

became oddly lonely as he dried her tears.
Became like all the other little rooms on earth
light finds hard to penetrate.

Rooms where people yell and hurt each other.
And afterwards feel pain, and loneliness.
Uncertainty. The need to comfort.

Sweet Light

After the winter, grieving and dull,
I flourished here all spring. Sweet light

began to fill my chest. I pulled up
a chair. Sat for hours in front of the sea.

Listened to the buoy and learned
to tell the difference between a bell,

and the sound of a bell. I wanted
everything behind me. I even wanted

to become inhuman. And I did that.
I know I did. (She'll back me up on this.)

I remember the morning I closed the lid
on memory and turned the handle.

Locking it away forever.
Nobody knows what happened to me

out here, sea. Only you and I know.
At night, clouds form in front of the moon.

By morning they're gone. And that sweet light
I spoke of? That's gone too.

The Garden

In the garden, small laughter from years ago.
Lanterns burning in the willows.
The power of those four words, "I loved a woman."
Put that on the stone beside his name.
God keep you and be with you.

Those horses coming into the stretch at Ruidoso!
Mist rising from the meadow at dawn.
From the veranda, the blue outlines of the mountains.
What used to be within reach, out of reach.
And in some lesser things, just the opposite is true.

Order anything you want! Then look for the man
with the limp to go by. He'll pay.
From a break in the wall, I could look down
on the shanty lights in the Valley of Kidron.
Very little sleep under strange roofs. His life far away.

Playing checkers with my dad. Then he hunts up
the shaving soap, the brush and bowl, the straight
razor, and we drive to the county hospital. I watch him
lather my grandpa's face. Then shave him.
The dying body is a clumsy partner.

Drops of water in your hair.
The dark yellow of the fields, the black and blue rivers.
Going out for a walk means you intend to return, right?
Eventually.
The flame is guttering. Marvelous.

The meeting between Goethe and Beethoven
took place in Leipzig in 1812. They talked into the night
about Lord Byron and Napoleon.
She got off the road and from then on it was nothing
but hardpan all the way.

*

She took a stick and in the dust drew the house where
they'd live and raise their children.
There was a duck pond and a place for horses.
To write about it, one would have to write in a way
that would stop the heart and make one's hair stand on end.

Cervantes lost a hand in the Battle of Lepanto.
This was in 1571, the last great sea battle fought
in ships manned by galley slaves.
In the Unuk River, in Ketchikan, the backs of the salmon
under the street lights as they come through town.

Students and young people chanted a requiem
as Tolstoy's coffin was carried across the yard
of the stationmaster's house at Astapovo and placed
in the freight car. To the accompaniment of singing,
the train slowly moved off.

A hard sail and the same stars everywhere.
But the garden is right outside my window.
Don't worry your heart about me, my darling.
We weave the thread given to us.
And Spring is with me.

Son

Awakened this morning by a voice from my childhood
that says *Time to get up*, I get up.
All night long, in my sleep, trying
to find a place where my mother could live
and be happy. *If you want me to lose my mind*,
the voice says *okay. Otherwise,*
get me out of here! I'm the one to blame
for moving her to this town she hates. Renting
her the house she hates.
Putting those neighbors she hates so close.
Buying the furniture she hates.

Why didn't you give me money instead, and let me spend it?
I want to go back to California, the voice says.
I'll die if I stay here. Do you want me to die?
There's no answer to this, or to anything else
in the world this morning. The phone rings
and rings. I can't go near it for fear
of hearing my name once more. The same name
my father answered to for 53 years.
Before going to his reward.
He died just after saying "Take this
into the kitchen, son."
The word *son* issuing from his lips.
Wobbling in the air for all to hear.

Kafka's Watch

from a letter

I have a job with a tiny salary of 80 crowns, and
an infinite eight to nine hours of work.
I devour the time outside the office like a wild beast.
Someday I hope to sit in a chair in another
country, looking out the window at fields of sugarcane
or Mohammedan cemeteries.
I don't complain about the work so much as about
the sluggishness of swampy time. The office hours
cannot be divided up! I feel the pressure
of the full eight or nine hours even in the last
half hour of the day. It's like a train ride
lasting night and day. In the end you're totally
crushed. You no longer think about the straining
of the engine, or about the hills or
flat countryside, but ascribe all that's happening
to your watch alone. The watch which you continually hold
in the palm of your hand. Then shake. And bring slowly
to your ear in disbelief.

III

The Lightning Speed of the Past

The corpse fosters anxiety in men who believe
in the Last Judgment, and those who don't.
— ANDRÉ MALRAUX

He buried his wife, who'd died in
misery. In misery, he
took to his porch, where he watched
the sun set and the moon rise.
The days seemed to pass, only to return
again. Like a dream in which one thinks,
I've already dreamt that.

Nothing, having arrived, will stay.
With his knife he cut the skin
from an apple. The white pulp, body
of the apple, darkened
and turned brown, then black,
before his eyes. The worn-out face of death!
The lightning speed of the past.

Vigil

They waited all day for the sun to appear. Then,
late in the afternoon, like a good prince,
it showed itself for a few minutes.
Blazing high over the benchland that lies at the foot
of the peaks behind their borrowed house.
Then the clouds were drawn once more.

*

They were happy enough. But all evening
the curtains made melancholy gestures,
swishing in front of the open windows. After dinner
they stepped onto the balcony.
Where they heard the river plunging in the canyon and,
closer, the creak of trees, sigh of boughs.

The tall grasses promised to rustle forever.
She put her hand on his neck. He touched her cheek.
Then bats came from all sides to harry them back.
Inside, they closed the windows. Kept their distance.
Watched a procession of stars. And, once in a while,
creatures that flung themselves in front of the moon.

In the Lobby of the Hotel del Mayo

The girl in the lobby reading a leather-bound book.
The man in the lobby using a broom.
The boy in the lobby watering plants.
The desk clerk looking at his nails.
The woman in the lobby writing a letter.
The old man in the lobby sleeping in his chair.
The fan in the lobby revolving slowly overhead.
Another hot Sunday afternoon.

Suddenly, the girl lays her finger between the pages of
    her book.
The man leans on his broom and looks.
The boy stops in his tracks.
The desk clerk raises his eyes and stares.
The woman quits writing.
The old man stirs and wakes up.
What is it?

Someone is running up from the harbor.
Someone who has the sun behind him.
Someone who is barechested.
Waving his arms.

It's clear something terrible has happened.
The man is running straight for the hotel.
His lips are working themselves into a scream.
Everyone in the lobby will recall their terror.
Everyone will remember this moment for the rest of their lives.

Bahia, Brazil

The wind is level now. But pails of rain
fell today, and the day before,
and the day before that, all the way back
to Creation. The buildings
in the old slave quarter are dissolving,
and nobody cares. Not the ghosts
of the old slaves, or the young.
The water feels good on their whipped backs.
They could cry with relief.

No sunsets in this place. Light one minute,
and then the stars come out.
We could look all night in vain
for the Big Dipper. Down here
the Southern Cross is our sign.
I'm sick of the sound of my own voice!
Uneasy, and dreaming
of rum that could split my skull open.

There's a body lying on the stairs.
Step over it. The lights in the tower
have gone out. A spider hops from the man's
hair. This life. I'm saying it's one
amazing thing after the other.

*

Lines of men in the street,
as opposed to lines of poetry.
Choose! Are you guilty or not guilty?
What else have you? he answered.
Well, say the house was burning.
Would you save the cat or the Rembrandt?
That's easy. I don't have a Rembrandt,
and I don't have a cat. But I have
a sorrel horse back home
that I want to ride once more
into the high country.

Soon enough we'll rot under the earth.
No truth to this, just a fact.
We who gave each other so much
happiness while alive –
we're going to rot. But we won't
rot in this place. Not here.
Arms shackled together.
Jesus, the very idea of such a thing!
This life. These shackles.
I shouldn't bring it up.

The Phenomenon

I woke up feeling wiped out. God knows
where I've been all night, but my feet hurt.
Outside my window, a phenomenon is taking place.
The sun and moon hang side-by-side over the water.
Two sides of the same coin. I climb from bed
slowly, much as an old man might maneuver
from his musty bed in midwinter, finding it difficult
for a moment even to make water! I tell myself
this has to be a temporary condition.
In a few years, no problem. But when I look out
the window again, there's a sudden swoop of feeling.

Once more I'm arrested with the beauty of this place.
I was lying if I ever said anything to the contrary.
I move closer to the glass and see it's happened
between this thought and that. The moon
is gone. Set, at last.

Wind

FOR RICHARD FORD

Water perfectly calm. Perfectly amazing.
Flocks of birds moving
restlessly. Mystery enough in that, God knows.

You ask if I have the time. I do.
Time to go in. Fish not biting
anyway. Nothing doing anywhere.

When, a mile away, we see wind
moving across the water. Sit quiet and
watch it come. Nothing to worry about.

Just wind. Not so strong. Though strong enough.
You say, "Look at that!"
And we hold on to the gunwales as it passes.

I feel it fan my face and ears. Feel it
ruffle my hair – sweeter, it seems,
than any woman's fingers.

Then turn my head and watch
it move on down the Strait,
driving waves before it.

Leaving waves to flop against
our hull. The birds going crazy now.
Boat rocking from side to side.

*

"Jesus," you say, "I never saw anything like it."
"Richard," I say —
"You'll never see that in Manhattan, my friend."

Migration

A late summer's day, and my friend on the court
with his friend. Between games, the other remarks
how my friend's step seems not to have any spring
to it. His serve isn't so hot, either.
"You feeling okay?" he asks. "You had a checkup
lately?" Summer, and the living is easy.
But my friend went to see a doctor friend of his.
Who took his arm and gave him three months, no longer.

When I saw him a day later, it
was in the afternoon. He was watching TV.
He looked the same, but — how should I say it? —
different. He was embarrassed about the TV
and turned the sound down a little. But he couldn't
sit still. He circled the room, again and again.
"It's a program on animal migration," he said, as if this
might explain everything.
I put my arms around him and gave him a hug.
Not the really big hug I was capable of. Being afraid
that one of us, or both, might go to pieces.
And there was the momentary, crazy and dishonorable
    thought —
this might be catching.

I asked for an ashtray, and he was happy
to range around the house until he found one.
We didn't talk. Not then. Together we finished watching
the show. Reindeer, polar bears, fish, waterfowl,

butterflies and more. Sometimes they went from one
continent, or ocean, to another. But it was hard
to pay attention to the story taking place on screen.
My friend stood, as I recall, the whole time.

Was he feeling okay? He felt fine. He just couldn't
seem to stay still, was all. Something came into his eyes
and went away again. "What in hell are they talking about?"
he wanted to know. But didn't wait for an answer.
Began to walk some more. I followed him awkwardly
from room to room while he remarked on the weather,
his job, his ex-wife, his kids. Soon, he guessed,
he'd have to tell them . . . something.
"Am I really going to die?"

What I remember most about that awful day
was his restlessness, and my cautious hugs — *hello, goodbye.*
He kept moving until
we reached the front door and stopped.
He peered out, and drew back as if astounded
it could be light outside. A bank of shadow
from his hedge blocked the drive. And shadow fell
from the garage onto his lawn. He walked me to the car.
Our shoulders bumped. We shook hands, and I hugged him
once more. Lightly. Then he turned and went back,
passing quickly inside, closing the door. His face
appeared behind the window, then was gone.

He'll be on the move from now on. Traveling night and day,
without cease, all of him, every last exploding piece
of him. Until he reaches a place only he knows about.
An Arctic place, cold and frozen. Where he thinks,
This is far enough. This is the place.
And lies down, for he is tired.

Sleeping

He slept on his hands.
On a rock.
On his feet.
On someone else's feet.
He slept on buses, trains, in airplanes.
Slept on duty.
Slept beside the road.
Slept on a sack of apples.
He slept in a pay toilet.
In a hayloft.
In the Super Dome.
Slept in a Jaguar, and in the back of a pickup.
Slept in theaters.
In jail.
On boats.
He slept in line shacks and, once, in a castle.
Slept in the rain.
In blistering sun he slept.
On horseback.
He slept in chairs, churches, in fancy hotels.
He slept under strange roofs all his life.
Now he sleeps under the earth.
Sleeps on and on.
Like an old king.

The River

I waded, deepening, into the dark water.
Evening, and the push
and swirl of the river as it closed
around my legs and held on.
Young grilse broke water.
Parr darted one way, smolt another.
Gravel turned under my boots as I edged out.

Watched by the furious eyes of king salmon.
Their immense heads turned slowly,
eyes burning with fury, as they hung
in the deep current.
They were there. I felt them there,
and my skin prickled. But
there was something else.
I braced with the wind on my neck.
Felt the hair rise
as something touched my boot.
Grew afraid at what I couldn't see.
Then of everything that filled my eyes –
that other shore heavy with branches,
the dark lip of the mountain range behind.
And this river that had suddenly
grown black and swift.
I drew breath and cast anyway.
Prayed nothing would strike.

The Best Time of the Day

Cool summer nights.
Windows open.
Lamps burning.
Fruit in the bowl.
And your head on my shoulder.
These the happiest moments in the day.

Next to the early morning hours,
of course. And the time
just before lunch.
And the afternoon, and
early evening hours.
But I do love

                *

these summer nights.
Even more, I think,
than those other times.
The work finished for the day.
And no one who can reach us now.
Or ever.

Scale

FOR RICHARD MARIUS

It's afternoon when he takes off
his clothes and lies down.
Lights his cigarette. Ashtray
balanced over his heart.
The chest rising, then
sinking
as he draws, holds it,
and lets the smoke out in spurts.
The shades are drawn. His eyelids
closing. It's like after sex,
a little. But only a little.
Waves thrash below the house.
He finishes the cigarette.
All the while thinking
of Thomas More who,
according to Erasmus, "liked eggs"
and never lay with his second wife.

The head stares down at its trunk
until it thinks it has it
memorized and could recognize
it anywhere, even in death.
But now the desire to sleep
has left him, utterly.

He is still remembering More
and his hair shirt. After thirty years of wear
he handed it over, along with his cloak,
before embracing his executioner.

He gets up to raise the shades.
Light slices the room in two.
A boat slowly rounds the hook
with its sails lowered.
There's a milky haze
over the water. A silence there.
It's much too quiet.
Even the birds are still.
Somewhere, off in another room,
something has been decided.
A decision reached, papers signed
and pushed aside.

He keeps on staring at the boat.
The empty rigging, the deserted deck.
The boat rises. Moves closer.
He peers through the glasses.
The human figure, the music
it makes, that's what's missing
from the tiny deck.
A deck no broader than a leaf.
So how could it support a life?

Suddenly, the boat shudders.
Stops dead in the water.
He sweeps the glasses over the deck.
But after a while his arms grow
unbearably heavy. So he drops them,
just as he would anything unbearable.
He lays the glasses on the shelf.
Begins dressing. But the image

of the boat stays. Drifting.
Stays awhile longer. Then bobs away.
Forgotten about as he takes up
his coat. Opens the door. Goes out.

Company

This morning I woke up to rain
on the glass. And understood
that for a long time now
I've chosen the corrupt when
I had a choice. Or else,
simply, the merely easy.
Over the virtuous. Or the difficult.
This way of thinking happens
when I've been alone for days.
Like now. Hours spent
in my own dumb company.
Hours and hours
much like a little room.
With just a strip of carpet to walk on.

Yesterday

Yesterday I dressed in a dead man's
woolen underwear. Then drove to the end
of an icy road where I passed
some time with Indian fishermen.
I stepped into water over my boots.
Saw four pintails spring from the creek.
Never mind that my thoughts were elsewhere
and I missed the perfect shot.
Or that my socks froze. I lost track
of everything and didn't make it back
for lunch. You could say

it wasn't my day. But it was!
And to prove it I have this little bite
she gave me last night. A bruise
coloring my lip today, to remind me.

The Schooldesk

The fishing in Lough Arrow is piss-poor.
Too much rain, too much high water.
They say the mayfly hatch has come
and gone. All day I stay put
by the window of the borrowed cottage
in Ballindoon, waiting for a break
in the weather. A turf fire smokes
in the grate, though no romance
in this or anything else
here. Just outside the window an old iron
and wood schooldesk keeps me company.
Something is carved into the desk under
the inkwell. It doesn't matter
what; I'm not curious. It's enough
to imagine the instrument
that gouged those letters.

                My dad is dead,
and Mother slips in and out of her mind.
I can't begin to say how bad it is
for my grown-up son and daughter.
They took one long look at me
and tried to make all my mistakes.
More's the pity. Bad luck for them,
my sweet children. And haven't I mentioned
my first wife yet? What's wrong with me
that I haven't? Well, I can't anymore.
Shouldn't, anyway. She claims
I say too much as it is.

Says she's happy now, and grinds her teeth.
Says the Lord Jesus loves her,
and she'll get by. That love
of my life over and done with. But what
does that say about my life?
My loved ones are thousands of miles away.
But they're in this cottage too,
in Ballindoon. And in every
hotel room I wake up in these days.

The rain has let up.
And the sun has appeared and small
clouds of unexpected mayflies,
proving someone wrong. We move
to the door in a group, my family and I.
And go outside. Where I bend over the desk
and run my fingers across its rough surface.
Someone laughs, someone grinds her teeth.
And someone, someone is pleading with me.
Saying, "For Christ's sake, don't
turn your back on me."

An ass and cart pass down the lane.
The driver takes the pipe from his mouth
and raises his hand.
There's the smell of lilacs in the damp air.
Mayflies hover over the lilacs,
and over the heads of my loved ones.
Hundreds of mayflies.
I sit on the bench. Lean
over the desk. I can remember
myself with a pen. In the beginning,
looking at pictures of words.
Learning to write them, slowly,
one letter at a time. Pressing down.
A word. Then the next.
The feeling of mastering something.

The excitement of it.
Pressing hard. At first
the damage confined to the surface.
But then deeper.

These blossoms. Lilacs.
How they fill the air with sweetness!
Mayflies in the air as the cart
goes by — as the fish rise.

Cutlery

Trolling the coho fly twenty feet behind the boat,
under moonlight, when the huge salmon hit it!
And lunged clear of the water. Stood, it seemed,
on its tail. Then fell back and was gone.
Shaken, I steered on into the harbor as if
nothing had happened. But it had.
And it happened in just the way I've said.
I took the memory with me to New York,
and beyond. Took it wherever I went.
All the way down here onto the terrace
of the Jockey Club in Rosario, Argentina.
Where I look out onto the broad river
that throws back light from the open windows
of the dining room. I stand smoking a cigar,
listening to the murmuring of the officers
and their wives inside; the little clashing
sound of cutlery against plates. I'm alive
and well, neither happy nor unhappy,
here in the Southern Hemisphere. So I'm all the more
astonished when I recall that lost fish rising,
leaving the water, and then returning.
The feeling of loss that gripped me then
grips me still. How can I communicate what I feel
about any of this? Inside, they go on

conversing in their own language.
                    I decide to walk
alongside the river. It's the kind of night
that brings men and rivers close.
I go for a ways, then stop. Realizing
that I haven't been close. Not
in the longest time. There's been
this waiting that's gone along with me
wherever I go. But the hope widening now
that something will rise up and splash.
I want to hear it, and move on.

The Pen

The pen that told the truth
went into the washing machine
for its trouble. Came out
an hour later, and was tossed
in the dryer with jeans
and a western shirt. Days passed
while it lay quietly on the desk
under the window. Lay there
thinking it was finished.
Without a single conviction
to its name. It didn't have
the will to go on, even if it'd wanted.
But one morning, an hour or so
before sunrise, it came to life
and wrote:
"The damp fields asleep in moonlight."
Then it was still again.
Its usefulness in this life
clearly at an end.

*

He shook it and whacked it
on the desk. Then gave up
on it, or nearly.
Once more though, with the greatest
effort, it summoned its last
reserves. This is what it wrote:
"A light wind, and beyond the window
trees swimming in the golden morning air."

He tried to write some more
but that was all. The pen
quit working forever.
By and by it was put
into the stove along with
other junk. And much later
it was another pen,
an undistinguished pen
that hadn't proved itself
yet, that facilely wrote:
"Darkness gathers in the branches.
Stay inside. Keep still."

The Prize

He was never the same, they said, after that.
And they were right. He left home, glad for his life.
Fell under the spell of Italian opera.
A gout stool was built into the front of his sedan chair.
His family went on living in a hut without a chimney.
One season very much like another for them.
What did they know?
A river wound through their valley.
At night the candles flickered, blinking like eyelashes.
As though tobacco smoke burned their eyes.
But nobody smoked in that stinking place.
Nobody sang or wrote cantatas.

When he died it was they who had to identify the body.
It was terrible!
His friends couldn't remember him.
Not even what he'd looked like the day before.
His father spat and rode off to kill squirrels.
His sister cradled his head in her arms.
His mother wept and went through his pockets.
Nothing had changed.
He was back where he belonged.
As though he'd never left.
Easy enough to say he should have declined it.
But would you?

An Account

He began the poem at the kitchen table,
one leg crossed over the other.
He wrote for a time, as if
only half interested in the result. It wasn't
as if the world didn't have enough poems.
The world had plenty of poems. Besides,
he'd been away for months.
He hadn't even *read* a poem in months.
What kind of life was this? A life
where a man was too busy even to read poems?
No life at all. Then he looked out the window,
down the hill to Frank's house.
A nice house situated near the water.
He remembered Frank opening his door
every morning at nine o'clock.
Going out for his walks.
He drew nearer the table, and uncrossed his legs.

*

Last night he'd heard an account
of Frank's death from Ed, another neighbor.
A man the same age as Frank,
and Frank's good friend. Frank
and his wife watching TV. *Hill Street Blues*.
Frank's favorite show. When he gasps
twice, is thrown back in his chair —
"as if he'd been electrocuted." That fast,
he was dead. His color draining away.
He was grey, turning black. Betty runs
out of the house in her robe. Runs
to a neighbor's house where a girl knows
something about CPR. *She's* watching
the same show! They run back
to Frank's house. Frank totally black now,
in his chair in front of the TV.
The cops and other desperate characters
moving across the screen, raising their voices,
yelling at each other, while this neighbor girl
hauls Frank out of his chair onto the floor.
Tears open his shirt. Goes to work.
Frank being the first real-life victim
she's ever had.

                She places her lips
on Frank's icy lips. A dead man's lips. Black lips.
And black his face and hands and arms.
Black too his chest where the shirt's been torn,
exposing the sparse hairs that grew there.
Long after she must've known better, she goes on
with it. Pressing her lips against his
unresponsive lips. Then stopping to beat on him
with clenched fists. Pressing her lips to his again,
and then again. Even after it's too late and it
was clear he wasn't coming back, she went on with it.
This girl, beating on him with her fists, calling

him every name she could think of. Weeping
when they took him away
from her. And someone thought to turn off
the images pulsing across the screen.

The Meadow

In the meadow this afternoon, I fetch
any number of crazy memories. That
undertaker asking my mother did she
want to buy the entire suit to bury my dad in,
or just the coat? I don't
have to provide the answer to this,
or anything else. But, hey, he went
into the furnace wearing his britches.

This morning I looked at his picture.
Big, heavyset guy in the last year
of his life. Holding a monster salmon
in front of the shack where he lived
in Fortuna, California. My dad.
He's nothing now. Reduced to a cup of ashes,
and some tiny bones. No way
is this any way
to end your life as a man.
Though as Hemingway correctly pointed out,
all stories, if continued far enough,
end in death. Truly.

Lord, it's almost fall.
A flock of Canada geese passes
high overhead. The little mare lifts
her head, shivers once, goes back
to grazing. I think I will lie down
in this sweet grass. I'll shut my eyes
and listen to wind, and the sound of wings.

Just dream for an hour, glad to be here
and not there. There's that. But also
the terrible understanding
that men I loved have left
for some other, lesser place.

Loafing

I looked into the room a moment ago,
and this is what I saw –
my chair in its place by the window,
the book turned facedown on the table.
And on the sill, the cigarette
left burning in its ashtray.
Malingerer! my uncle yelled at me
so long ago. He was right.
I've set aside time today,
same as every day,
for doing nothing at all.

Sinew

The girl minding the store.
She stands at the window
picking a piece of pork
from her teeth. Idly
watching the men in serge suits,
waistcoats, and ties,
dapping for trout on Lough Gill,
near the Isle of Innisfree.
The remains of her midday meal
congealing on the sill.
The air is still and warm.
A cuckoo calls.

*

Close in, a man in a boat,
wearing a hat, looks
toward shore, the little store,
and the girl. He looks, whips
his line, and looks some more.
She leans closer to the glass.
Goes out then to the lakeside.
But it's the cuckoo in the bush
that has her attention.

The man strikes a fish,
all business now.
The girl goes on working
at the sinew in her teeth.
But she watches this well-dressed
man reaching out
to slip a net under his fish.

In a minute, shyly, he floats near.
Holds up his catch for the girl's pleasure.
Doffs his hat. She stirs and smiles
a little. Raises her hand.
A gesture which starts the bird
in flight, toward Innisfree.

The man casts and casts again.
His line cuts the air. His fly
touches the water, and waits.
But what does this man
really care for trout?
What he'll take
from this day is the memory of
a girl working her finger
inside her mouth as their glances
meet, and a bird flies up.

They look at each other and smile.
In the still afternoon.
With not a word lost between them.

Waiting

Left off the highway and
down the hill. At the
bottom, hang another left.
Keep bearing left. The road
will make a Y. Left again.
There's a creek on the left.
Keep going. Just before
the road ends, there'll be
another road. Take it
and no other. Otherwise,
your life will be ruined
forever. There's a log house
with a shake roof, on the left.
It's not that house. It's
the next house, just over
a rise. The house
where trees are laden with
fruit. Where phlox, forsythia,
and marigold grow. It's
the house where the woman
stands in the doorway
wearing sun in her hair. The one
who's been waiting
all this time.
The woman who loves you.
The one who can say,
"What's kept you?"

IV

The Debate

This morning I'm torn
between responsibility to
myself, duty
to my publisher, and the pull
I feel toward the river
below my house. The winter-
run steelhead are in,
is the problem. It's
nearly dawn, the tide
is high. Even as
this little dilemma
occurs, and the debate
goes on, fish
are starting into the river.
Hey, I'll live, and be happy,
whatever I decide.

Its Course

The man who took 38 steelhead out
of this little river
last winter (his name is Bill Zitter,
"last name in the directory")
told me the river's changed its course
dramatically, he would even say
radically, since he first moved here,
he and his wife. It used to flow
"yonder, where those houses are."
When salmon crossed that shoal at night,
they made a noise like water boiling

in a cauldron, a noise like you were
scrubbing something on a washboard.
"It could wake you up from a deep sleep."
Now, there's no more salmon run.
And he won't fish for steelhead
this winter, because Mrs Zitter's
eaten up with cancer. He's needed
at home. The doctors expect
she'll pass away before the New Year.

"Right where you're living," he goes on,
"that used to be a motorcycle run.
They'd come from all over the county
to race their bikes. They'd tear up
that hill and then go down
the other side. But they were
just having fun. Young guys. Not
like those gangs today, those bad apples."
I wished him luck. Shook his hand.
And went home to my house, the place
they used to race motorcycles.

Later, at the table in my room, looking
out over the water, I give some thought
to just what it is I'm doing here.
What it is I'm after in this life.
It doesn't seem like much,
in the end. I remembered what he'd said
about the young men
and their motorcycles.
Those young men who must be old men
now. Zitter's age, or else
my age. Old enough, in either case.
And for a moment I imagine
the roar of the engines as they surge
up this hill, the laughter and
shouting as they spill, swear, get up,

shake themselves off, and walk
their bikes to the top.
Where they slap each other on the back
and reach in the burlap bag for a beer.
Now and then one of them gunning it
for all it's worth, forcing his way
to the top, and then going lickety-
split down the other side!
Disappearing in a roar, in a cloud of dust.
Right outside my window is where
all this happened. We vanish soon enough.
Soon enough, eaten up.

September

September, and somewhere the last
of the sycamore leaves
have returned to earth.

Wind clears the sky of clouds.

What's left here? Grouse, silver salmon,
and the struck pine not far from the house.
A tree hit by lightning. But even now
beginning to live again. A few shoots
miraculously appearing.

Stephen Foster's "Maggie by My Side"
plays on the radio.

I listen with my eyes far away.

The White Field

Woke up feeling anxious and bone-lonely.
Unable to give my attention to anything
beyond coffee and cigarettes. Of course,
the best antidote for this is work.
"What is your duty? What each day requires,"
said Goethe, or someone like him.
But I didn't have any sense of duty.
I didn't feel like doing anything.
I felt as if I'd lost my will, and my memory.
And I had. If someone had come along
at that minute, as I was slurping coffee, and said,
"Where were you when I needed you?
How have you spent your life? What'd you do
even two days ago?" What could I have said?
I'd only have gawped. Then I tried.
Remembered back a couple of days.
Driving to the end of that road with Morris.
Taking our fishing gear from the jeep.
Strapping on snowshoes, and walking across the white field
toward the river. Every so often
turning around to look at the strange tracks
we'd left. Feeling glad enough to be alive
as we kicked up rabbits, and ducks passed over.

Then to come upon Indians standing in the river
in chest-high waders! Dragging a net for steelhead
through the pool we planned to fish.
The hole just above the river's mouth.
Them working in relentless silence. Cigarettes
hanging from their lips. Not once
looking up or otherwise acknowledging
our existence.

*

"Christ almighty," Morris said.
"This is for the birds." And we snowshoed back
across the field, cursing our luck, cursing Indians.
The day in all other respects unremarkable.
Except when I was driving the jeep
and Morris showed me the three-inch scar
across the back of his hand from the hot stove
he'd fallen against in elk camp.

But this happened the day before yesterday.
It's yesterday that got away, that slipped through
the net and back to sea.

Yet hearing those distant voices down the road just now,
I seem to recall everything. And I understand
that yesterday had its own relentless logic.
Just like today, and all the other days in my life.

Shooting

I wade through wheat up to my belly,
cradling a shotgun in my arms.
Tess is asleep back at the ranch house.
The moon pales. Then loses face completely
as the sun spears up over the mountains.

Why do I pick this moment
to remember my aunt taking me aside that time
and saying, *What I am going to tell you now
you will remember every day of your life?*
But that's all I can remember.

I've never been able to trust memory. My own
or anyone else's. I'd like to know what on earth
I'm doing here in this strange regalia.
It's my friend's wheat – this much is true.
And right now, his dog is on point.

*

Tess is opposed to killing for sport,
or any other reason. Yet not long ago she
threatened to kill me. The dog inches forward.
I stop moving. I can't see or hear
my breath any longer.

Step by tiny step, the day advances. Suddenly,
the air explodes with birds.
Tess sleeps through it. When she wakes,
October will be over. Guns and talk
of shooting behind us.

The Window

A storm blew in last night and knocked out
the electricity. When I looked
through the window, the trees were translucent.
Bent and covered with rime. A vast calm
lay over the countryside.
I knew better. But at that moment
I felt I'd never in my life made any
false promises, nor committed
so much as one indecent act. My thoughts
were virtuous. Later on that morning,
of course, electricity was restored.
The sun moved from behind the clouds,
melting the hoarfrost.
And things stood as they had before.

Heels

Begin nude, looking for the socks
worn yesterday and maybe
the day before, etc. They're not
on your feet, but they can't

have gone far. They're under the bed!
You take them up and give them
a good shaking to free the dust.
Shaking's no more than they deserve.
Now run your hand down the limp,
shapeless things. These blue,
brown, black, green, or grey socks.
You feel you could put your arm into one
and it wouldn't make a particle
of difference. So why not do this
one thing you're inclined to do?
You draw them on over your fingers
and work them up to the elbow.
You close and open your fists. Then
close them again, and keep them that way.
Now your hands are like heels
that could stamp
on things. Anything.
You're heading for the door
when a draft of air hits your ankles
and you're reminded of those wild swans
at Coole, and the wild swans at places
you've never heard of, let alone
visited. You understand now
just how far away you are from all that
as you fumble with the closed door.
Then the door opens! You wanted it
to be morning, as expected
after a night's uneasy sleep.
But stars are overhead, and the moon
reels above dark trees.
You raise your arms and gesture.
A man with socks over his hands
under the night sky.
It's like, but not like, a dream.

The Phone Booth

She slumps in the booth, weeping
into the phone. Asking a question
or two, and weeping some more.
Her companion, an old fellow in jeans
and denim shirt, stands waiting
his turn to talk, and weep.
She hands him the phone.
For a minute they are together
in the tiny booth, his tears
dropping alongside hers. Then
she goes to lean against the fender
of their sedan. And listens
to him talk about arrangements.

I watch all this from my car.
I don't have a phone at home, either.
I sit behind the wheel,
smoking, waiting to make
my own arrangements. Pretty soon
he hangs up. Comes out and wipes his face.
They get in the car and sit
with the windows rolled up.
The glass grows steamy as she
leans into him, as he puts
his arm around her shoulders.
The workings of comfort in that cramped, public place.

I take my small change over
to the booth, and step inside.
But leaving the door open, it's
so close in there. The phone still warm to the touch.
I hate to use a phone
that's just brought news of death.
But I have to, it being the only phone
for miles, and one that might
listen without taking sides.

I put in coins and wait.
Those people in the car wait too.
He starts the engine then kills it.
Where to? None of us able
to figure it. Not knowing
where the next blow might fall,
or why. The ringing at the other end
stops when she picks it up.
Before I can say two words, the phone
begins to shout, "I told you it's over!
Finished! You can go
to hell as far as I'm concerned!"

I drop the phone and pass my hand
across my face. I close and open the door.
The couple in the sedan roll
their windows down and
watch, their tears stilled
for a moment in the face of this distraction.
Then they roll their windows up
and sit behind the glass. We
don't go anywhere for a while.
And then we go.

Cadillacs and Poetry

New snow onto old ice last night. Now,
errand-bound to town, preoccupied with the mudge
in his head, he applied his brakes too fast.
And found himself in a big car out of control,
moving broadside down the road in the immense
stillness of the winter morning. Headed
inexorably for the intersection.
The things that were passing through his mind?
The news film on TV of three alley cats

and a rhesus monkey with electrodes implanted
in their skulls; the time he stopped to photograph
a buffalo near where the Little Big Horn
joined the Big Horn; his new graphite rod
with the Limited Lifetime Warranty;
the polyps the doctor'd found on his bowel;
the Bukowski line that flew
through his mind from time to time:
We'd all like to pass by in a 1995 Cadillac.
His head a hive of arcane activity.
Even during the time it took his car
to slide around on the highway and point him
back in the direction he'd come from.
The direction of home, and relative security.
The engine was dead. The immense stillness
descended once more. He took off his woolen cap
and wiped his forehead. But after a moment's
consideration, started his car, turned around
and continued on into town.
More carefully, yes. But thinking all the while
along the same lines as before. Old ice, new snow.
Cats. A monkey. Fishing. Wild buffalo.
The sheer poetry in musing on Cadillacs
that haven't been built yet. The chastening effect
of the doctor's fingers.

Simple

A break in the clouds. The blue
outline of the mountains.
Dark yellow of the fields.
Black river. What am I doing here,
lonely and filled with remorse?

*

I go on casually eating from the bowl
of raspberries. If I were dead,
I remind myself, I wouldn't
be eating them. It's not so simple.
It is that simple.

The Scratch

I woke up with a spot of blood
over my eye. A scratch
halfway across my forehead. But
I'm sleeping alone these days.
Why on earth would a man raise his hand
against himself, even in sleep?
It's this and similar questions
I'm trying to answer this morning.
As I study my face in the window.

Mother

My mother calls to wish me a Merry Christmas.
And to tell me if this snow keeps on
she intends to kill herself. I want to say
I'm not myself this morning, please
give me a break. I may have to borrow a psychiatrist
again. The one who always asks me the most fertile
of questions, "But what are you *really* feeling?"
Instead, I tell her one of our skylights
has a leak. While I'm talking, the snow is
melting onto the couch. I say I've switched to All-Bran
so there's no need to worry any longer
about me getting cancer, and her money coming to an end.
She hears me out. Then informs me
she's leaving *this goddamn place*. Somehow. The only time
she wants to see it, or me again, is from her coffin.

Suddenly, I ask if she remembers the time Dad
was dead drunk and bobbed the tail of the Labrador pup.
I go on like this for a while, talking about
those days. She listens, waiting her turn.
It continues to snow. It snows and snows
as I hang on the phone. The trees and rooftops
are covered with it. How can I talk about this?
How can I possibly explain what I'm feeling?

The Child

Seeing the child again.
Not having seen him
for six months. His face
seems broader than last time.
Heavier. Almost coarse.
More like his father's now.
Devoid of mirth. The eyes
narrowed and without
expression. Don't expect
gentleness or pity
from this child, now or ever.
There's something rough,
even cruel, in the grasp
of his small hand.
I turn him loose.
His shoes scuff against
each other as he makes for the door.
As it opens. As he gives his cry.

The Fields

The worms crawl in,
the worms crawl out.
The worms play pinochle
in your snout.
— CHILDHOOD DITTY

I was nearsighted and had to get up close
so I could see it in the first place: the earth
that'd been torn with a disk or plow.
But I could smell it, and I didn't like it.
To me it was gruesome, suggesting death
and the grave. I was running once and fell
and came up with a mouthful. That
was enough to make me want to keep my distance
from fields just after they'd been sliced open
to expose whatever lay teeming underneath.
And I never cared anything for gardens, either.
Those over-ripe flowers in summer bloom.
Or spuds lying just under the surface
with only part of their faces showing.
Those places I shied away from, too. Even today
I can do without a garden. But something's changed.

There's nothing I like better now than to walk into
a freshly turned field and kneel and let the soft dirt
slide through my fingers. I'm lucky to live
close to the fields I'm talking about.
I've even made friends with some of the farmers.
The same men who used to strike me
as unfriendly and sinister.
So what if the worms come sooner or later?
And what's it matter if the winter snow piles up
higher than fences, then melts and drains away
deep into the earth to water what's left of us?
It's okay. Quite a lot was accomplished here, after all.

I gambled and lost, sure. Then gambled some more,
and won. My eyesight is failing. But if I move
up close and look carefully, I can see all kinds of life
in the earth. Not just worms, but beetles, ants, ladybugs.
Things like that. I'm gladdened, not concerned with the sight.
It's nice to walk out into a field any day
that I want and not feel afraid. I love to reach
down and bring a handful of dirt right up under my nose.
And I can push with my feet and feel the earth give
under my shoes. I can stand there quietly
under the great balanced sky, motionless.
With this impulse to take off my shoes.
But just an impulse. More important,
this not moving. And then
Amazing! to walk that opened field —
and keep walking.

After Reading Two Towns in Provence

FOR M. F. K. FISHER

I went out for a minute and
left your book on the table.
Something came up. Next morning,
at a quarter to six,
dawn began. Men had already
gone into the fields to work.
Windrows of leaves lay
alongside the track.
Reminding me of fall.
I turned to the first page
and began to read.

*

I spent the entire morning
in your company, in Aix,
in the South of France.
When I looked up,
it was twelve o'clock.

And they all said I'd never find a place
for myself in this life!
Said I'd never be happy,
not in this world, or the next.
That's how much they knew.
Those dopes.

Evening

I fished alone that languid autumn evening.
Fished as darkness kept coming on.
Experiencing exceptional loss and then
exceptional joy when I brought a silver salmon
to the boat, and dipped a net under the fish.
Secret heart! When I looked into the moving water
and up at the dark outline of the mountains
behind the town, nothing hinted then
I would suffer so this longing
to be back once more, before I die.
Far from everything, and far from myself.

The Rest

Clouds hang loosely over this mountain range
behind my house. In a while, the light
will go and the wind come up
to scatter these clouds, or some others,
across the sky.
                    I drop to my knees,

roll the big salmon onto its side
on the wet grass, and begin to use
the knife I was born with. Soon
I'll be at the table in the living room,
trying to raise the dead. The moon
and the dark water my companions.
My hands are silvery with scales.
Fingers mingling with the dark blood.
Finally, I cut loose the massive head.
I bury what needs burying
and keep the rest. Take one last look
at the high blue light. Turn
toward my house. My night.

Slippers

The four of us sitting around that afternoon.
Caroline telling her dream. How she woke up
barking this one night. And found her little dog,
Teddy, beside the bed, watching.
The man who was her husband at the time
watched too as she told of the dream.
Listened carefully. Even smiled. But
there was something in his eyes. A way
of looking, and a look. We've all had it . . .
Already he was in love with a woman
named Jane, though this is no judgment
on him, or Jane, or anyone else. Everyone went on
to tell a dream. I didn't have any.
I looked at your feet, tucked up on the sofa,
in slippers. All I could think to say,
but didn't, was how those slippers were still warm
one night when I picked them up
where you'd left them. I put them beside the bed.
But a quilt fell and covered them
during the night. Next morning, you looked

everywhere for them. Then called downstairs,
"I found my slippers!" This is a small thing,
I know, and between us. Nevertheless,
it has moment. Those lost slippers. And
that cry of delight.
It's okay that this happened
a year or more ago. It could've been
yesterday, or the day before. What difference?
Delight, and a cry.

Asia

It's good to live near the water.
Ships pass so close to land
a man could reach out
and break a branch from one of the willow trees
that grow here. Horses run wild
down by the water, along the beach.
If the men on board wanted, they could
fashion a lariat and throw it
and bring one of the horses on deck.
Something to keep them company
for the long journey East.

From my balcony I can read the faces
of the men as they stare at the horses,
the trees, and two-story houses.
I know what they're thinking
when they see a man waving from a balcony,
his red car in the drive below.
They look at him and consider themselves
lucky. What a mysterious piece
of good fortune, they think, that's brought
them all this way to the deck of a ship
bound for Asia. Those years of doing odd jobs,
or working in warehouses, or longshoring,

or simply hanging out on the docks,
are forgotten about. Those things happened
to other, younger men,
if they happened at all.

                        The men on board
raise their arms and wave back.
Then stand still, gripping the rail,
as the ship glides past. The horses
move from under the trees and into the sun.
They stand like statues of horses.
Watching the ship as it passes.
Waves breaking against the ship.
Against the beach. And in the mind
of the horses, where
it is always Asia.

The Gift

FOR TESS

Snow began falling late last night. Wet flakes
dropping past windows, snow covering
the skylights. We watched for a time, surprised
and happy. Glad to be here, and nowhere else.
I loaded up the wood stove. Adjusted the flue.
We went to bed, where I closed my eyes at once.
But for some reason, before falling asleep,
I recalled the scene at the airport
in Buenos Aires the evening we left.
How still and deserted the place seemed!
Dead quiet except the sound of our engines
as we backed away from the gate and
taxied slowly down the runway in a light snow.
The windows in the terminal building dark.
No one in evidence, not even a ground crew. "It's as if
the whole place is in mourning," you said.

I opened my eyes. Your breathing said
you were fast asleep. I covered you with an arm
and went on from Argentina to recall a place
I lived in once in Palo Alto. No snow in Palo Alto.
But I had a room and two windows looking onto the
 Bayshore Freeway.
The refrigerator stood next to the bed.
When I became dehydrated in the middle of the night,
all I had to do to slake that thirst was reach out
and open the door. The light inside showed the way
to a bottle of cold water. A hot plate
sat in the bathroom close to the sink.
When I shaved, the pan of water bubbled
on the coil next to the jar of coffee granules.

I sat on the bed one morning, dressed, clean-shaven,
drinking coffee, putting off what I'd decided to do. Finally
dialed Jim Houston's number in Santa Cruz.
And asked for 75 dollars. He said he didn't have it.
His wife had gone to Mexico for a week.
He simply didn't have it. He was coming up short
this month. "It's okay," I said. "I understand."
And I did. We talked a little
more, then hung up. He didn't have it.
I finished the coffee, more or less, just as the plane
lifted off the runway into the sunset.
I turned in the seat for one last look
at the lights of Buenos Aires. Then closed my eyes
for the long trip back.

This morning there's snow everywhere. We remark on it.
You tell me you didn't sleep well. I say
I didn't either. You had a terrible night. "Me too."
We're extraordinarily calm and tender with each other
as if sensing the other's rickety state of mind.
As if we knew what the other was feeling. We don't,

of course. We never do. No matter.
It's the tenderness I care about. That's the gift
this morning that moves and holds me.
Same as every morning.

A New Path
to the Waterfall

GIFT

A day so happy.
Fog lifted early, I worked in the garden.
Hummingbirds were stopping over honeysuckle flowers.
There was no thing on earth I wanted to possess.
I knew no one worth my envying him.
Whatever evil I had suffered, I forgot.
To think that once I was the same man did not embarrass me.
In my body I felt no pain.
When straightening up, I saw the blue sea and sails.

— CZESLAW MILOSZ

I

Wet Picture

Those beautiful days
when the city resembles a die, a fan and a bird song
or a scallop shell on the seashore
> *— goodbye, goodbye, pretty girls,*
> *we met today*
and will not ever meet again.

The beautiful Sundays
when the city resembles a football, a card and an ocarina
or a swinging bell
> *— in the sunny street*
> *the shadows of passers-by were kissing*
and people walked away, total strangers.

Those beautiful evenings
when the city resembles a rose, a chessboard, a violin
or a crying girl
> *— we played dominoes,*
> *black-dotted dominoes with the thin girls in the bar,*
> *watching their knees,*

> *which were emaciated*
> *like two skulls with the silk crowns of their garters*
> *in the desperate kingdom of love.*

— JAROSLAV SEIFERT
(translated by Ewald Osers)

Thermopylae

Back at the hotel, watching her loosen, then comb out
her russet hair in front of the window, she deep in private
    thought,
her eyes somewhere else, I am reminded for some reason of
    those
Lacedaemonians Herodotus wrote about, whose duty
it was to hold the Gates against the Persian army. And who
did. For four days. First, though, under the disbelieving
eyes of Xerxes himself, the Greek soldiers sprawled as if
uncaring, outside their timber-hewn walls, arms stacked,
combing and combing their long hair, as if it were
simply another day in an otherwise unremarkable campaign.
When Xerxes demanded to know what such display signified,
he was told, *When these men are about to leave their lives*
they first make their heads beautiful.
       She lays down her bone-handle comb and moves closer
to the window and the mean afternoon light. Something, some
creaking movement from below, has caught her
attention. A look, and it lets her go.

Two Worlds

In air heavy
with odor of crocuses,

sensual smell of crocuses,
I watch a lemon sun disappear,

a sea change blue
to olive black.

I watch lightning leap from Asia as
sleeping,

my love stirs and breathes and
sleeps again,

*

part of this world and yet
part that.

Smoke and Deception

When after supper Tatyana Ivanovna sat quietly down
and took up her knitting, he kept his eyes fixed on her
fingers and chatted away without ceasing.
    "Make all the haste you can to live, my friends . . ." he said.
"God forbid you should sacrifice the present for the future!
There is youth, health, fire in the present; the future is smoke
and deception! As soon as you are twenty,
begin to live."
    Tatyana Ivanovna dropped a knitting-needle.

— ANTON CHEKHOV
"The Privy Councillor"

In a Greek Orthodox Church
near Daphne

Christ broods over our heads
as you comment on this, on that.
Your voice
is borne through those empty chambers still.

Halt with desire, I follow
outside where we wonderingly examine
ruined walls. Wind
rises to meet the evening.

Wind, you're much overdue.
Wind, let me touch you.
Evening, you've been expected all day.
Evening, hold us and cover us.

And evening sinks down at last.
And wind runs to the four corners of the body.
And walls are gone.
And Christ broods over our heads.

For the Record

The papal nuncio, John Burchard, writes calmly
that dozens of mares and stallions
were driven into a courtyard of the Vatican
so the Pope Alexander VI and his daughter,
Lucretia Borgia, could watch from a balcony
"with pleasure and much laughter"
the equine coupling going on below.
When this spectacle was over
they refreshed themselves, then waited
while Lucretia's brother, Caesar,
shot down ten unarmed criminals
who were herded into the same courtyard.
Remember this the next time you see
the name *Borgia,* or the word *Renaissance.*
I don't know what I can make of this,
this morning. I'll leave it for now.
Go for that walk I planned earlier, hope maybe
to see those two herons sift down the cliffside
as they did for us earlier in the season
so we felt alone and freshly
put here, not herded, not
driven.

Transformation

Faithless, we have come here
this morning on empty stomachs
and hearts.
I open my hands to quiet
their stupid pleading, but
they begin to drip
onto the stones.
A woman beside me slips
on those same stones, striking
her head in the Grotto.
Behind me my love with the camera
records it all on color film down
to the finest detail.

But see!
The woman groans, rises slowly
shaking her head: she blesses
those very stones while we escape
through a side door.
Later we play the entire film again and
again. I see the woman keep falling
and getting up, falling and
getting up, Arabs evil-eyeing
the camera. I see myself striking
one pose after the other.

Lord, I tell you
I am without purpose here
in the Holy Land.
My hands grieve in this
bright sunlight.
They walk back and forth along
the Dead Sea shore
with a thirty-year-old man.
Come, Lord. Shrive me.
Too late I hear the film running,

taking it all down.
I look into the camera.
My grin turns to salt. Salt
where I stand.

Threat

Today a woman signaled me in Hebrew.
Then she pulled out her hair, swallowed it
and disappeared. When I returned home,
shaken, three carts stood by the door with
fingernails showing through the sacks of grain.

Conspirators

No sleep. Somewhere near here in the woods, fear
envelops the hands of the lookout.

The white ceiling of our room
has lowered alarmingly with dark.

Spiders come out to plant themselves
on every coffee mug.

Afraid? I know if I put out my hand
I will touch an old shoe three inches long
with bared teeth.

Sweetheart, it's time.
I know you're concealed there behind
that innocent handful of flowers.

Come out.
Don't worry, I promise you.

Listen . . .
There is the rap on the door.

*

But the man who was going to deliver this
instead points a gun at your head.

This Word Love

I will not go when she calls
even if she says *I love you*,
especially that,
even though she swears
and promises nothing
but love love.

The light in this room
covers every
thing equally;
even my arm throws no shadow,
it too is consumed with light.

But this word *love* –
this word grows dark, grows
heavy and shakes itself, begins
to eat, to shudder and convulse
its way through this paper
until we too have dimmed in
its transparent throat and still
are riven, are glistening, hip and thigh, your
loosened hair which knows
no hesitation.

Don't Run

Nadya, pink-cheeked, happy, her eyes shining with tears
in expectation of something extraordinary, circled
in the dance, her white dress billowing and showing glimpses
of her slim, pretty legs in their flesh-tinted
stockings. Varya, thoroughly contented, took Podgorin by the arm

and said to him under her breath with significant expression:
"Misha, don't run away from your happiness. Take it
while it offers itself to you freely, later you will be running
after it, but you won't overtake it."

— ANTON CHEKHOV
"A Visit to Friends"

Woman Bathing

Naches River. Just below the falls.
Twenty miles from any town. A day
of dense sunlight
heavy with odors of love.
How long have we?
Already your body, sharpness of Picasso,
is drying in this highland air.
I towel down your back, your hips,
with my undershirt.
Time is a mountain lion.
We laugh at nothing,
and as I touch your breasts
even the ground-
          squirrels
are dazzled.

II

The Name

I got sleepy while driving and pulled in under a tree at the side of the road. Rolled up in the back seat and went to sleep. How long? Hours. Darkness had come.

    All of a sudden I was awake, and didn't know who I was. I'm fully conscious, but that doesn't help. Where am I? WHO am I? I am something that has just woken up in a back seat, throwing itself around in panic like a cat in a gunnysack. Who am I?

    After a long while my life comes back to me. My name comes to me like an angel. Outside the castle walls there is a trumpet blast (as in the Leonora Overture) and the footsteps that will save me come quickly quickly down the long staircase. It's me coming! It's me!

    But it is impossible to forget the fifteen-second battle in the hell of nothingness, a few feet from a major highway where the cars slip past with their lights on.

— TOMAS TRANSTRÖMER
(*translated by Robert Bly*)

Looking for Work [2]

I have always wanted brook trout
for breakfast.

Suddenly, I find a new path
to the waterfall.

I begin to hurry.
Wake up,

my wife says,
you're dreaming.

    *

But when I try to rise,
the house tilts.

Who's dreaming?
It's noon, she says.

My new shoes wait by the door,
gleaming.

The World Book Salesman

He holds conversation sacred
though a dying art. Smiling,
by turns he is part toady,
part *Oberführer.* Knowing when
is the secret.
Out of the slim briefcase come
maps of all the world;
                deserts, oceans,
photographs, artwork –
it is all there, all there
for the asking
as the doors swing open, crack
or slam.

In the empty
rooms each evening, he eats
alone, watches television, reads
the newspaper with a lust
that begins and ends in the fingertips.
There is no God,
and conversation is a dying art.

The Toes

This foot's giving me nothing
but trouble. The ball,
the arch, the ankle — I'm saying
it hurts to walk. But
mainly it's these toes
I worry about. Those
"terminal digits" as they're
otherwise called. How true!
For them no more delight
in going headfirst
into a hot bath, or
a cashmere sock. Cashmere socks,
no socks, slippers, shoes, Ace
bandage — it's all one and the same
to these dumb toes.
They even looked zonked out
and depressed, as if
somebody'd pumped them full
of Thorazine. They hunch there
stunned and mute — drab, lifeless
things. What in hell is going on?
What kind of toes are these
that nothing matters any longer?
Are these really *my*
toes? Have they forgotten
the old days, what it was like
being alive then? Always first
on line, first onto the dance floor
when the music started.
First to kick up their heels.
Look at them. No, don't.
You don't want to see them,
those slugs. It's only with pain
and difficulty they can recall

the other times, the good times.
Maybe what they really want
is to sever all connection
with the old life, start over,
go underground, live alone
in a retirement manor
somewhere in the Yakima Valley.
But there was a time
they used to strain
with anticipation
simply
curl with pleasure
at the least provocation,
the smallest thing.
The feel of a silk dress
against the fingers, say.
A becoming voice, a touch
behind the neck, even
a passing glance. Any of it!
The sound of hooks being
unfastened, stays coming
undone, garments letting go
onto a cool, hardwood floor.

The Moon, the Train

The moon, the landscape, the train.
We are moving steadily along the south shore
of the lake, past the spas and sanitoriums.
The conductor comes through the club car to tell us
that if we look to the left – there, where those
lights are shining – we will see a lighted tennis
court, and it's probable, even at this hour, we'll
find Franz Kafka on the court. He's crazy about
tennis and can't get enough of it. In a minute, sure

enough – there's Kafka, dressed in whites,
playing doubles against a young man and woman.
An unidentified young woman is Kafka's partner. Which
pair is ahead? Who is keeping score? The ball goes back
and forth, back and forth. Everyone seems to be playing perfectly,
intently. None of the players even bothers to look up
at the passing train. Suddenly the track curves
and begins to go through a woods. I turn in the seat
to look back, but either the lights on the court have been
extinguished suddenly, or the train car is in such
a position that everything behind us is darkness.
It is at this moment that all the patrons left in the club car
decide to order another drink, or something to snack on.
Well, and why not? Kafka was a vegetarian and a teetotaler
himself, but that shouldn't crimp anyone's style. Besides,
no one in the train car seems to show the slightest
interest in the game, or who was playing on the court under
the lights. I was going forward to a new and different
life, and I was really only half interested myself, my
thoughts being somewhere else. Nevertheless, I thought it
was something that was of some slight interest and should be
pointed out; and I was glad the conductor had done so.

      "So that was Kafka," someone behind me spoke up.
      "So," somebody else replied. "So what? I'm Perlmutter.
Pleased to meet you. Let's have a drink." And saying this, he
took a deck of cards out of his shirt pocket and began to shuffle
them back and forth on the table in front of him. His huge
hands were red and chapped; they seemed to want to
devour the cards whole. Once more the track curves
and begins to go through a woods.

Two Carriages

Again the flying horses, the strange voice of drunken Nicanor,
the wind and the persistent snow which got into one's eyes, one's
mouth, and every fold of one's fur coat. . . . The wind whistled,
the coachmen shouted; and while this frantic uproar was going on,
I recalled all the details of that strange wild day, unique in my
life, and it seemed to me that I really had gone out of my mind
or become a different man. It was as though the man I had been
till that day were already a stranger to me. . . . A quarter of an hour
later his horses fell behind and the sound of his bells was
lost in the roar of the snowstorm.

— ANTON CHEKHOV
"The Wife"

Miracle

They're on a one-way flight, bound from LAX
to SFO, both of them drunk and strung-out
having just squirmed through the hearing,
their second bankruptcy in seven years.
And who knows what, if anything, was said
on the plane, or who said it?
It could have been accumulation
of the day's events, or years on years
of failure and corruption that triggered violence.

Earlier, turned inside out, crucified and left
for dead, they'd been dropped like so much
garbage in front of the terminal. But
once inside they found their bearings,
took refuge in an airport lounge where they tossed
back doubles under a banner that read *Go Dodgers!*
They were plastered, as usual, as they buckled
into their seats and, as always, ready to assume
it was the universal human condition, this battle

waged continually with forces past all reckoning,
forces beyond mere human understanding.

But she's cracking. She can't take any more
and soon, without a word, she turns
in her seat and drills him. Punches him and
punches him, and he takes it.
Knowing deep down he deserves it ten times over –
whatever she wants to dish out – he is being
deservedly beaten for something, there are
good reasons. All the while his head is pummeled,
buffeted back and forth, her fists falling
against his ear, his lips, his jaw, he protects
his whiskey. Grips that plastic glass as if, yes,
it's the long-sought treasure right there
on the tray in front of him.

She keeps on until his nose begins to bleed
and it's then he asks her to stop. *Please, baby,
for Christ's sake, stop.* It may be his plea
reaches her as a faint signal from another
galaxy, a dying star, for this is what it is,
a coded sign from some other time and place
needling her brain, reminding her of something
so lost it's gone forever. In any event, she stops
hitting him, goes back to her drink. Why
does she stop? Because she remembers
the fat years preceding the lean? All that history
they'd shared, sticking it out together, the two
of them against the world? No way. If she'd truly
remembered everything and those years had dropped
smack into her lap all at once,
she would've killed him on the spot.

Maybe her arms are tired, that's why she stops.
Say she's tired then. So she stops. He picks up
his drink almost as if nothing's happened
though it has, of course, and his head aches

and reels with it. She goes back to her whiskey
without a word, not even so much as the usual
"bastard" or "son of a bitch." Dead quiet.
He's silent as lice. Holds the drink
napkin under his nose to catch the blood,
turns his head slowly to look out.

Far below, the small steady lights in houses
up and down some coastal valley. It's
the dinner hour down there. People pushing
up to a full table, grace being said,
hands joined together under roofs so solid
they will never blow off those houses — houses where,
he imagines, decent people live and eat, pray
and pull together. People who, if they left
their tables and looked up from the dining
room windows, could see a harvest moon and,
just below, like a lighted insect, the dim glow
of a jetliner. He strains to see over
the wing and beyond, to the myriad lights
of the city they are rapidly approaching,
the place where they live with others of their kind,
the place they call home.

He looks around the cabin. Other people,
that's all. People like themselves
in a way, male or female, one sex
or the other, people not entirely unlike
themselves — hair, ears, eyes, nose, shoulders,
genitals — my God, even the clothes they wear
are similar, and there's that identifying strap
around the middle. But he knows he and she
are not like those others though he'd like it,
and she too, if they were.

Blood soaks his napkin. His head rings and rings
but he can't answer it. And what would he say
if he could? *I'm sorry they're not in. They left*

here, and there too, years ago. They tear
through the thin night air, belted in, bloody husband
and wife, both so still and pale they could be
dead. But they're not, and that's part of
the miracle. All this is one more giant step
into the mysterious experience of their lives.
Who could have foretold any of it years back when,
their hands guiding the knife, they made
that first cut deep into the wedding cake?
Then the next. Who would have listened?
Anyone bringing such tidings of the future
would have been scourged from the gate.

The plane lifts, then banks sharply. He touches
her arm. She lets him. She even takes his hand.
They were made for each other, right? It's fate.
They'll survive. They'll land and pull themselves
together, walk away from this awful fix –
they simply have to, they must.
There's lots in store for them yet, so many fierce
surprises, such exquisite turnings. It's now
they have to account for, the blood
on his collar, the dark smudge of it
staining her cuff.

My Wife

My wife has disappeared along with her clothes.
She left behind two nylon stockings, and
a hairbrush overlooked behind the bed.
I should like to call your attention
to these shapely nylons, and to the strong
dark hair caught in the bristles of the brush.
I drop the nylons into the garbage sack; the brush
I'll keep and use. It is only the bed
that seems strange and impossible to account for.

Wine

Reading a life of Alexander the Great, Alexander
whose rough father, Philip, hired Aristotle to tutor
the young scion and warrior, to put some polish
on his smooth shoulders. Alexander who, later
on the campaign trail into Persia, carried a copy of
The Iliad in a velvet-lined box, he loved that book so
much. He loved to fight and drink, too.
I came to that place in the life where Alexander, after
a long night of carousing, a wine-drunk (the worst kind of drunk –
hangovers you don't forget), threw the first brand
to start a fire that burned Persepolis, capital of the Persian Empire
(ancient even in Alexander's day).
Razed it right to the ground. Later, of course,
next morning – maybe even while the fire roared – he was
remorseful. But nothing like the remorse felt
the next evening when, during a disagreement that turned ugly
and, on Alexander's part, overbearing, his face flushed
from too many bowls of uncut wine, Alexander rose drunkenly to
    his feet,
grabbed a spear and drove it through the breast
of his friend, Cletus, who'd saved his life at Granicus.

For three days Alexander mourned. Wept. Refused food. "Refused
to see to his bodily needs." He even promised
to give up wine forever.
(I've heard such promises and the lamentations that go with them.)
Needless to say, life for the army came to a full stop
as Alexander gave himself over to his grief.
But at the end of those three days, the fearsome heat
beginning to take its toll on the body of his dead friend,
Alexander was persuaded to take action. Pulling himself together
and leaving his tent, he took out his copy of Homer, untied it,
began to turn the pages. Finally he gave orders that the funeral
rites described for Patroklos be followed to the letter:
he wanted Cletus to have the biggest possible send-off.

And when the pyre was burning and the bowls of wine were
passed his way during the ceremony? Of course, what do you
think? Alexander drank his fill and passed
out. He had to be carried to his tent. He had to be lifted, to be put
into his bed.

After the Fire

The little bald old man, General Zhukov's cook, the very one
whose cap had been burnt, walked in. He sat down and
listened. Then he, too, began to reminisce and tell stories.
Nikolay, sitting on the stove with his legs hanging down,
listened and asked questions about the dishes
that were prepared for the gentry in the old days.
They talked about chops, cutlets, various soups and sauces, and
the cook, who remembered everything very well, mentioned dishes
that were no longer prepared; there was one, for instance – a dish
made of bulls' eyes, that was called "waking up
in the morning."

– ANTON CHEKHOV
"Peasants"

III

What lasts is what you start with.

— CHARLES WRIGHT
from *A Journal of Southern Rivers*

The Kitchen

At Sportsmen's Park, near Yakima, I crammed a hook
with worms, then cast it toward the middle
of the pond, hoping for bass. Bullfrogs scraped the air
invisibly. A turtle, flapjack-sized, slid
from a lily pad while another pulled itself onto
the same pad, a little staging area. Blue sky, warm
afternoon. I pushed a forked branch
into the sandy bank, rested the pole in the fork,
watched the bobber for a while, then beat off.
Grew sleepy then and let my eyes close.
Maybe I dreamed. I did that back then. When
suddenly, in my sleep, I heard a plop, and my eyes
flew open. My pole was gone!
I saw it tearing a furrow through
the scummy water. The bobber appeared, then
disappeared, then showed itself once more
skimming the surface, then gone under again.
What could I do? I bellowed, and bellowed some more.
Began to run along the bank, swearing to God
I would not touch myself again if He'd let me
retrieve that pole, that fish. Of course
there was no answer, not a sign.
I hung around the pond a long time
(the same pond that'd take my friend a year later),

once in a while catching a glimpse of my bobber,
now here, now there. Shadows grew fat
and dropped from trees into the pond. Finally
it was dark, and I biked home.

My dad was drunk
and in the kitchen with a woman not his wife, nor
my mother either. This woman was, I swear, sitting
on his lap, drinking a beer. A woman
with part of a front tooth
missing. She tried to grin as she rose
to her feet. My dad stayed where he was, staring at me
as if he didn't recognize his own get. *Here,
what is it, boy?* he said. *What happened,
son?* Swaying against the sink, the woman wet her lips
and waited for whatever was to happen next.
My dad waited too, there in his old place
at the kitchen table, the bulge in his pants
subsiding. We all waited and wondered
at the stuttered syllables, the words made to cling
as anguish that poured from my raw young mouth.

Songs in the Distance

Because it was a holiday, they bought a herring at the tavern
and made a soup of the herring head. At midday
they sat down to have tea and went on drinking it until
they were all perspiring: they looked actually swollen with
tea; and then they attacked the soup, all helping themselves
out of one pot. The herring itself Granny hid away.
In the evening a potter was firing pots on the slope. Down
below in the meadow the girls got up a round dance
and sang songs . . . and in the distance the singing sounded soft
and melodious. In and about the tavern the peasants were

making a racket. They sang with drunken voices, discordantly,
and swore at one another. . . . And the girls and children listened
to the swearing without turning a hair; it was evident
that they had been used to it from their cradles.

— ANTON CHEKHOV
"Peasants"

Suspenders

Mom said I didn't have a belt that fit and
I was going to have to wear suspenders to school
next day. Nobody wore suspenders to second grade,
or any other grade for that matter. She said,
You'll wear them or else I'll use them on you. I don't
want any more trouble. My dad said something then. He
was in the bed that took up most of the room in the cabin
where we lived. He asked if we could be quiet and settle this
in the morning. Didn't he have to go in early to work in
the morning? He asked if I'd bring him
a glass of water. It's all that whiskey he drank, Mom said. He's
dehydrated.

      I went to the sink and, I don't know why, brought him
a glass of soapy dishwater. He drank it and said, That sure
tasted funny, son. Where'd this water come from?
Out of the sink, I said.
I thought you loved your dad, Mom said.
I do, I do, I said, and went over to the sink and dipped a glass
into the soapy water and drank off two glasses just
to show them. I love Dad, I said.
Still, I thought I was going to be sick then and there. Mom said,
I'd be ashamed of myself if I was you. I can't believe you'd
do your dad that way. And, by God, you're going to wear those
suspenders tomorrow, or else. I'll snatch you bald-headed if you
give me any trouble in the morning. I don't want to wear
      suspenders,

I said. You're going to wear suspenders, she said. And with that
she took the suspenders and began to whip me around the bare legs
while I danced in the room and cried. My dad
yelled at us to stop, for God's sake, stop. His head was killing him,
and he was sick at his stomach from soapy dishwater
besides. That's thanks to this one, Mom said. It was then somebody
began to pound on the wall of the cabin next to ours. At first it
sounded like it was a fist — *boom-boom-boom* — and then
whoever it was switched to a mop or a broom
handle. For Christ's sake, go to bed over there! somebody yelled.
Knock it off! And we did. We turned out the lights and
got into our beds and became quiet. The quiet that comes to a house
where nobody can sleep.

What You Need to Know for Fishing

The angler's coat and trowsers should be of cloth,
not too thick and heavy, for if they be the sooner wet
they will be the sooner dry. Water-proof velveteens,
fustians, and mole-skins — rat catcher's costume —
ought never to be worn by the angler for if
he should have to swim a mile or two on any occasion
he would find them a serious weight once thoroughly
saturated with water. And should he have a stone
of fish in his creel, it would be safest not to make
the attempt. An elderly gentleman of my acquaintance
suggests the propriety of anglers wearing *cork* jackets
which, if strapped under the shoulders, would enable
the wearer to visit any part of a lake where,
in warm weather, with an umbrella over his head,
he might enjoy his sport, cool and comfortable, as if
"in a sunny pleasure dome with caves of ice."
This same gentleman thinks that a bottle of *Reading* sauce,

a box of "peptic pills," and a portable frying-pan
ought to form part of every angler's travelling equipage.

— STEPHEN OLIVER
from *Scenes and Recollections of Fly Fishing in
Northumberland, Cumberland and Westmoreland* (1834)

Oyntment to Alure Fish to the Bait

Take Mans Fat and Cats Fat, of each half an Ounce;
Mummy finely poudred, three Drams; Cummin-seed
finely poudred, one Dram; distilled Oyl of Annise
and Spike, of each six Drops; Civet two Grains,
and Camphir four Grains. Make an Oyntment.
When you Angle, annoint eight Inches of the Line
next the Hook therewith, and keep it in
a pewter Box. When you use this Oyntment
never Angle with less than three hairs next Hook
because if you Angle with but one hair
it will not stick on. Take the Bones or Scull
of a Dead-man, at the opening of a Grave,
and beat the same into pouder, and put this pouder
in the Moss wherein you keep your worms. But
others like Grave-earth as well. Now
go find your water.

— JAMES CHETHAM
from *The Angler's Vade Mecum* (1681)

The Sturgeon

Narrow-bodied, iron head like the flat side
of a lance,
          mouth underneath,
the sturgeon is a bottom-feeder

and can't see well.
Mosslike feelers hang down over
the slumbrous lips,
and its dorsal fins and plated backbone
mark it out
something left over from another world.
The sturgeon
lives alone, confines itself
to large, freshwater rivers, and takes
100 years getting around to its first mating.

        Once with my father
at the Central Washington State Fair
I saw a sturgeon that weighed 900 pounds
winched up in a corner
of the Agricultural Exhibit Building.
I will not forget that.
A card gave the name in italics,
also a sketch, as they say,
of its biography –
    which my father read
    and then read aloud.

The largest are netted
in the Don River
somewhere in Russia.
These are called White Sturgeon
and no one can be sure
just how large they are.
The next biggest ones recorded
are trapped at the mouth
of the Yukon River in Alaska
and weigh upwards of 1,900 pounds.

     *

This particular specimen
        – I am quoting –
was killed in the exploratory dynamiting
that went on in the summer of 1951
at Celilo Falls on the Columbia River.
I remember my father told me
a story then about three men he knew long ago in Oregon
who hooked what must have been the largest in the world.
                So big, he said,
                they fastened a team of horses
                to it – the cable or chain, whatever
                they were using for line –
                and for a while, even the horses
                were at a standstill.

I don't remember much else –
maybe it got away
even then – just my father there beside me
leaning on his arms over the railing, staring, the two of us
staring up at that great dead fish,
and that marvelous story of his, all
surfacing, now and then.

Night Dampness

I am sick and tired of the river, the stars
that strew the sky, this heavy funereal silence.
To while away the time, I talk to my coachman, who
looks like an old man. . . . He tells me that this dark, forbidding river
abounds in sterlet, white salmon, eel-pout, pike, but there is no one
to catch the fish and no tackle to catch it with.

– ANTON CHEKHOV
"Across Siberia"

Another Mystery

That time I tagged along with my dad to the dry cleaners –
What'd I know then about Death? Dad comes out carrying
a black suit in a plastic bag. Hangs it up behind the back seat
of the old coupe and says, "This is the suit your grandpa
is going to leave the world in." What on earth
could he be talking about? I wondered.
I touched the plastic, the slippery lapel of that coat
that was going away, along with my grandpa. Those days it was
just another mystery.

Then there was a long interval, a time in which relatives departed
this way and that, left and right. Then it was my dad's turn.
I sat and watched him rise up in his own smoke. He didn't own
a suit. So they dressed him gruesomely
in a cheap sports coat and tie,
for the occasion. Wired his lips
into a smile as if he wanted to reassure us, *Don't worry, it's*
not as bad as it looks. But we knew better. He was dead,
wasn't he? What else could go wrong? (His eyelids
were sewn closed, too, so he wouldn't have to witness
the frightful exhibit.) I touched
his hand. Cold. The cheek where a little stubble had
broken through along the jaw. Cold.

Today I reeled this clutter up from the depths.
Just an hour or so ago when I picked up my own suit
from the dry cleaners and hung it carefully behind the back seat.
I drove it home, opened the car door and
lifted it out into sunlight. I stood there a minute
in the road, my fingers crimped on the wire hanger. Then
tore a hole through the plastic to the other side. Took one of
the empty sleeves between my fingers and held it –
the rough, palpable fabric.
I reached through to the other side.

IV

Return to Kraków in 1880

So I returned here from the big capitals,
To a town in a narrow valley under the cathedral hill
With royal tombs. To a square under the tower
And the shrill trumpet sounding noon, breaking
Its note in half because the Tartar arrow
Has once again struck the trumpeter.
And pigeons. And the garish kerchiefs of women selling flowers.
And groups chattering under the Gothic portico of the church.
My trunk of books arrived, this time for good.
What I know of my laborious life: it was lived.
Faces are paler in memory than on daguerreotypes.
I don't need to write memos and letters every morning.
Others will take over, always with the same hope,
The one we know is senseless and devote our lives to.
My country will remain what it is, the backyard of empires,
Nursing its humiliation with provincial daydreams.
I leave for a morning walk tapping with my cane:
The places of old people are taken by new old people
And where the girls once strolled in their rustling skirts,
New ones are strolling, proud of their beauty.
And children trundle hoops for more than half a century.
In a basement a cobbler looks up from his bench,
A hunchback passes by with his inner lament,
Then a fashionable lady, a fat image of the deadly sins.
So the Earth endures, in every petty matter
And in the lives of men, irreversible.
And it seems a relief. To win? To lose?
What for, if the world will forget us anyway.

— CZESLAW MILOSZ
(*translated by Milosz and Robert Hass*)

Sunday Night

Make use of the things around you.
This light rain
Outside the window, for one.
This cigarette between my fingers,
These feet on the couch.
The faint sound of rock-and-roll,
The red Ferrari in my head.
The woman bumping
Drunkenly around in the kitchen . . .
Put it all in,
Make use.

The Painter & the Fish

All day he'd been working like a locomotive.
I mean he was *painting*, the brush strokes
coming like clockwork. Then he called
home. And that was that. That was all she
wrote. He shook like a leaf. He started
smoking again. He lay down and got back
up. Who could sleep if your woman sneered
and said time was running out? He drove
into town. But he didn't go drinking.
No, he went walking. He walked past a mill
called "the mill." Smell of fresh-cut
lumber, lights everywhere, men driving
jitneys and forklifts, driving themselves.
Lumber piled to the top of the warehouse,
the whine and groan of machinery. Easy
enough to recollect, he thought. He went
on, rain falling now, a soft rain that wants
to do its level best not to interfere
with anything and in return asks only
that it not be forgotten. The painter

turned up his collar and said to himself
he wouldn't forget. He came to a lighted
building where, inside a room, men played
cards at a big table. A man wearing
a cap stood at the window and looked
out through the rain as he smoked
a pipe. That was an image he didn't
want to forget either, but then
with his next thought he
shrugged. What was the point?

He walked on until he reached the jetty
with its rotten pilings. Rain fell
harder now. It hissed as it struck
the water. Lightning came and went.
Lightning broke across the sky
like memory, like revelation. Just
when he was at the point of despair,
a fish came up out of the dark
water under the jetty and then fell back
and then rose again in a flash
to stand on its tail and shake itself!
The painter could hardly credit
his eyes, or his ears! He'd just
had a sign — faith didn't enter
into it. The painter's mouth flew
open. By the time he'd reached home
he'd quit smoking and vowed never
to talk on the telephone again.
He put on his smock and picked up
his brush. He was ready to begin
again, but he didn't know if one
canvas could hold it all. Never
mind. He'd carry it over
onto another canvas if he had to.
It was all or nothing. Lightning, water,
fish, cigarettes, cards, machinery,

the human heart, that old port.
Even the woman's lips against
the receiver, even that.
The curl of her lip.

At Noon

You are served "duck soup" and nothing more. But you
can hardly swallow this broth; it is a turbid liquid
in which bits of wild duck and guts
imperfectly cleaned are swimming. . . .
It is far from tasty.

— ANTON CHEKHOV
"Across Siberia"

Artaud

Among the hieroglyphs, the masks, the unfinished poems,
the spectacle unfolds: *Antonin et son double*.
They are at work now, calling up the old demons.
The enchantments, etc. The tall, scarred-looking
one at the desk, the one with the cigarette and
no teeth to speak of, is prone to
boldness, to a certain excess
in speech, in gesture. The other is cautious,
watches carefully his opportunity, is effacing even. But
at certain moments still hints broadly, impatiently
of his necessarily arrogant existence.

Antonin, sure enough, there are no more masterpieces.
But your hands trembled as you said it,
and behind every curtain there is always, as you
knew, a rustling.

Caution

Trying to write a poem while it was still dark out,
he had the unmistakable feeling he was being watched.
Laid down the pen and looked around. In a minute,
he got up and moved through the rooms of his house.
He checked the closets. Nothing, of course.
Still, he wasn't taking any chances.
He turned off the lamps and sat in the dark.
Smoking his pipe until the feeling had passed
and it grew light out. He looked down
at the white paper before him. Then got up
and made the rounds of his house once more.
The sound of his breathing accompanying him.
Otherwise nothing. Obviously.
Nothing.

One More

He arose early, the morning tinged with excitement,
eager to be at his desk. He had toast and eggs, cigarettes
and coffee, musing all the while on the work ahead, the hard
path through the forest. The wind blew clouds across
the sky, rattling the leaves that remained on the branches
outside his window. Another few days for them and they'd
be gone, those leaves. There was a poem there, maybe;
he'd have to give it some thought. He went to
his desk, hesitated for a long moment, and then made
what proved to be the most important decision
he'd make all day, something his entire flawed life
had prepared him for. He pushed aside the folder of poems —
one poem in particular still held him in its grip after
a restless night's sleep. (But, really, what's one more, or
less? So what? The work would keep for a while yet,
wouldn't it?) He had the whole wide day opening before him.
Better to clear his decks first. He'd deal with a few items

of business, even some family matters he'd let go far
too long. So he got cracking. He worked hard all day – love
and hate getting into it, a little compassion (very little), some
fellow-feeling, even despair and joy.
There were occasional flashes of anger rising, then
subsiding, as he wrote letters, saying "yes" or "no" or "it
depends" – explaining why, or why not, to people out there
at the margin of his life or people he'd never seen and never
would see. Did they matter? Did they give a damn?
Some did. He took some calls too, and made some others, which
in turn created the need to make a few more. So-and-so, being
unable to talk now, promised to call back next day.

Toward evening, worn out and clearly (but mistakenly, of course)
feeling he'd done something resembling an honest day's work,
he stopped to take inventory and note the couple of
phone calls he'd have to make next morning if
he wanted to stay abreast of things, if he didn't want to
write still more letters, which he didn't. By now,
it occurred to him, he was sick of all business, but he went on
in this fashion, finishing one last letter that should have been
answered weeks ago. Then he looked up. It was nearly dark outside.
The wind had laid. And the trees – they were still now, nearly
stripped of their leaves. But, finally, his desk was clear,
if he didn't count that folder of poems he was
uneasy just to look at. He put the folder in a drawer, out
of sight. That was a good place for it, it was safe there and
he'd know just where to go to lay his hands on it when he
felt like it. Tomorrow! He'd done everything he could do
today. There were still those few calls he'd have to make,
and he forgot who was supposed to call him, and there were a
few notes he was required to send due to a few of the calls,
but he had it made now, didn't he? He was out of the woods.
He could call today a day. He'd done what he had to do.
What his duty told him he should do. He'd fulfilled his sense of
obligation and hadn't disappointed anybody.

*

But at that moment, sitting there in front of his tidy desk,
he was vaguely nagged by the memory of a poem he'd wanted
to write that morning, and there was that other poem
he hadn't gotten back to either.

So there it is. Nothing much else needs be said, really. What
can be said for a man who chooses to blab on the phone
all day, or else write stupid letters
while he lets his poems go unattended and uncared for,
              abandoned –
or worse, unattempted. This man doesn't deserve poems
and they shouldn't be given to him in any form.
              His poems, should he ever produce any more,
ought to be eaten by mice.

At the Bird Market

There is no deceiving the bird-fancier. He sees and
understands his bird from a distance. "There is no relying on
that bird," a fancier will say,
looking into a siskin's beak, and counting the feathers
on its tail. "He sings now, it's true, but what
of that? I sing in company too. No, my boy, shout, sing
to me without company; sing in solitude, if
you can. . . . Give me
the quiet one!"

– ANTON CHEKHOV
"The Bird Market"

His Bathrobe Pockets
Stuffed with Notes

Talking about her brother, Morris, Tess said:
"The night always catches him. He never
believes it's coming."

That time I broke a tooth on barbecued ribs.
I was drunk. We were all drunk.

The early sixteenth-century Belgian painter called,
for want of his real name,
"The Master of the Embroidered Leaf."

Begin the novel with the young married couple
getting lost in the woods, just after the picnic.

Those dead birds on the porch when I opened up
the house after being away for three months.

The policeman whose nails were bitten to the quick.

Aunt Lola, the shoplifter, rolled her own dad
and other drunks as well.

Dinner at Doug and Amy's. Steve ranting, as usual,
about Bob Dylan, the Vietnam War, granulated sugar,
silver mines in Colorado. And, as usual, just
as we sit down the phone rings and is passed around
the table so everyone can say something. (It's Jerry.)
The food grows cold. No one is hungry anyway.

"We've sustained damage, but we're still able
to maneuver." Spock to Captain Kirk.

Remember Haydn's 104 symphonies. Not all of them
were great. But there were 104 of them.

The rabbi I met on the plane that time who gave me comfort
just after my marriage had broken up for good.

Chris's story about going to an AA meeting where
a well-to-do family comes in – "freaked out,"
her words – because they've just been robbed at gunpoint.

Three men and a woman in wet suits. The door to their
motel room is open and they are watching TV.

"I am disbanding the fleet and sending it back
to Macedonian shores."

Richard Burton
Alexander the Great

Don't forget when the phone was off the hook
all day, every day.

The bill collector (in Victoria, B.C.) who asks
the widow if she'd like it if the bailiff dug up
her husband and repossessed the suit he was buried in.

"Your bitter grief is proof enough."

Mozart, Act II, Scene 2
La Clemenza di Tito

The woman in El Paso who wants to give us her furniture.
But it's clear she is having a nervous breakdown.
We're afraid to touch it. Then we take the bed, and a chair.

Duke Ellington riding in the back of his limo, somewhere
in Indiana. He is reading by lamplight. Billy Strayhorn
is with him, but asleep. The tires hiss on the pavement.
The Duke goes on reading and turning the pages.

I've got — how much longer?

Enough horsing around!

The March into Russia

Just when he had given up thinking
he'd ever write another line of poetry,
she began brushing her hair.
And singing that Irish folk song
he liked so much.
That one about Napoleon and
his "bonnie bunch of roses, oh!"

Some Prose on Poetry

Years ago – it would have been 1956 or 1957 – when I was a teenager, married, earning my living as a delivery boy for a pharmacist in Yakima, a small town in eastern Washington, I drove with a prescription to a house in the upscale part of town. I was invited inside by an alert but very elderly man wearing a cardigan sweater. He asked me to please wait in his living room while he found his checkbook.

There were a lot of books in that living room. Books were everywhere, in fact, on the coffee table and end tables, on the floor next to the sofa – every available surface had become the resting place for books. There was even a little library over against one wall of the room. (I'd never seen a *personal* library before; rows and rows of books arranged on built-in shelves in someone's private residence.) While I waited, eyes moving around, I noticed on his coffee table a magazine with a singular and, for me, startling name on its cover: *Poetry.* I was astounded, and I picked it up. It was my first glimpse of a "little magazine," not to say a poetry magazine, and I was dumbstruck. Maybe I was greedy: I picked up a book, too, something called *The Little Review Anthology*, edited by Margaret Anderson. (I should add that it was a mystery to me then just what "edited by" meant.) I fanned the pages of the magazine and, taking still more liberty, began to leaf through the pages of the book. There were lots of poems in the book, but also prose pieces and what looked like remarks or even pages of commentary on each of the selections. What on earth *was* all this? I wondered. I'd never before seen a book like it – nor, of course, a magazine like *Poetry.* I looked from one to the other of these publications, and secretly coveted each of them.

When the old gentleman had finished writing out his check, he said, as if reading my heart, "Take that book with you, sonny. You might find something in there you'll like. Are you interested in poetry? Why don't you take the magazine too? Maybe you'll write something yourself someday. If you do, you'll need to know where to send it."

Where to send it. Something – I didn't know just what, but I felt something momentous happening. I was eighteen or nineteen years old, obsessed with the need to "write something," and by then I'd made a few clumsy attempts at poems. But it had never really occurred to me that there might be a place where one actually sent these efforts in hopes they would be read and even, just possibly – incredibly, or so it seemed – considered for publication. But right there in my hand was visible proof that there were responsible people somewhere out in the great world who produced, sweet Jesus, a monthly magazine of poetry. I was staggered. I felt, as I've said, in the presence of revelation. I thanked the old gentleman several times over, and left his house. I took his check to my boss, the pharmacist, and I took *Poetry* and *The Little Review* book home with me. And so began an education.

Of course, I can't recall the names of any of the contributors to that issue of the magazine. Most likely there were a few distinguished older poets alongside new, "unknown" poets, much the same situation that exists within the magazine today. Naturally, I hadn't heard of anyone in those days – or read anything either, for that matter, modern, contemporary or otherwise. I do remember I noted the magazine had been founded in 1912 by a woman named Harriet Monroe. I remember the date because that was the year my father had been born. Later that night, bleary from reading, I had the distinct feeling my life was in the process of being altered in some significant and even, forgive me, magnificent way.

In the anthology, as I recall, there was serious talk about "modernism" in literature, and the role played in advancing modernism by a man bearing the strange name of Ezra Pound. Some of his poems, letters and lists of rules – the do's and don't's for writing – had been included in the anthology. I was told that, early in the life of *Poetry*, this Ezra Pound had served as foreign editor for the magazine – the same magazine which had on that day passed into my hands. Further, Pound had been instrumental in introducing the work of a large number of new poets to Monroe's magazine, as well as to *The Little Review*, of course; he was, as everyone knows, a tireless editor and promoter – poets with names like H. D., T. S. Eliot, James Joyce, Richard Aldington, to cite only a handful. There was discussion and analysis of poetry movements; imagism, I remember, was one of these movements. I learned that, in addition to *The Little Review*, *Poetry* was one of the magazines hospitable to imagist writing. By then I was reeling. I don't see how I could have slept much that night.

This was back in 1956 or 1957, as I've said. So what excuse is there for the fact that it took me twenty-eight years or more to finally send off some work to *Poetry*? None. The amazing thing, the crucial factor, is that when I did send something, in 1984, the magazine was still around, still alive and well, and edited, as always, by responsible people whose goal it was to keep this unique enterprise running and in sound order. And one of those people wrote to me in his capacity as editor, praising my poems, and telling me the magazine would publish six of them in due course.

Did I feel proud and good about this? Of course I did. And I believe thanks are due in part to that anonymous and lovely old gentleman who gave me his copy of the magazine. Who was he? He would have to be long dead now and the contents of his little library dispersed to wherever small, eccentric, but probably not in the end very valuable collections go – the second-hand bookstores. I'd told him that day I would read his magazine and read the book, too, and I'd get back to him about what I thought. I didn't do that, of course. Too many other things intervened; it was a promise easily given and broken the moment the door closed behind me. I never saw him again, and I don't know his name. I can only say this encounter really happened, and in much the way I've described. I was just a pup then, but nothing can explain, or explain away, such a moment: the moment when the very thing I needed most in my life – call it a polestar – was casually, generously given to me. Nothing remotely approaching that moment has happened since.

Poems

They've come every day this month.
Once I said I wrote them because
I didn't have time for anything
else. Meaning, of course, better
things — things other than mere
poems and verses. Now I'm writing
them because I want to.
More than anything because
this is February
when normally not much of anything
happens. But this month
the larches have blossomed,
and the sun has come out
every day. It's true my lungs
have heated up like ovens.
And so what if some people
are waiting for the other shoe
to drop, where I'm concerned.
Well, here it is then. Go ahead.
Put it on. I hope it fits
like a shoe.
Close enough, yes, but supple
so the foot has room to breathe
a little. Stand up. Walk
around. Feel it? It will go
where you're going, and be there
with you at the end of your trip.
But for now, stay barefoot. Go
outside for a while, and play.

Letter

Sweetheart, please send me the notebook I left
on the bedside table. If it isn't *on* the table,
look under the table. Or even under the bed! It's
somewhere. If it isn't a notebook, it's just
a few lines scribbled on some scraps
of paper. But I know it's there. It has to do
with what we heard that time from our doctor friend, Ruth,
about the old woman, eighty-some years old,
"dirty and caked with grime" – the doctor's words – so lacking
in concern for herself that her clothes had stuck
to her body and had to be peeled
from her in the Emergency Room. "I'm so
ashamed. I'm sorry," she kept saying. The smell
of the clothing burned Ruth's eyes! The old woman's fingernails
had grown out and begun to curl in
toward her fingers. She was fighting for breath, her eyes
rolled back in her fright. But she was able, even so, to give
some of her story to Ruth. She'd been a Madison Avenue
debutante, but her father disowned her after
she went to Paris to dance in the Folies Bergère.
Ruth and some of the other Emergency Room staff thought
          she was
hallucinating. But she gave them the name of her estranged
          son who
was gay and who ran a gay bar in that same city. He confirmed
everything. Everything the old woman said was true.
Then she suffered a heart attack and died in Ruth's arms.

But I want to see what else I noted from all I heard.
I want to see if it's possible to recreate what it was like
sixty years ago when this young woman stepped off the boat
in Le Havre, beautiful, poised, determined to make it
on the stage at the Folies Bergère, able
to kick over her head and hop at the same time, to wear feathers
and net stockings, to dance and dance, her arms linked with

the arms of other young women at the Folies Bergère, to
        high-step it
at the Folies Bergère. Maybe it's
in that notebook with the blue cloth cover, the one
you gave me when we came home from Brazil. I can see
my handwriting next to the name of my winning horse at the track
near the hotel: *Lord Byron*. But the woman, not the dirt, that
doesn't matter, nor even that she weighed nearly 300 pounds.
Memory doesn't care where it lives and mocks
the body. "I understood something about identity once," Ruth
said, recalling her training days, "all of us young medical students
gaping at the hands of a corpse. That's
where the humanness
stays longest – the hands." And the woman's hands. I made a note
at the time, as if I could see them anchored on her
slim hips, the same hands
Ruth let go of, then couldn't forget.

The Young Girls

Forget all experiences involving wincing.
And anything to do with chamber music.
Museums on rainy Sunday afternoons, etcetera.
The old masters. All that.
Forget the young girls. Try and forget them.
The young girls. And all that.

V

Yet why not say what happened?

— ROBERT LOWELL
from *Epilogue*

The Offending Eel

His former wife called while he was in the south
of France. It was his *chance of a lifetime*,
she suggested, addressing herself
to his answering machine. A celebration
was under way, friends arriving, even as he listened once again
to her voice, confidential yet fortified, too, with
some heady public zeal:

> *I'm going under fast. But that's not*
> *the point, that's not why*
> *I'm calling. I'm telling you, it's a heaven-sent*
> *opportunity to make a lot of money!*
> *Call me when you get home for details.*

She hung up, in that distant three weeks ago, then called
right back, unable to contain herself.

> *Honey, listen. This is not another*
> *crazy scheme. This, I repeat, is*
> *the real thing. It's a game*
> *called Airplane. You start off*
> *in the economy section then work*
> *your way forward to the co-pilot's seat,*
> *or maybe even the pilot's seat!*
> *You'll get there if*
> *you're lucky, and you are*
> *lucky, you always have*
> *been. You'll make a lot of*
> *money. I'm not kidding. I'll*
> *fill you in on details, but you have to*
> *call me.*

It was sunset, late evening. It was the season
when the grain had begun to head and the fields
were fair with flowers — flowers beginning to nod
as night came on and on, night which really did wear its
"cloak of darkness." Tables were being laid outside; candles
lit and placed in the blossoming pear trees
where, shortly, they would assist the moon
to light the homecoming festivities.

He continued listening to her high, manic voice
on the tape. *Call me*, it said, again and again.
But he wouldn't be calling. He couldn't.
He knew better. They'd been through all that.
His heart which, a few minutes before this message,
had been full and passionate and, for a few minutes anyway,
forgetful and unguarded, shrank in its little place
until it was only a fist-sized muscle joylessly
discharging its duties. What could he do?
She was going to die one of these days and
he was going to die too. This much they knew
and still agreed on. But though many things
had happened in his life, and none more or less
strange than this last-ditch offer of great profit
on her airplane, he'd known for a long time
they would die in separate lives and far from each other,
despite oaths exchanged when they were young.
One or the other of them — she, he felt with dread
certainty — might even die raving, completely
gone off. This seemed a real possibility now.
Anything could happen. What could be done?
Nothing. Nothing, nothing, nothing.
He couldn't even talk to her any longer.
Not only that — he was afraid to. He
deemed her insane. *Call me*, she said.

No, he wouldn't be calling. He stood there
thinking. Then swerved wildly and remembered
back a couple of days. Finding that passage

in the book as he blasted across the Atlantic
at 1,100 m.p.h., 55,000 feet above it all.
Some young knight riding over the drawbridge
to claim his prize, his bride, a woman he'd never
laid eyes on, one who waited anxiously
inside the keep, combing and combing her long tresses.
The knight rode slowly, splendidly, falcon on his wrist,
gold spurs a-jingle, a sprig of plantagenesta
in his scarlet bonnet. Behind him
many riders, a long row of polished helmets, sun
striking the breastplates of those cavaliers.
Everywhere banners unfurling in the warm breeze,
banners spilling down the high stone walls.

He'd skipped ahead a little and suddenly found
this same man, a prince now, grown disillusioned
and unhappy, possessed of a violent disposition –
drunk, strangling, in the middle of a page,
on a dish of eels. Not a pretty picture.
His cavaliers, who'd also grown coarse
and murderous, they could do nothing except
pound on his back, vainly push greasy fingers
down his throat, vainly hoist him off the floor
by his ankles until he quit struggling.
His face and neck suffused with the colors of sunset.

They let him down then, one of his fingers
still cocked and frozen, aimed at his breast
as if to say *there*. Just there it lodges.
Just over the heart's where this offending eel
can be found. The woman in the story dressed herself
in widow's weeds then dropped from sight, disappeared
into the tapestry. It's true these people
were once real people. But who now remembers?
Tell me, horse, what rider? What banners? What
strange hands unstrapped your bucklers?
Horse, what rider?

Sorrel

Through the open window he could see a flock of ducks
with their young. Waddling and stumbling, they were hurrying
down the road, apparently on their way to the pond. One
duckling picked up a piece of gut that was lying on
the ground, tried to swallow it, choked
on it and raised an alarmed squeaking. Another
duckling ran up, pulled the gut out of its beak and choked on
the thing too. . . . At some distance from the fence,
in the lacy shadow cast on the grass by the young lindens,
the cook Darya was wandering about, picking sorrel
for a vegetable soup.

— ANTON CHEKHOV
"An Unpleasantness"

The Attic

Her brain is an attic where things
were stored over the years.

From time to time her face appears
in the little windows near the top of the house.

The sad face of someone who has been locked up
and forgotten about.

Margo

His name was Tug. Hers, Margo.
Until people, seeing what was happening,
began calling her Cargo.
Tug and Cargo. He had drive,
they said. Lots of hair on his face
and arms. A big guy. Commanding
voice. She was more laid-back. A blond.

Dreamy. (Sweet and dreamy.) She broke
loose, finally. Sailed away
under her own power. Went to places
pictured in books, and some
not in any book, or even on the map.
Places she, being a girl, and cargo,
never dreamed of getting to.
Not on her own, anyway.

On an Old Photograph of My Son

It's 1974 again, and he's back once more. Smirking,
a pair of coveralls over a white tee-shirt,
no shoes. His hair, long and blond, falls
to his shoulders like his mother's did
back then, and like one of those young Greek
heroes I was just reading about. But
there the resemblance ends. On his face
the contemptuous expression of the wise guy,
the petty tyrant. I'd know that look anywhere.
It burns in my memory like acid. It's
the look I never hoped I'd live to see
again. I want to forget that boy
in the picture – that jerk, that bully!

What's for supper, mother dear? Snap to!
Hey, old lady, jump, why don't you? Speak
when spoken to. I think I'll put you in
a headlock to see how you like it. I like
it. I want to keep you on
your toes. Dance for me now. Go ahead,
bag, dance. I'll show you a step or two.
Let me twist your arm. Beg me to stop, beg me
to be nice. Want a black eye? You got it!

*

Oh, son, in those days I wanted you dead
a hundred – no, a thousand – different times.
I thought all that was behind us. Who in hell
took this picture, and
why'd it turn up now,
just as I was beginning to forget?
I look at your picture and my stomach cramps.
I find myself clamping my jaws, teeth on edge, and
once more I'm filled with despair and anger.
Honestly, I feel like reaching for a drink.
That's a measure of your strength and power, the fear
and confusion you still inspire. That's
how mighty you once were. Hey, I hate this
photograph. I hate what became of us all.
I don't want this artifact in my house another hour!
Maybe I'll send it to your mother, assuming
she's still alive somewhere and the post can reach
her this side of the grave. If so, she'll have
a different reaction to it, I know. Your youth and
beauty, that's all she'll see and exclaim over.
My handsome son, she'll say. My boy wonder.
She'll study the picture, searching for her likeness
in the features, and mine. (She'll find them, too.)
Maybe she'll weep, if there are any tears left.
Maybe – who knows? – she'll even wish for those days
back again! Who knows anything anymore?

But wishes don't come true, and it's a good thing.
Still, she's bound to keep your picture out
on the table for a while and make over you
for a time. Then, soon, you'll go
into the big family album along with the other crazies –
herself, her daughter and me, her former husband. You'll be
safe in there, cheek to jowl with all your victims. But don't
worry, my boy – the pages turn, my son. We all
do better in the future.

Five O'Clock in the Morning

As he passed his father's room, he glanced in at the door.
Yevgraf Ivanovitch, who had not taken off his clothes or gone
to bed, was standing by the window, drumming on the panes.

"Goodbye, I am going," said his son.

"Goodbye . . . the money is on the round table," his father
answered without turning around.

A cold, hateful rain was falling as the laborer drove him
to the station. . . . The grass seemed darker than ever.

– ANTON CHEKHOV
"Difficult People"

Summer Fog

To sleep and forget everything for a few hours . . .
To wake to the sound of the foghorn in July.
To look out the window with a heavy heart and see fog
hanging in the pear trees, fog clogging the intersection,
shrouding the neighborhood like a disease invading a healthy
body. To go on living when she has stopped living . . .

A car eases by with its lights on, and the clock is
turned back to five days ago, the ringing and ringing that brought me
back to this world and news of her death, she who'd simply been
away, whose return had been anticipated with baskets
of raspberries from the market. (Starting from this day
forward, I intend to live my life differently. For one thing,
I won't ever answer the phone again at five in the morning. I knew
better, too, but still I picked up the receiver and said that fateful
word, "Hello." The next time I'll simply let it ring.)
First, though, I have her funeral to get through. It's today, in a
matter of hours. But the idea of a cortege creeping through this fog
to the cemetery is unnerving, and ridiculous, everyone in the town
with their lights on anyway, even the tourists. . . .

May this fog lift and burn off before three this afternoon! Let us
be able, at least, to bury her under sunny skies, she who worshiped
the sun. Everyone knows she is taking part
in this dark masque today only because she has no choice.
She has lost the power of choice! How she'd
hate this! She who loved in April *deciding*
to plant the sweetpeas and who staked them before
they could climb.

I light my first cigarette of the day and turn away from
the window with a shudder. The foghorn sounds again, filling me
with apprehension, and then, then stupendous
grief.

Hummingbird

FOR TESS

Suppose I say *summer*,
write the word "hummingbird,"
put it in an envelope,
take it down the hill
to the box. When you open
my letter you will recall
those days and how much,
just how much, I love you.

Out

Out of the black mouth of the big king
salmon comes pouring the severed heads of herring,
cut on the bias, slant-wise —
near perfect handiwork of the true
salmon fisherman, him and his slick, sharp bait knife.
Body of the cut herring affixed then eighteen inches behind
a flashing silver spoon, heads tossed over
the side, to sink and turn

in the mottled water. How they managed it, those heads,
to reappear so in our boat – most amazingly! – pouring forth
from the torn mouth, this skewed version, misshapen chunks
of a bad fairy tale, but one where no wishes will be
granted, no bargains struck nor promises kept.

We counted nine of those heads, as if to count was already
to tell it later. "Jesus," you said, "Jesus," before
tossing them back overboard where they belonged.
I started the motor and again we dropped our plugged herring-
baited hooks into the water. You'd been telling stories
about logging for Mormons on Prince of Wales Island (no booze,
no swearing, no women. Just *no*, except for work
and a paycheck). Then you fell quiet, wiped the knife
on your pants and stared toward Canada, and beyond.
All morning you'd wanted to tell me something and now you
began to tell me; how
your wife wants you out of her life, wants
you gone, wants you to just disappear.
Why don't you disappear and just don't ever
come back? she'd said. "Can you beat it? I think she hopes
a spar will take me out." Just then there's one hell of a strike.
The water boils as line goes out. It keeps
going out.

Downstream

At noon we have rain, which washes away the snow,
and at dusk, when I stand on the river bank and watch
the approaching boat contend with the current,
a mixture of rain and snow comes down. . . . We go downstream,
keeping close to a thicket of purple willow shrubs. The men
at the oars tell us that only ten minutes ago a boy in a cart
saved himself from drowning by catching hold of
a willow shrub; his team went under. . . .
The bare willow shrubs bend toward the water with

a rustling sound, the river suddenly grows dark. . . . If
there is a storm we shall have to spend the night among
the willows and in the end get drowned, so why not go on?
We put the matter to a vote and decide to row on.

— ANTON CHEKHOV
"Across Siberia"

The Net

Toward evening the wind changes. Boats
still out on the bay
head for shore. A man with one arm
sits on the keel of a rotting-away
vessel, working on a glimmering net.
He raises his eyes. Pulls at something
with his teeth, and bites hard.
I go past without a word.
Reduced to confusion
by the variableness of this weather,
the importunities of my heart. I keep
going. When I turn back to look
I'm far enough away
to see that man caught in a net.

Nearly

The two brothers, Sleep and Death, they unblinkingly called
themselves, arrived at our house around nine in the evening,
             just as
the light was fading. They unloaded all their paraphernalia
in the driveway, what they'd need for killing bees, hornets —
             yellow-
jackets as well. A "dusky" job, one had said on the phone. Those
invaders, we told ourselves, had become such a nuisance.

Frightening, too. An end to it! And *them*, we decided: we'll write
finish to their short-lived career as pollen-gatherers, honey-
makers. Not a decision taken lightly, or easily. Annihilation
            on such
an undreamt-of scale, a foreign thing to us. We moved

to the window to look down to the drive where the men,
            one older,
one younger, stood smoking, watching a few late stragglers find
their way to the hole under the eave. Those bees trying to
beat the sun as it tipped over the horizon, the air turning
            colder now,
the light gradually fainter. We raised our eyes and, through the
glass, could see a dozen, two dozen, a tiny fist
of them, waiting in a swirl their turn to enter their newfound
city. We could hear rustling, like scales, like wings chaffing
behind the wall, up near the ceiling. Then the sun disappeared

entirely, it was dark. All bees inside. One of the brothers, Sleep, it
must have been, he was the younger, positioned the ladder
in the drive, under the southwest corner. A few words we couldn't
catch were exchanged, then Death pulled on his oversized
            gloves and
began his climb up the ladder, slowly, balancing on his back
a heavy cannister held papoose-like by a kind of harness. In
            one hand
was a hose, for killing. He passed our lighted window on his
            way up,
glancing briefly, incuriously, into the living room. Then he stopped,
about even with our heads, only his boots showing where he
            stood on
a rung of the ladder. We tried to act as if nothing out of

the ordinary were happening. You picked up a book, sat in your
favorite chair, pretended to concentrate. I put on a record. It was
dark out, darker, as I've said, but there remained a saffron flush in
the western sky, like blood just under the skin. Saffron, that
            hoarded

spice you said drove the harvesters in Kashmir nearly mad, the
fields ripe with the smell of it. An ecstasy, you said. You turned a
page, as if you'd read a page. The record played and
played. Then came the hiss-hiss of spray as Death pressed
the trigger of his device again and again and again. From the drive
below, Sleep called up, "Give it to them some more, those
bastards." And then, "That's good. That ought to do it, by God.
      Come
down now." Pretty soon they left, those slicker-coated men, and we

never had to see them or talk to them again. You took a glass of
wine. I smoked a cigarette. That domestic sign mingling with
the covetous reek that hung like a vapor near the cast-iron stove.
What an evening! you said, or I said. We never spoke of it after that.
It was as if something shameful had occurred.
Deep in the night, still awake as the house sailed west, tracking
the moon, we came together in the dark like knives, like wild
animals, fiercely, drawing blood even – something we referred to
next morning as "love-making." We didn't tell each other of our
dreams. How could we? But once in the night, awake, I heard the
house creak, almost a sigh, then creak again. Settling, I think
it's called.

VI

Foreboding

"I have a foreboding. . . . I'm oppressed
by a strange, dark foreboding. As though
the loss of a loved one awaited me."

    "Are you married, Doctor? You have a family?"

    "Not a soul. I'm alone, I haven't even any
friends. Tell me, madam, do you believe in forebodings?"

    "Oh, yes, I do."

— ANTON CHEKHOV
"Perpetuum Mobile"

Quiet Nights

I go to sleep on one beach,
wake up on another.

Boat all fitted out,
tugging against its rope.

Sparrow Nights

There are terrible nights with thunder, lightning, rain, and
wind, such as are called among the people "sparrow nights."
There has been one such night in my personal life. . . .

I woke up after midnight and leaped suddenly out of bed.
It seemed to me for some reason that I was just immediately
going to die. Why did it seem so? I had no sensation
in my body that suggested my immediate death, but my soul
was oppressed with terror, as though I had suddenly seen
a vast menacing glow of fire.

I rapidly struck a light, drank some water straight out of
the decanter, then hurried to the open window.
The weather outside was magnificent.
There was a smell of hay and some other
very sweet scent. I could see the spikes of the fence,
the gaunt, drowsy trees by the window, the road,
the dark streak of woodland,
there was a serene, very bright moon in the sky and not a single
cloud, perfect stillness, not one
leaf stirring. I felt that everything was looking at me and
waiting for me to die. . . . My spine was
cold; it seemed to be drawn
inwards, and I felt as though death
were coming upon me stealthily from behind. . . .

— ANTON CHEKHOV
"A Dreary Story"

Lemonade

When he came to my house months ago to measure
my walls for bookcases, Jim Sears didn't look like a man
who'd lose his only child to the high waters
of the Elwha River. He was bushy-haired, confident,
cracking his knuckles, alive with energy, as we
discussed tiers, and brackets, and this oak stain
compared to that. But it's a small town, this town,
a small world here. Six months later, after the bookcases
have been built, delivered and installed, Jim's
father, a Mr Howard Sears, who is "covering for his son"
comes to paint our house. He tells me – when I ask, more
out of small-town courtesy than anything, "How's Jim?" –
that his son lost Jim Jr in the river last spring.
Jim blames himself. "He can't get over it,
neither," Mr Sears adds. "Maybe he's gone on to lose

his mind a little too," he adds, pulling on the bill
of his Sherwin-Williams cap.

      Jim had to stand and watch as the helicopter
grappled with, then lifted, his son's body from the river
with tongs. "They used like a big pair of kitchen tongs
for it, if you can imagine. Attached to a cable. But God always
takes the sweetest ones, don't He?" Mr Sears says. He has
His own mysterious purposes." "What do *you* think about it?"
I want to know. "I don't want to think," he says. "We
can't ask or question His ways. It's not for us to know.
I just know He taken him home now, the little one."

He goes on to tell me Jim Sr's wife took him to thirteen foreign
countries in Europe in hopes it'd help him get over it. But
it didn't. He couldn't. "Mission unaccomplished," Howard says.
Jim's come down with Parkinson's disease. What next?
He's home from Europe now, but still blames himself
for sending Jim Jr back to the car that morning to look for
that thermos of lemonade. They didn't need any lemonade
that day! Lord, lord, what was he thinking of, Jim Sr has said
a hundred – no, a thousand – times now, and to anyone who will
still listen. If only he hadn't made lemonade in the first
place that morning! What could he have been thinking about?
Further, if they hadn't shopped the night before at Safeway, and
if that bin of yellowy lemons hadn't stood next to where they
kept the oranges, apples, grapefruit and bananas.
That's what Jim Sr had really wanted to buy, some oranges
and apples, not lemons for lemonade, forget lemons, he hated
lemons – at least now he did – but Jim Jr, he liked lemonade,
always had. He wanted lemonade.

"Let's look at it this way," Jim Sr would say, "those lemons
had to come from someplace, didn't they? The Imperial Valley,
probably, or else over near Sacramento, they raise lemons
there, right?" They had to be planted and irrigated and
watched over and then pitched into sacks by field workers and
weighed and then dumped into boxes and shipped by rail or
truck to this god-forsaken place where a man can't do anything

but lose his children! Those boxes would've been off-loaded
from the truck by boys not much older than Jim Jr himself.
Then they had to be uncrated and poured all yellow and
lemony-smelling out of their crates by those boys, and washed
and sprayed by some kid who was still living, walking around town,
living and breathing, big as you please. Then they were carried
into the store and placed in that bin under that eye-catching sign
that said Have You Had Fresh Lemonade Lately? As Jim Sr's
reckoning went, it harks all the way back to first causes, back to
the first lemon cultivated on earth. If there hadn't been any lemons
on earth, and there hadn't been any Safeway store, well, Jim would
still have his son, right? And Howard Sears would still have his
grandson, sure. You see, there were a lot of people involved
in this tragedy. There were the farmers and the pickers of lemons,
the truck drivers, the big Safeway store. . . . Jim Sr, too, he was ready
to assume his share of responsibility, of course. He was the most
guilty of all. But he was still in his nosedive, Howard Sears
told me. Still, he had to pull out of this somehow and go on.
Everybody's heart was broken, right. Even so.

Not long ago Jim Sr's wife got him started in a little
wood-carving class here in town. Now he's trying to whittle bears
and seals, owls, eagles, seagulls, anything, but
he can't stick to any one creature long enough to finish
the job, is Mr Sears's assessment. The trouble is, Howard Sears
goes on, every time Jim Sr looks up from his lathe, or his
carving knife, he sees his son breaking out of the water downriver,
and rising up – being reeled in, so to speak – beginning to turn and
turn in circles until he was up, way up above the fir trees, tongs
sticking out of his back, and then the copter turning and swinging
upriver, accompanied by the roar and whap-whap of
the chopper blades. Jim Jr passing now over the searchers who
line the bank of the river. His arms are stretched out from his sides,
and drops of water fly out from him. He passes overhead once more,
closer now, and then returns a minute later to be deposited, ever
so gently laid down, directly at the feet of his father. A man
who, having seen everything now – his dead son rise from the river

in the grip of metal pinchers and turn and turn in circles flying
above the tree line – would like nothing more now than
to just die. But dying is for the sweetest ones. And he remembers
sweetness, when life was sweet, and sweetly
he was given that other lifetime.

Such Diamonds

It was a glorious morning. The sun was shining brightly and
cleaving with its rays the layers of white snow
still lingering here and there. The snow as it took leave of
the earth glittered with such diamonds that it hurt the eyes
to look, while the young winter corn was hastily thrusting up
its green beside it. The rooks floated with dignity over
the fields. A rook would fly, drop
to earth, and give several hops before standing firmly
on its feet. . . .

— ANTON CHEKHOV
"A Nightmare"

Wake Up

In June, in the Kyborg Castle, in the canton
of Zurich, in the late afternoon, in the room
underneath the chapel, in the dungeon,
the executioner's block hunches on the floor next
to the Iron Maiden in her iron gown. Her serene features
are engraved with a little noncommittal smile. If
you ever once slipped inside her she closed her spiked
interior on you like a demon, like one
possessed. Embrace – that word on the card next to
the phrase "no escape from."
     Over in a corner stands the rack, a dreamlike
contrivance that did all it was called on to do, and more,
no questions asked. And if the victim passed out

too soon from pain, as his bones were being broken
one by one, the torturers simply threw a bucket of water
on him and woke him up. Woke him again,
later, if necessary. They were thorough. They knew
what they were doing.

      The bucket is gone, but there's an old cherrywood
crucifix up on the wall in a corner of the room:
Christ hanging on his cross, of course, what else?
The torturers were human after all, yes? And who
knows – at the last minute their victim might see
the light, some chink of understanding, even acceptance of
his fate might break, might pour into his nearly molten
heart. *Jesu Christo, my Savior.*

      I stare at the block. Why not? Why not indeed?
Who hasn't ever wanted to stick his neck out without fear
of consequence? Who hasn't wanted to lay his life on the line,
then draw back at the last minute?
Who, secretly, doesn't lust after every experience?
It's late. There's nobody else in the dungeon but us,
she and me, the North Pole and the South. I drop down
to my knees on the stone floor, grasp my hands behind
my back, and lay my head on the block. Inch it forward
into the pulse-filled groove until my throat fits the shallow
depression. I close my eyes, draw a breath. A deep breath.
The air thicker somehow, as if I can almost taste it.
For a moment, calm now, I feel I could almost drift off.

      Wake up, she says, and I do, turn my head over to see
her standing above me with her arms raised. I see the axe too,
the one she pretends to hold, so heavy it's all she
can do to hold it up over her shoulder. Only kidding,
she says, and lowers her arms, and the idea-of-axe, then
grins. I'm not finished yet, I say. A minute later, when I
do it again, put my head back down on the block, in
the same polished groove, eyes closed, heart racing
a little now, there's no time for the prayer forming in my
throat. It drops unfinished from my lips as I hear her
sudden movement. Feel flesh against my flesh as the sharp

wedge of her hand comes down unswervingly to the base of
my skull and I tilt, nose over chin into the last
of sight, of whatever sheen or rapture I can grasp to take
with me, wherever I'm bound.

   You can get up now, she says, and
I do. I push myself up off my knees, and I look at her,
neither of us smiling, just shaky
and not ourselves. Then her smile and my arm going
around her hips as we walk into the next corridor
needing the light. And outside then, in the open, needing more.

What the Doctor Said

He said it doesn't look good
he said it looks bad in fact real bad
he said I counted thirty-two of them on one lung before
I quit counting them
I said I'm glad I wouldn't want to know
about any more being there than that
he said are you a religious man do you kneel down
in forest groves and let yourself ask for help
when you come to a waterfall
mist blowing against your face and arms
do you stop and ask for understanding at those moments
I said not yet but I intend to start today
he said I'm real sorry he said
I wish I had some other kind of news to give you
I said Amen and he said something else
I didn't catch and not knowing what else to do
and not wanting him to have to repeat it
and me to have to fully digest it
I just looked at him
for a minute and he looked back it was then
I jumped up and shook hands with this man who'd just given me
something no one else on earth had ever given me
I may even have thanked him habit being so strong

Let's Roar, Your Honor

To scream with pain, to cry, to summon help, to call
generally – all that is described here as "roaring."
In Siberia not only bears roar, but sparrows and mice as well.
"The cat got it, and it's roaring," they say of a mouse.

— ANTON CHEKHOV
"Across Siberia"

Proposal

I ask her and then she asks me. We each
accept. There's no back and forth about it. After nearly eleven years
together, we know our minds and more. And this postponement, it's
ripened too. Makes sense now. I suppose we should be
in a rose-filled garden or at least on a beautiful cliff overhanging
the sea, but we're on the couch, the one where sleep
sometimes catches us with our books open, or
some old Bette Davis movie unspools
in glamorous black and white – flames in the fireplace dancing
menacingly in the background as she ascends the marble
staircase with a sweet little snub-nosed
revolver, intending to snuff her ex-lover, the fur coat
he bought her draped loosely over her shoulders. Oh lovely, oh lethal
entanglements. In such a world
to be true.

A few days back some things got clear
about there not being all those years ahead we'd kept
assuming. The doctor going on finally about "the shell" I'd be
leaving behind, doing his best to steer us away from the vale of
tears and foreboding. "But he loves his life," I heard a voice say.
Hers. And the young doctor, hardly skipping a beat, "I know.
I guess you have to go through those seven stages. But you end
up in acceptance."

*

After that we went to lunch in a little café we'd never
been in before. She had pastrami. I had soup. A lot
of other people were having lunch too. Luckily
nobody we knew. We had plans to make, time pressing down
on us like a vise, squeezing out hope to make room for
the everlasting – that word making me want to shout "Is there
an Egyptian in the house?"

Back home we held on to each other and, without
embarrassment or caginess, let it all reach full meaning. This
was it, so any holding back had to be stupid, had to be
insane and meager. How many ever get to this? I thought
at the time. It's not far from here to needing
a celebration, a joining, a bringing of friends into it,
a handing out of champagne and
Perrier. "Reno," I said. "Let's go to Reno and get married."
In Reno, I told her, it's marriages
and remarriages twenty-four hours a day seven days a week. No
waiting period. Just "I do." And "I do." And if you slip
the preacher ten bucks extra, maybe he'll even furnish
a witness. Sure, she'd heard all

those stories of divorcees tossing their wedding rings into
the Truckee River and marching up to the altar ten minutes later
with someone new. Hadn't she thrown her own last wedding band
into the Irish Sea? But she agreed. Reno was just
the place. She had a green cotton dress I'd bought her in Bath.
She'd send it to the cleaners.
We were getting ready, as if we'd found an answer to
that question of what's left
when there's no more hope: the muffled sound of dice coming
        down
the felt-covered table, the click of the wheel,
the slots ringing on into the night, and one more, one
more chance. And then that suite we engaged for.

Cherish

From the window I see her bend to the roses
holding close to the bloom so as not to
prick her fingers. With the other hand she clips, pauses and
clips, more alone in the world
than I had known. She won't
look up, not now. She's alone
with roses and with something else I can only think, not
say. I know the names of those bushes

given for our late wedding: Love, Honor, Cherish —
this last the rose she holds out to me suddenly, having
entered the house between glances. I press
my nose to it, draw the sweetness in, let it cling — scent
of promise, of treasure. My hand on her wrist to bring her close,
her eyes green as river-moss. Saying it then, against
what comes: *wife*, while I can, while my breath, each hurried petal
can still find her.

Gravy

No other word will do. For that's what it was. Gravy.
Gravy, these past ten years.
Alive, sober, working, loving and
being loved by a good woman. Eleven years
ago he was told he had six months to live
at the rate he was going. And he was going
nowhere but down. So he changed his ways
somehow. He quit drinking! And the rest?
After that it was *all* gravy, every minute
of it, up to and including when he was told about,
well, some things that were breaking down and
building up inside his head. "Don't weep for me,"
he said to his friends. "I'm a lucky man.
I've had ten years longer than I or anyone
expected. Pure gravy. And don't forget it."

No Need

I see an empty place at the table.
Whose? Who else's? Who am I kidding?
The boat's waiting. No need for oars
or a wind. I've left the key
in the same place. You know where.
Remember me and all we did together.
Now, hold me tight. That's it. Kiss me
hard on the lips. There. Now
let me go, my dearest. Let me go.
We shall not meet again in this life,
so kiss me goodbye now. Here, kiss me again.
Once more. There. That's enough.
Now, my dearest, let me go.
It's time to be on the way.

Through the Boughs

Down below the window, on the deck, some ragged-looking
birds gather at the feeder. The same birds, I think,
that come every day to eat and quarrel. *Time was, time was,*
they cry and strike at each other. It's nearly time, yes.
The sky stays dark all day, the wind is from the west and
won't stop blowing. . . . Give me your hand for a time. Hold on
to mine. That's right, yes. Squeeze hard. Time was we
thought we had time on our side. *Time was, time was,*
those ragged birds cry.

Afterglow

The dusk of evening comes on. Earlier a little rain
had fallen. You open a drawer and find inside
the man's photograph, knowing he has only two years
to live. He doesn't know this, of course,

that's why he can mug for the camera.
How could he know what's taking root in his head
at that moment? If one looks to the right
through boughs and tree trunks, there can be seen
crimson patches of the afterglow. No shadows, no
half-shadows. It is still and damp. . . .
The man goes on mugging. I put the picture back
in its place along with the others and give
my attention instead to the afterglow along the far ridge,
light golden on the roses in the garden.
Then, I can't help myself, I glance once more
at the picture. The wink, the broad smile,
the jaunty slant of the cigarette.

Late Fragment

And did you get what
you wanted from this life, even so?
I did.
And what did you want?
To call myself beloved, to feel myself
beloved on the earth.

Appendixes

Appendix 1

Uncollected Poems: *No Heroics, Please*

The Brass Ring

Whatever became of that brass ring
supposed to go with the merry-go-round?
The brass one that all the poor-but-happy
young girls and boys were always snagging just
at the Magic Moment? I've asked around: Do you know
anything about the brass ring . . . ? I said to my neighbor.
I asked my wife, and I even asked the butcher (who I think
is from a foreign country and should know).
         No one knows, it seems.
Then I asked a man who used to work for a carnival. Years ago,
he said, it was different then. Even the grown-ups rode.
He remembered a young woman in Topeka, Kansas. It was
in August. She held hands with the man who rode
the horse next to her, who had a moustache and
who was her husband. The young woman laughed
all the time, he said. The husband laughed
too, even though he had a moustache. But
all that is another story. He didn't
say anything about a brass ring.

Beginnings

Once
there was a plumb-line
sunk deep into the floor
of a spruce valley
nr Snohomish
in the Cascades
that passed under

Mt Rainier, Mt Hood,
and the Columbia River
and came up
somewhere
in the Oregon rainforest
wearing
a fern leaf.

On the Pampas Tonight

On the pampas tonight a gaucho
on a tall horse slings
a bolas towards the sunset, west
into the Pacific.
Juan Perón sleeps in Spain
with General Franco,
the President barbecues
in Asia . . .

I wish to settle deeper
into the seasons,
to become like a pine tree
or a reindeer,
observe the slow grind and creep of glaciers
into northern fjords,
stand against this nemesis,
this dry weather.

Those Days

FOR C.M.

Yes I remember those days,
Always young, always June or July;
Molly, her skirt rucked up over
Her knees, I in my logger-boots

My arm round her little waist,
We laughing, doing
                onetwothree – glide!
                onetwothree – glide!
                    in the warm kitchen,
Fish chowder or venison steaks
On the stove, roses stroking
The bedroom window.
Across the pasture, the Nisqually River
We listened to at night.
                    Oh how I wish
I could be like those Chinook salmon,
Thrusting, leaping the falls,
Returning!
Not chunks and flakes and drift
                drift

The Sunbather, to Herself

A kind of
airy dullness;
head is a puddle,
heart & fingers –
all extremities –
glow
under your indifferent
touch.

Now old sun,
husband,
pour into me,
be rough
with me,
strengthen me
against that other,
that bastard.

No Heroics, Please

Zhivago with a fine moustache,
A wife and son. His poet's eyes
Witness every kind of suffering,
His doctor's hands are kept busy.
"The walls of his heart were paper-thin,"
Comrade-General half-brother Alec Guinness
Says to Lara, whom Zhivago has loved
And made pregnant.

But at that moment,
The group from the topless bar
Next the theater begins to play.
The saxophone climbs higher and higher,
Demanding our attention. The drums
And the bass are also present,
But it is the rising and falling saxophone
That drains away the strength
To resist.

Adultery

A matinee that Saturday
          afternoon *Sound of Music*
     Your coat on the empty seat
                    beside me
               your hand in my lap
          we are transported
               to Austria
     There
          somewhere along the Rhine
     In any of these old
               beautiful towns
          we could live quietly
                    a hundred years

Later
             you put on an apron
        fix me a cup of tea with a slice of lemon
                             on Radio Monitor
                    Herb Alpert
                       and the Tijuana Brass
               play *Zorba the Greek*
                          We also overhear
                 part of a conversation
                       with Dizzy Dean
               On the floor
          beside the bed *Esquire*
                        Frank Sinatra
        surrounded by flaming cigarette lighters
            Tacitus
                        Maxim Gorky
                 under the ashtray
Your head on my arm
        we smoke cigarettes
                    and talk of Lake Louise
                    Banff National Park
                    the Olympic
          Peninsula
                    places
                 neither of us has seen
                       Outside
        heat lightning
                 the first heavy drops of rain
             strike the patio
                       Listen
                 How splendid these gifts

Poem on My Birthday, July 2

    "and we kept going
    up and up and up
    and your brother
    had a headache
    from the al-titude
    and we kept going
    up and up and he said,
    'where we going, dad?'
    and I said, up."

just pleasant to sit here
this morning drinking fresh coffee
wearing a clean shirt. taking stock?
what does that mean? mum dead,
dad has sclerosis. sclerosis,
a hell of a word. what is tomorrow?
tuesday? ha. my wife wants
to bake me a cake. she says. most
of my birthdays I've had to work.
that means. birthdays? I remember
                    the road into jameson lake:
                    hardpan, switchback, dogwood
                    scraping the fenders and trailing
                    along the canvas top of the jeep
                    until, past timberline, we left
                    the woods and road behind
                    and nothing ahead but steep ridges
                    sided with wildflowers and bunchgrass,
                    then over the highest ridge
                    into jameson valley,
                    and the lake still frozen.
that was a giggle. ice fishing
in july. high country, indeed.

Return

George Mensch's cattle
have dunged-up the living room,
windows have fallen out
and the back porch
has caved in around the kitchen:
I move through each filthy room
like a finance company.

For the Egyptian Coin Today,
Arden, Thank You

As I stare at the smoothly worn portrait of
The Sphinx, surrounded by a strange fading landscape,
I recall the remoteness of my own hands pulling
Themselves awake this morning, shaky, ready to begin
Their terrible round of questioning.

In the Trenches
with Robert Graves

The latin winds of Majorca
are far away still. Here,
machineguns traverse each night. By day,
high-explosives, barbed wire, snipers . . .
Rats work their way in and out
of the fallen. The corpses are like lorries,
the rats drive them deeper
into the mud. Behind the lines,
on both sides, officers and men queue
for a last fuck. All but Graves, anyhow.
First the hawk must grow in a man, a spur
to sex. We live
in difficult times.

The Man Outside

There was always the inside and
the outside. Inside, my wife,
my son and daughters, rivers
of conversation, books, gentleness
and affection.

But then one night outside
my bedroom window someone –
something, breathes, shuffles.
I rouse my wife and terrified
I shudder in her arms till morning.

That space outside my bedroom
window! The few flowers that grow
there trampled down, the Camel
cigarette butts underfoot –
I am not imagining things.

The next night and the next
it happens, and I rouse my wife
and again she comforts me and
again she rubs my legs tense
with fright and takes me in her embrace.

But then I begin to demand more
and more of my wife. In shame she
parades up and down the bedroom floor,
I driving her like a loaded wheel-
barrow, the carter and the cart.

Finally, tonight, I touch my wife lightly
and she springs awake anxious
and ready. Lights on, nude, we sit
at the vanity table and stare frantically
into the glass. Behind us, two lips,
the reflection of a glowing cigarette.

Seeds

FOR CHRISTI

I exchange nervous glances
with the man who sells
my daughter watermelon seeds.

The shadow of a bird passes
over all our hands.

The vendor raises his whip &
hurries away behind his old horse
towards Beersheba.

You offer me my choice of seeds.
Already you have forgotten the man
the horse
the watermelons themselves &
the shadow was something unseen
between the vendor & myself.

I accept your gift here
on the dry roadside.
I reach out my hand to receive
your blessing.

Betrayal

like bad credit
begins with the fingers
their lies

The Contact

Mark the man I am with.
He is soon to lose
His left hand, his balls, his
Nose and handsome moustache.

Tragedy is everywhere
Oh Jerusàlem.

He raises his tea cup.
Wait.
We enter the cafe.
He raises his tea cup.
We sit down together.
He raises his tea cup.
Now.

I nod.

Faces!

His eyes, crossed,
Fall slowly out of his head.

Something Is Happening

Something is happening to me
if I can believe my
senses this is not just
another distraction dear
I am tied up still
in the same old skin
the pure ideas and ambitious yearnings
the clean and healthy cock
at all costs
but my feet are beginning

to tell me things about
themselves
about their new relationship to
my hands heart hair and eyes

Something is happening to me
if I could I would ask you
have you ever felt anything similar
but you are already so far
away tonight I do not think
you would hear besides
my voice has also been affected

Something is happening to me
do not be surprised if
waking someday soon in this bright
Mediterranean sun you look
across at me and discover
a woman in my place
or worse
a strange whitehaired man
writing a poem
one who can no longer form words
who is simply moving his lips
trying
to tell you something

A Summer in Sacramento

we have been looking at cars lately
my wife has in mind
a 1972 Pontiac Catalina conv
bucket seats power everything
but I've had my eye on a little
red & white 71 Olds Cutlass
A/C R&H wsw tires
low mileage & 500 cheaper

but I like convertibles too
we've never owned a really good car

most of our bills are paid
& we can afford another car
still
a couple of grand is a lot of money
& a yr ago we wd have taken it
& fled to Mexico

the rent's due Thursday
but we can pay it
by God there's nothing like
being able to meet your responsibilities

on my birthday May 25
we spent 60 dollars or more
on dinner wine cocktails
& a movie
at dinner we cd hardly find anything to talk about
though we smiled at each other
frequently

we've gone to a lot of movies the last few months

this Friday night
I am to meet a girl I have been seeing
now & then since Christmas
nothing serious
on my part
but we make it well together
& I'm flattered
with the little attentions she shows me
& flattered too
she wants to marry me
if I will get a Reno divorce soon

I will have to think about it

a few days ago
an attractive woman I'd never seen before
who called herself Sue Thompson
a neighbor
came to the door & told me
her 15 yr old foster son had been observed
raising my 7 yr old daughter's dress

the boy's juvenile parole officer wd like
to ask my daughter some questions

last night at still another movie
an older man took me by the shoulder
in the lobby asked me –
where're you going Fred? –
shitman I said
you have the wrong fella

when I woke up this morning
I cd still feel his hand there

almost

Reaching

He knew he was
in trouble when,
in the middle
of the poem,
he found himself
reaching
for his thesaurus
and then
Webster's
in that order.

Soda Crackers

You soda crackers! I remember
when I arrived here in the rain,
whipped out and alone.
How we shared the aloneness
and quiet of this house.
And the doubt that held me
from fingers to toes
as I took you out
of your cellophane wrapping
and ate you, meditatively,
at the kitchen table
that first night with cheese,
and mushroom soup. Now,
a month later to the day,
an important part of us
is still here. I'm fine.
And you – I'm proud of you, too.
You're even getting remarked
on in print! Every soda cracker
should be so lucky.
We've done all right for
ourselves. Listen to me.
I never thought
I could go on like this
about soda crackers.
But I tell you
the clear sunshiny
days are here, at last.

Appendix 2

Introduction by Tess Gallagher to
A New Path to the Waterfall (1989)

This is a last book and last things, as we learn, have rights of their own. They don't need us, but in our need of them we commemorate and make more real that finality which encircles us, and draws us again into that central question of any death: What is life for? Raymond Carver lived and wrote his answer: "I've always squandered," he told an interviewer, no doubt steering a hard course away from the lofty and noble. It was almost a law, Carver's law, not to save up things for some longed-for future, but to use up the best that was in him each day and to trust that more would come. Even the packaging of the cigarettes he smoked bore the imprint of his oath in the imperative: NOW.

This was an injunction that would bear down on us with increasing intensity as we attempted to finish this book. In an episode eerily like that which preceded the death of Chekhov, to whom he had recently paid tribute in his story "Errand", Ray had been diagnosed with lung cancer after spitting up blood in September 1987. There would follow ten months of struggle during which the cancer would reoccur as a brain tumor in early March. After twice swerving away from recommendations for brain surgery by several doctors, he would undergo seven weeks of intense, full-brain radiation. After a short respite, however, tumors would again be found in his lungs in early June.

These are the facts of that time, enough to have made realists out of us if we hadn't been realists already. Nonetheless, much as Chekhov had kept reading the train schedules away from the town in which he would die, Ray kept working, planning, believing in the importance of the time he had left, and also believing that he might, through some loop in fate, even get out of this. An errand list I found in his shirt pocket later read "eggs, peanut butter, hot choc" and then, after a space, "Australia? Antarctica??" The insistent nature of Ray's belief in his own capacity to recover from reversals during the course of his illness gave us both strength. In his journal he wrote: "When hope is gone, the ultimate sanity is to grasp at straws." In this way he lived hope as a function of gesture, a reaching for or toward, while the object of promise stayed rightly illusory. The alternative was acceptance of death, which at age fifty was impossible for him. Another journal entry revealed his anguish as the pace of the disease quickened: "I wish I had a while. Not five years – or even three years – I couldn't ask for that long, but if I had even a year. If I knew I had a year."

In January 1988 Ray began keeping a journal under the inspiration of Stephen Spender's *Journals: 1939–1983*, but with the discovery of his brain tumor it broke off suddenly in March, though he would start again in another notebook later. Our attentions were turned instead to the task of drafting a short essay to appear in the commencement booklet for the University of Hartford, where Ray was to accept a Doctorate of Letters in May.

During much of this time I had been clinging to the stories of Chekhov, reading one after the other of the Ecco Press volumes, and now I offered two passages to Ray from *Ward No. 6* to illustrate the epigraph from Saint Teresa ("Words lead to deeds . . . they prepare the soul, make it ready, and move it to tenderness"), which he'd used from my book of poems to begin his essay. Ray incorporated the passages from Chekhov into his piece, and this was the beginning of an important spiritual accompaniment which began to run through our days, and which eventually would play an important part in the writing of this book.

The fervor with which we both seized on these particular moments in *Ward No. 6* came, I think, directly out of the ordeal we were undergoing with Ray's health, and this was particularly true of the second passage in which two characters, a disaffected doctor and an imperious postmaster, his elder, suddenly find themselves discussing the human soul:

> "And you do not believe in the immortality of the soul?"
>
> "No, honored Mihail Averyanitch; I do not believe it, and have no grounds for believing it."
>
> "I must own I doubt it too," Mihail Averyanitch admits. "And yet I have a feeling as though I should never die myself: 'Old fogey, it's time you were dead!' but there is a little voice in my soul that says: 'Don't believe it; you won't die.'"

In his framing of the passage Ray underscored the power of "words which linger as deeds" and out of which "a little voice in the soul" is born. He seemed almost grateful to observe how in the Chekhov story "the way we have dismissed certain concepts about life, about death, suddenly gives over unexpectedly to belief of an admittedly fragile but insistent nature".

I continued to bring Chekhov into our days by reading a story first thing in the morning and then telling it to Ray when I came down for breakfast. I would give the story in as true a fashion as I could, and Ray would inevitably become engaged by it and have to read it for himself that afternoon. By evening we could discuss it.

Another of Ray's influences came from one of the books he'd been reading early in the year, Czeslaw Milosz's *Unattainable Earth*, and it began to affect his idea of the form and latitude his own book might discover. In the interests of what he called "a more spacious form", Milosz had incorporated prose quotes from Casanova's *Memoirs*, snippets from Baudelaire, from his uncle Oscar Milosz, Pascal, Goethe and other thinkers and writers who'd affected him as he was writing his poems. He also includes his own musings, which take the form of confessions, questionings and insights. Ray was very much attracted to the inclusiveness of Milosz's approach. His own reading at the time included García Lorca, Jaroslav Seifert, Tomas Tranströmer, Lowell, *The Selected Poems* of Milosz and a rereading of Tolstoy's *The Death of Ivan Ilych*. From these he selected whole poems, which we later used as section heads for the book.

But in early June, when the devastating news of tumors in the lungs again was given to us, it was to Chekhov we instinctively turned to restore our steadfastness. One night I looked at certain passages I had bracketed in the stories and realized that they seemed to be speaking toward poems of Ray's which I'd been helping him revise and typing into the computer. On impulse I went to the typewriter and shaped some of these excerpts into lines and gave them titles. When I showed the results to Ray, it was as if we'd discovered another Chekhov inside Chekhov. But because I'd been looking at the passages with Ray's poems in mind, there was the sense that Chekhov had stepped toward us, and that while he remained in his own time, he seemed also to have become our contemporary. The world of headlong carriage races through snowstorms and of herring-head soup, of a dish made of bulls' eyes, of cooks picking sorrel for vegetable soup, of peasant children raised not to flinch at the crude language of their drunken parents – this world was at home with the world of Raymond Carver, in which a man puts his head on the executioner's block while touring a castle only to have the hand of his companion come down on his neck like an axe, a world in which a drunken father is caught in the kitchen by his son with a strange woman in a heavily sexual context, and in which we watch as a drowned child is carried above the trees in the tongs of a helicopter.

Once we'd discovered the poet in Chekhov, Ray began to mark passages he wanted to include and to type them up himself. The results were something between poems and prose, and this pleased us because some of Ray's new poems blurred the boundaries between poem and story, just as his stories had often taken strength from dramatic and poetic strategies. Ray had so collapsed the distance between his language and thought that the resulting transparency of method allowed distinctions between genres to dissolve without violence or a feeling of trespass. The story given as poem could unwind without having to pretend to intensities of phrasing or language that might have impeded the force of the story itself, yet the story could pull at the attention of the reader in another way for having been conceived as poetry.

In order to work at all on the book during what was a bewildering time for us, we made the decision not to tell anyone about the cancer's recurrence in the lungs. Instead of giving over to visitors and a parade of sorrowful goodbyes we could keep our attention on the things we wanted to do. And one of the things we decided to do was to celebrate our eleven years together by getting married in Reno, Nevada, on June 17. The wedding was what Ray called a "high tacky affair" and it took place across from the courthouse in the Heart of Reno Chapel, which had a huge heart in the window spiked with small golden light bulbs and a sign that read SE HABLA ESPANOL. Afterwards we went gambling in the casinos and I headed into a phenomenal three-day winning streak at roulette.

When we returned home Ray wrote "Proposal", which carries the urgency of that time, the raw sense of life lived without guile, or that cushion of hope we count on to extend life past the provisional. Our having married anchored us in a new way and it seemed we had knowingly saved this occasion to give ourselves solace, and perhaps also to allow us to toss back our heads once more in a rippling cosmic laugh as from that "gay and empty journey" Kafka writes of.

This was also the time during which Ray wrote "Gravy". The idea for the poem had come from a conversation we'd had while sitting on the deck facing the Strait of Juan de Fuca, taking stock. "You remember telling me how you almost died before you met me?" I asked him. "It could've ended back then and we'd never even have met. None of this would have happened." We sat there quietly, just marveling at what we'd been allowed. "It's all been gravy," Ray said. "Pure gravy."

Many of the poems Ray had accumulated toward the book had been drafted during July and late August the summer before. Nearly a year later, in early July, enough finished poems had accumulated that we decided I should begin to arrange them into sections and to shape the book. I had done this with each of Ray's collections of poetry and also with most of his fiction. My perhaps primitive way of ordering a manuscript was to scatter the pages out on the living-room floor and crawl on my hands and knees among them, reading and sensing what should come next, moving by intuition and story and emotion.

We had decided to try to include the Chekhov passages. The stories had been so integral to our spiritual survival that, as with Milosz's inclusion of Whitman in his book, Chekhov seemed a companion soul, as if Ray had somehow won permission through a lifetime of admiration to take up his work with the audacity of love.

One night I remember watching with Ray a composer being interviewed on television, and the composer was exclaiming that Tchaikovsky had lifted whole passages from Beethoven and offered them as his own. When someone had challenged him about this he had said simply, "I have a right. I love him." Ray had jotted down this exchange, and I think this right-of-love figured heavily into his decision to bring Chekhov so boldly into conjunction with his own work. The Chekhov passages also bound Ray's poetry to his fiction, his last collection having ended with the tribute of "Errand". The Chekhov selections seemed to fall very naturally into place in the manuscript, keying and amplifying in a tonal and emotional way the poems Ray had been writing. At times, through Chekhov, Ray was able to give himself and others instructions for the difficult task of continuing under the certainty of loss ("Downstream"), or he could admit fears he might have stifled in order to keep the upper hand in his waiting game with cancer ("Foreboding" and "Sparrow Nights").

The book, as we finalized my arrangement, fell into six sections. It began with poems retrieved from earlier publications, poems which, for one reason and another, had not been joined with more recent work. So just as Ray was bringing the time of Chekhov to bear on his work, he was carrying forward poems from his earlier life, and perhaps affecting both lives in their imaginative composition. I think in this regard that a passage he had marked in Milosz's *Unattainable Earth* may illuminate Ray's inner objectives:

> Jeanne, a disciple of Karl Jaspers, taught me the philosophy of freedom, which consists in being aware that a choice made now, today, projects itself backwards and changes our past actions.

There was an urge in Ray's writing, in both the poems and stories, to revisit certain evocative scenes and characters in his life, to wrest from them if not release, then at least a telling anatomy of the occasion. In this book the early love poems hint at a dark element which is realized more fully in recent poems such as "Miracle", "The Offending

Eel" and "Wake Up". The son as an oppressive figure in former poems and in the stories "Elephant" and "The Compartment" reappears in "On an Old Photograph of My Son", and although the pain is freshly present, there is the redeeming knowledge at the end of the poem that "we all do better in the future". The theme of the dead child, which was explored so poignantly in his story "A Small, Good Thing", is revived in the poem "Lemonade", in which a child, sent by the father for a thermos of lemonade, drowns in the river.

The second section introduced a series of poems whose territory was suggested by Tomas Tranströmer's poem, "The Name", about a loss of identity. Perhaps the best way to characterize these poems is by their dis-ease, the way in which a wildness, a strangeness, can erupt and carry us into realms of unreason with no way to turn back. Here the verbally abusive woman of his story "Intimacy" is joined by the physically abusive woman of "Miracle". Drinking continued to motivate the rituals of disintegration in the poems about his first marriage, and he inventoried the havoc it had caused as if it had occurred only yesterday.

Childhood innocence is abruptly sundered in the third section with "The Kitchen", which recalls the story "Nobody Said Anything". There are poems in which the unknown is left fully intact, as in "The Sturgeon" and "Another Mystery". The violence of working-class family life in "Suspenders" plays off a section from Chekhov about peasant life and the brutalizing of the sensibilities of children.

The hard question Milosz asks in "Return to Kraków in 1880" at the front of the fourth section – "To win? To lose? / What for, if the world will forget us anyway?" – challenges the poet's sense of memory as an entrustment. And for Ray, of course, in facing his death the idea of whether one's memory would persist importantly in the survival of one's writing was also present. His poems suggest that an artist's obsessions and signs, fragmentary and intermittent as they may be, exist in a world of necessity that transcends anyone else's need of them. At the same time, poems like "One More" and "His Bathrobe Pockets Stuffed with Notes" reveal humorously the haphazard nature of creation itself, and indeed the amazement that anything worthwhile should accumulate from such a scattershot process. There is also a prose record in this section of Ray's first intimations of the literary life when he's handed a copy of *Poetry* by an elderly man whose home he enters as a delivery boy. Here, as in "Errand", it is the ordinary moment which illuminates the most extraordinary things. A magazine passes from one hand to another and the young would-be writer discovers, to his surprise, a world in which writing and reading poems is believed to be a creditable endeavor.

The juxtaposition of contemporary time with the era of knights and chivalry in "The Offending Eel" is one we've seen before in the story "What We Talk about When We Talk about Love", and also in the more recent "Blackbird Pie". Such counterpointing seems to allow the contemporary material a fresh barbarism. In light of the Lowell quote that begins the fifth section – "Yet why not say what happened?"– we look with fluorescent starkness into the unrelenting, obsessive magnetism of "the real", its traps and violences.

The poem "Summer Fog" in the same section was made all the more extraordinary for me because of something Ray said when he first gave me the poem to read. He told me he was sorry he wouldn't be there to do the things for me that I was doing for him. "I've tried something here," he said. "I don't know if it works." What he had tried was to leap ahead into the time of my death, and to imagine his grief as a gift to me against my own approaching solitude. It seems all the more moving that this was done at a time when his own death was, in the words of the poem, the "stupendous grief" we were feeling together.

The last section of the book deals with the stages of his awareness as his health worsened and he moved toward death. In "Gravy", as I've mentioned, he displaces the devastating significance of death in the present by inserting the memory of a prior death narrowly avoided, when in 1976–7 he had nearly died of alcoholism. So in effect he uses his coming death as proof of a former escape; and death, he realized, once displaced by such an excess of living during the ten productive years he'd been allowed, could never be quite the same. Nevertheless, the introductory passages from Chekhov ("Foreboding" and "Sparrow Nights") acknowledge an inner panic. Along with the matter-of-factness of "What the Doctor Said" and the "practicing" for death in "Wake Up", there is the defiance of "Proposal", and the two poems which rehearse the final goodbye – "No Need" and "Through the Boughs". I hadn't realized until three weeks after Ray's death, as I went over the manuscript to enter corrections Ray had made before we'd taken the final trip to Alaska, that I had perfectly, though unwittingly, enacted the instructions of "No Need" the night before his death. The three kisses which had been meant as "Good night" had, at the time, carried the possibility that Ray would not wake again. "Don't be afraid," I'd said. "Just go into your sleep now" and, finally, "I love you" – to which he had answered, "I love you too. You get some sleep now." He never opened his eyes again, and at 6:20 the next morning he stopped breathing.

The "jaunty" slant of the cigarette in the self-portrait "Afterglow" belies the consequences which have made this a last glance. Maybe it's as close as Ray would let himself come to irony at a time when a lesser writer might have carved out a sad, edgy little empire with it. In the final poem, "Late Fragment", the voice has earned a more elevated coda. There is the sense that central to the effort of the life, of the writing, has been the need to be beloved and that one's own willingness to award that to the self – to "call myself beloved" and, beyond that, to "feel myself beloved on the earth" – has somehow been achieved. For a recovering alcoholic, this self-recognition and the more generalized feeling of love he was allowing himself was no small accomplishment. Ray knew he had been graced and blessed and that his writing had enabled him to reach far beyond the often mean circumstances from which he and those he wrote about had come, and also that through his writing those working-class lives had become a part of literature. On a piece of scrap paper near his typewriter he had written: "Forgive me if I'm thrilled with the idea, but just now I thought that every poem I write ought to be called 'Happiness'." And he was, in spite of not agreeing to such an early death, in the keeping of a grateful equanimity when we talked during those long summer evenings of what our life together as writers, lovers and helpmates had been.

By mid-July his last book was finished and I had found its title, taken from an early poem called "Looking for Work". We didn't discuss the title; we just knew it was right. We had been given a rather incredible gift shortly after our wedding and this, I think, influenced us in our choice. Our painter friend, Alfredo Arreguin, had been working on a large painting about which mysterious, tantalizing hints had been leaked at intervals to us by his wife, Susan Lytle, also a painter. The day before our wedding reception, Alfredo and Susan arrived with the painting strapped to the top of their car. The painting, once hung in our living room, proved to be of several salmon leaping midair toward a vigorous, stylized waterfall. In the sky, what Ray would call "the ghost fish" were patterned into clouds heading in the opposite direction. The rocks in the background were inhabited as well, studded with prehistoric eyes.

Each morning we took our coffee in front of the painting where Ray could sometimes be seen sitting alone during the day, meditating. When I look at it now, his particular aliveness seems imbedded there in the pageantry of a cycle we had seen played out year after year in the river below our house. In the painting the fish are heading upstream, bowed eternally to the light in a fierce, determined flight above water, and above them the ghost fish float unimpeded in an opposing current, relieved of their struggle.

In Alaska, on one last fishing trip, we raised glasses of Perrier to toast the book, and ourselves, for having managed to finish it against so many odds. In the crucial last days of our work, guests had arrived for an extended stay and Ray's son had come from Germany. We'd kept working, parceling out the day, until the work was done. "Don't tell them we've finished," he said to me – "them" meaning the guests. "I need you here." So the book as pretext allowed us a few more precious mornings with each other before what would be the final onset of his illness. After our guests had left, we began making calls, trying desperately to arrange a trip to Russia to see Chekhov's grave and to visit the houses of Dostoyevsky and Tolstoy. There were places associated with Akhmatova that I wanted to find. Even though this wasn't to be, our planning in those last days was, in itself, a kind of dream-visit that lifted our spirits. Later, when Ray entered the hospital, we talked about what a great trip it would have been. "I'll go there," I said, "I'll go for us." "I'll get there before you," he said, and grinned. "I'm traveling faster."

After Ray's death at home in Port Angeles on August 2, the mail was heaped for weeks with letters and cards from people all over the world mourning his passing, sending me often very moving accounts of their having met him even briefly, things he'd said, acts of kindness performed, stories of his life before I had known him. Copies of obituaries also began to arrive from papers around the country, and one day I opened a packet from London with the obituary from the *Sunday Times*. The headline above the photograph of Ray with his hands in his jacket pockets reads simply: "The American Chekhov". From the *Guardian* there was the possessive "America's Chekhov". I seemed to be reading these *with* Ray, and to be carrying his knowing of it. Either headline would have been accolade enough to have made him humbly and deeply happy.

It seems important finally to say that Ray did not regard his poetry as simply a hobby or a pastime he turned to when he wanted a rest from fiction. Poetry was a spiritual necessity. The truths he came to through his poetry involved a dismantling of artifice to a degree not even Williams, whom he had admired early on, could have anticipated. He'd read Milosz's lines in "*Ars Poetica?*" and they'd appealed to him:

I have always aspired to a more spacious form
that would be free from the claims of poetry or prose
and would let us understand each other without exposing
the author or reader to sublime agonies.

In the very essence of poetry there is something indecent:
a thing is brought forth which we didn't know we had in us,
so we blink our eyes, as if a tiger had sprung out
and stood in the light, lashing his tail.

Ray used his poetry to flush the tiger from hiding. Further, he did not look on his writing life as the offering of products to a readership, and he was purposefully disobedient when pressures were put on him to write stories because that's where his reputation was centered and that's where the largest reward in terms of publication and audience lay. He didn't care. When he received the Mildred and Harold Strauss Living Award, given only to prose writers, he immediately sat down and wrote two books of poetry. He was not "building a career"; he was living a vocation and this meant that his writing, whether poetry or prose, was tied to inner mandates that insisted more and more on an increasingly unmediated apprehension of his subjects, and poetry was the form that best allowed this.

I can imagine that it might be tempting for those who loved Ray's fiction to the exclusion of his poetry to feel he had gone astray in giving so much of his time to poetry in the final years. But this would be to miss the gift of freshness his poems offer in a passionless era. Because judgments about the contribution of poets lag far behind those volunteered toward fiction writers in this country, it will likely be some time before Ray's impact as a poet can be adequately assessed. So far, the most astute essay on his poetry is Greg Kuzma's, published in the *Michigan Quarterly Review* (Spring 1988). It could be that Ray, in his own fashion, has done as much to challenge the idea of what poetry can be as he did to reinvigorate the short story. What is sure is that he wrote and lived his last ten years by his own design, and as his companion in that life, I'm glad to have helped him keep his poetry alive for the journey, for the comfort and soul making he drew from it so crucially in his too-early going.

TESS GALLAGHER

Appendix 3

Small Press Sources of Carver's Major Books

In his poetry as in his fiction Raymond Carver was a frequent contributor to little magazines and small presses. Carver was also an inveterate reviser and republisher of his work. To varying degrees these practices shape his four major poetry collections: *Fires* (1983), *Where Water Comes Together with Other Water* (1985), *Ultramarine* (1986), and *A New Path to the Waterfall* (1989). Each of these books includes poems previously published in one or more of Carver's small-press books.

Moreover, extensive revision and republishing occur within Carver's small-press publications. More than a dozen poems from his first book, *Near Klamath* (1968), reappear in his second, *Winter Insomnia* (1970). Eleven poems from those two books find their way into his third book of poetry, *At Night the Salmon Move* (1976). This recursive process culminates in *Fires: Essays, Poems, Stories*, a miscellany initially published by a small press (Capra), then reprinted by a major one (Vintage). Of the fifty poems in *Fires*, all but a dozen derive from *Near Klamath*, *Winter Insomnia*, and *At Night the Salmon Move*. As Carver explains in his afterword to *Fires*,* some poems have been revised so slightly that changes are nearly imperceptible. Others have been lengthened, shortened, rephrased, retitled – in effect, rewritten. Significant textual variants created by this process are recorded in the notes on individual poems.

Described below are the small-press books Raymond Carver drew on in creating his major poetry collections. In addition to the early books *Near Klamath* (1968), *Winter Insomnia* (1970), and *At Night the Salmon Move* (1976), the list includes the limited editions *This Water* (1985), *Early for the Dance* (1986), and *Those Days* (1987). First publication or subsequent reprinting of poems as broadsides, greeting cards, or poetry pamphlets is recorded in the notes on individual poems.

---

* In Britain this short essay appears as "On Rewriting" in *No Heroics, Please: Uncollected Writings* (pp. 107–10).

Near Klamath (1968)

Publication: [Sacramento, Calif.]: The English Club of Sacramento
State College, [1968].
Limitation: none.
Illustrations: none.
Dedication: none.
Epigraph:

> The more horses you yoke the quicker everything will go –
> not the rending of the block from its foundation, which is
> impossible, but the snapping of the traces and with that the gay
> and empty journey.
>
> Franz Kafka, *The Great Wall of China*

Contents: Because *Near Klamath* is unpaginated, page numbers are
given in brackets.

The Man Outside [31–2]
The Brass Ring [33]
These Fish [The Current] [34]

Winter Insomnia (1970)

Publication: Santa Cruz, Calif.: Kayak Books, 1970.
Limitation: 1,000 unsigned copies.
Illustrations: block prints by Robert McChesney.
Dedication: *For Dennis Schmitz*
Epigraph: same as in *Near Klamath* (above).
Contents:

Colophon: One thousand copies of this book designed and printed by George Hitchcock at the Kayak Press.

At Night the Salmon Move (1976)

Publication: Santa Barbara: Capra Press, 1976.
Limitation: 100 numbered copies signed by the author.
Illustrations: drawings by Marcia/maris.
Dedication: *For Jerry Davis and Amy Burk Wright*
Epigraph: none.
Contents:

Colophon: Designed for Capra Press by Noel Young in Santa Barbara, February 1976. Printed & bound by Mackintosh & Young. 100 copies were handbound by Emily Paine.

This Water (1985)

Publication: Concord, NH: William B. Ewert, 1985.
Limitation: 136 numbered copies signed by the author.
Illustrations: none.
Dedication: *for Tess*
Epigraph: none.
Contents:

The Trestle (7–8)
Harley's Swans (9–10)
Woolworth's, 1954 (11–13)
Wenas Ridge (14–15)
Our First House in Sacramento (16)
My Dad's Wallet (17–18)
Where Water Comes Together with Other Water (19)
A Haircut (20–1)

Colophon: This edition was designed by John Kristensen. It was printed letterpress from Optima type on Mohawk Superfine text and bound at the Firefly Press, Somerville, Massachusetts in January, 1985. Of 136 copies signed by the author, this is one of [either] 100 hand-sewn in paper wrappers [or] 36 specially bound in boards.

Early for the Dance (1986)

Publication: Concord, NH: William B. Ewert, 1986.
Limitation: 136 numbered copies signed by the author.
Illustrations: none.
Dedication: *for Tess*
Epigraph: none.
Contents:

Limits (7–8)
Migration (9–10)
Mother (11)
Its Course (12–13)
Powder-Monkey (14)
Egress (15–16)
The Mail (17)
The Autopsy Room (18)

Circulation (19–20)
The Meadow (21)

Colophon: This edition, designed by John Kristensen, was printed letterpress from Optima type on Mohawk Superfine text and bound at the Firefly Press, Somerville, Massachusetts in April, 1986. It is limited to 136 copies. Of these, 100 copies, numbered 1–100, are hand-sewn in paper wrappers and 36 deluxe copies, numbered I–XXXVI, are specially bound in cloth and paper over boards. All copies are signed by the author.

Those Days: Early Writings by Raymond Carver: Eleven Poems and a Story (1987)

Publication: Elmwood, Conn.: Raven Editions, 1987.
Limitation: 140 copies signed by the author.
Illustrations: tipped-in colorplate frontispiece by Ronald J. Sloan.
Dedication: *For Dick, Bill, Dennis, and Tess*
Epigraph: none.
Contents (poems):

Those Days (3)
On the Pampas Tonight (4)
Poem on My Birthday, July 2 (5–6)
Return (7)
The Sunbather, to Herself (8)
The Sturgeon (9–11)
No Heroics, Please (12)
Sunday Night (13)
My Wife (14)
Two Worlds (15)
In a Greek Orthodox Church near Daphne (16)

Colophon: First published by Raven Editions in 1987, *Those Days* is limited to 140 copies: numbered copies 1–100 are hand sewn and glued into paper wrappers; 26 copies lettered A–Z are hand bound in paper over boards; and 14 presentation copies *hors commerce* are hand bound in quarter leather with paper over boards. All copies are signed by the author. . . .

Appendix 4

A Note on *In a Marine Light*

In a Marine Light: Selected Poems (1987)

In a Marine Light is a selected and combined edition of *Where Water Comes Together with Other Water* (1985) and *Ultramarine* (1986). As such, it presents 112 poems from those two books arranged in a unique six-part sequence. *In a Marine Light* was published in England, and no corresponding American edition exists.

First edition: London: Collins Harvill, 1987. Publication date: 1 June 1987.
First paperback edition: London: Picador, 1988. Publication date: June 1988.
Dedication: Tess Gallagher
Epigraph:

> Light is my being, light in the kitchen,
> evening light, morning light.
> Light between despair and luminosity ...
> The nets that wavered in the light
> keep on shining from the sea.

> Pablo Neruda, *Isla Negra*

Contents:

I

III

IV

The notes to *Where Water Comes Together with Other Water* and *Ultramarine* indicate which poems from those two books were included in *In a Marine Light*. The following poems were not included in *In a Marine Light*:

Where Water Comes Together with Other Water

Ultramarine

Appendix 5

Bibliographical and Textual Notes

Abbreviations

1st   First magazine appearance or separate publication

ANP   *A New Path to the Waterfall* (New York: Atlantic Monthly Press, 1989)

ANTSM   *At Night the Salmon Move* (Santa Barbara, Calif.: Capra Press, 1976)

AUP   Advance uncorrected proof (publisher's paperbound uncorrected page proofs sent to review sources in advance of finished book)

F   *Fires* (Santa Barbara, Calif.: Capra Press, 1983)

EFTD   *Early for the Dance* (Concord, NH: William B. Ewert, 1986)

IAML   *In a Marine Light: Selected Poems* (London: Collins Harvill, 1987)

NHP   *No Heroics, Please: Uncollected Writings* (London: Harvill, 1991)

NK   *Near Klamath* (Sacramento, Calif.: English Club of Sacramento State College, 1968). *Note:* Because *NK* is unpaginated, page references to it are given in brackets.

RC   Raymond Carver

TD   *Those Days: Early Writings by Raymond Carver*, ed. William L. Stull (Elmwood, Conn.: Raven Editions, 1987)

TW   *This Water* (Concord, NH: William B. Ewert, 1985)

U   *Ultramarine* (New York: Random House, 1985)

WI   *Winter Insomnia* (Santa Cruz, Calif.: Kayak Books, 1970)

WWCT   *Where Water Comes Together with Other Water* (New York: Random House, 1986)

Notes

Fires: Essays, Poems, Stories

First edition: New York, NY: Santa Barbara, Calif.: Capra Press, 1983. A Noel Young Book. Simultaneously published in hardcover and paperback. Publication date: 14 Apr. 1983.

First signed, limited edition: "Printed April 1983 for Capra Press by the Kingsport Press. Two hundred & fifty copies have been numbered and signed by the author and bound into boards" (limitation leaf).

First expanded edition: New York, NY: Vintage Books, 1984. Adds "The *Paris Review* Interview". Publication date: 30 May 1984.

First English edition: London: Collins Harvill, 1985. Omits "The *Paris Review* Interview" and the "Afterword"; adds "My Father's Life" and "John Gardner: The Writer as Teacher". Publication date: 15 Apr. 1985.

Dedication: For Tess

Epigraph: From "Cows Grazing at Sunrise" by William Matthews, *Flood* (Boston: Little, Brown, 1982) 4.

Copy-text: First edition, first printing, collated and corrected against later editions and printings overseen by RC.

Small-press sources and separate publications: *NK, WI, ANTSM, Distress Sale* (Lord John, 1981), *Two Poems* (Scarab, 1982), *At Night the Salmon Move* (Capra, 1983), *Looking for Work/Downstream* (n.p., 1988).

3   DRINKING WHILE DRIVING: in *NK* [26], *WI* 55.

    1–2   It is August.
            I have not read a book in six months *NK, WI*
    8   go, / go *NK, WI*
    15   will / is going to *NK, WI*

3   LUCK: *1st* in *Kayak* [Santa Cruz, Calif.] 50 (May 1979): 40; in *The Poet's Choice*, a special issue of *Tendril* [Green Harbor, Mass.] 9 (1980): 43–4.

    4   drank, too, but they
            could handle it. *1st, Tendril*
    21   to take / and took *1st*
    28–9   at the starry sky –
            it was always starry then *1st, Tendril*
    38   morning. / morning, *1st, Tendril*
    39–40   I saw a woman sleeping on our lawn. *Tendril*
    42   then / and then *1st*
    54   no one / nobody *1st, Tendril*
    55   luck, I / luck I *Tendril*
    59–61   for a house where nobody
            was home, and all I could drink. *1st, Tendril*

5   DISTRESS SALE: *1st* in *Kayak* [Santa Cruz, Calif.] 49 (Oct. 1978): 16–17; separately published as a broadside (Northridge, Calif.: Lord John Press, 1981).

2–7   the child's canopy bed and vanity
table, the sofa, end tables and lamps,
the boxes of assorted books and records.
We carried out kitchen items,
a clock radio, hanging clothes, a big easy
chair that had been with them from the beginning *1st*

10   and they set themselves up around that
to do business. *1st*

12   I'm staying there with them trying to dry out *1st*

15   It's / It is *1st*

24–5   of clothing before moving on.
Everyone who wanders into this scene is embarrassed.
The man, my friend, sits at the table *1st*

32   This reduces us all. Is this what we've come to? *1st*

38   I reach for my wallet before I understand *1st*
I reach for my wallet and that is how I understand:
Lord John

6   YOUR DOG DIES: *1st* in *CutBank* [Univ. of Montana, Missoula] 1 (1973): 32; in *ANTSM* 25.

14   it / the dog afterwards *1st, ANTSM*

16   it / it, *1st*

25   hear / suddenly hear *1st*

7   PHOTOGRAPH OF MY FATHER IN HIS TWENTY-SECOND YEAR: *1st* in *Colorado Quarterly* [Univ. of Colorado, Boulder] 17.2 (Autumn 1968): 162; in *NK* [13], *WI* 17. All lines begin with capital letters in *1st, NK,* and *WI.*

6   denim / levi *1st*

7   1934 Ford / Ford *circa* 1934 *1st, NK, WI*

9   wear his old hat cocked over his ear, stick out his
tongue . . . *1st, NK, WI*

13   And the beer. *Father I loved you, 1st*
And the bottle of beer. Father, I loved you, *NK, WI*

14   Yet how can I say thank you, I who cannot hold my
liquor either *1st, NK, WI*

15   don't / do not *1st, NK, WI*

8   HAMID RAMOUZ (1818–1906): *1st* in *Mississippi Review* [Univ. of Southern Mississippi] 21 [7.3] (Fall 1978): 118.

1   began / started *1st*

3   gunshot / gutshot *1st*

8   BANKRUPTCY: in *NK* [7], *WI* 24. All lines begin with capital letters in *NK.*

9   THE BAKER: *1st* in *Kayak* [Santa Cruz, Calif.] 50 (May 1979): 41; separately published with "Louise" (see p. 46) in *Two Poems* (Salisbury, Md.: Scarab Press, 1982).

5–6   Pancho introduced his new girl friend
and her husband who was made to wear
his white apron, *1st*

8   him / him everything *1st*

<table>
<tr><td>17–18</td><td>The husband crossed himself,
took off his boots and
silently left the house 1st</td></tr>
<tr><td>22–3</td><td>humiliated, trying to save his life,
he is the hero of this poem. 1st</td></tr>
</table>

9   IOWA SUMMER: *1st* in *Chelsea* [New York, NY] 22–3 (June 1968): 57–8; in *NK* [2], *WI* 27. All lines begin with capital letters in *1st*, *NK*, and *WI*.

Title: "Iowa Summer 1967" *NK*, *WI*

<table>
<tr><td>7–12</td><td>It is only later, after they have gone,
I realize they have delivered a letter from my wife.
"What are you doing there?" my wife asks. "Are you
    drinking?"
I study the postmark for hours until it, too, begins to fade.
Someday, I hope to forget all this. 1st, NK, WI</td></tr>
</table>

10   ALCOHOL: *1st* in *New England Review* [Hanover, NH] 4.4 (Summer 1982): 530.

<table>
<tr><td>33–4</td><td>[stanza break between these lines in 1st]</td></tr>
<tr><td>35–6</td><td>You hear the song. 1st</td></tr>
</table>

11   FOR SEMRA, WITH MARTIAL VIGOR: *1st* in *Beloit Poetry Journal* [Ellsworth, Maine] 16.2 (Winter 1965–6): 17–19; in *NK* [20–3], *WI* 40–1.

<table>
<tr><td>6</td><td>things as well / things 1st, NK, WI</td></tr>
<tr><td>19–20</td><td>[stanza break between these lines in 1st]</td></tr>
<tr><td>33–4</td><td>O Semra Semra
Istanbul nee
Constantinople
Next to Paris she said 1st, NK</td></tr>
<tr><td>49–53</td><td>[omitted in WI]</td></tr>
<tr><td>50</td><td>goddamn / goddam 1st, NK</td></tr>
</table>

13   LOOKING FOR WORK [1]: in *WI* 16; see "Looking for Work" [2] in *ANP* (see p. 237); separately published with "Downstream" *ANP* (see p. 279) as a broadside (n.p.: 1988). The *F* version differs from the texts in *WI* and *ANP*, which are identical. The broadside, which otherwise agrees with *WI* and *ANP*, lacks the comma ending line 6 (likely a typographical error).

<table>
<tr><td>1</td><td>I've / I have WI, broadside, ANP</td></tr>
<tr><td>13</td><td>door. / door, WI, broadside, ANP</td></tr>
<tr><td>14</td><td>They are gleaming. / gleaming. WI, broadside, ANP</td></tr>
</table>

14   CHEERS: *1st* in *Esquire* [New York, NY] 86.1 (July 1976): 12; in *Prism International* [Univ. of British Columbia] 21.2 (Winter 1982): 28.

<table>
<tr><td>7–8</td><td>or else they call, Come out and play,
Raymond. 1st</td></tr>
<tr><td>13</td><td>dropped / stopped 1st</td></tr>
</table>

15   ROGUE RIVER JET-BOAT TRIP, GOLD BEACH, OREGON, JULY 4, 1977: *1st* in *Antioch Review* [Antioch Univ.] 36.3 (Summer 1978): 372.

Title: TRIP. / TRIP *1st*

<table>
<tr><td>2</td><td>marten, osprey / marten, mink, osprey 1st</td></tr>
<tr><td>4</td><td>family, / family 1st</td></tr>
</table>

12   do you / d'you *WI*
14   in / There in *WI*
16   closer, kneel / closer *WI*
18   *Corpse,* she whispers. The dog grins. *WI*
19–20 But I don't have time for games
      This morning and send her away *WI*

27   SUDDEN RAIN: *1st* in *Midwest Quarterly* [Pittsburg (Kans.) State Univ.] 14.1
(Oct. 1972): 63; in *ANTSM* 18.
      8   the narrow streets. / narrow streets *1st, ANTSM*
      9   and roll my eyes and clatter against stones. *1st, ANTSM*

28   BALZAC: *1st* in *Levee* [Sacramento State Univ.] 2.2 (Jan. 1967): 4; in *NK* [11],
Carolina Quarterly [Univ. of North Carolina, Chapel Hill] 21.3 (Fall 1969): 21, *WI* 34.
      3–4   the mist rising from his face and
            shoulders, the gown clinging *1st, NK, Carolina*
            Quarterly, WI
      7–8   [stanza break between these lines in *1st, NK, Carolina*
            Quarterly, WI]
      10   stroke / smooth *1st, NK*
      11   young / the young *1st, NK, Carolina Quarterly, WI*
      13   by, / by *1st, NK, Carolina Quarterly, WI*
      14–15 [stanza break between these lines in *1st, NK, Carolina*
            Quarterly, WI]
      20   early / fragile, early *1st, NK, Carolina Quarterly, WI*
      21–5 chamberpot. *1st, NK, Carolina Quarterly, WI*

28   COUNTRY MATTERS: *1st* in *Ploughshares* [Emerson College] 2.3 (1975): 92;
in *ANTSM* 19.
      1   grass, / grass *ANTSM*
      8   call. / call; *1st, ANTSM*
      9   Shreds / shreds *1st, ANTSM*
      10–11 float out onto the wintry air,
            but the girl does not turn her head, *1st, ANTSM*
      12   Cook / cook *1st, ANTSM*
      13   sill. / sill, *1st, ANTSM*
      13–14 In *1st* and *ANTSM* there is an additional line between
            these lines:

            their faces marred with tears, their hair *1st*
            their faces marred with tears, hair *ANTSM*

      14   knotted. He leans closer to hear the small *1st, ANTSM*
      15   whisperings, the broken / whispering, the unhappy *1st*
                              whisperings, the unhappy *ANTSM*

29   THIS ROOM: *1st* in *West Coast Review* [Simon Fraser Univ.] 2.1 (Spring 1967):
22; in *Grande Ronde Review* [Folsom, Calif.] 7 [2.1] (n.d. [1967]): 10, *WI* 51.
      4   Promises   promises *1st, Grande Ronde Review*
      7   parasols, / parasols *1st, Grande Ronde Review, WI*
      8   sea, / sea *1st, Grande Ronde Review, WI*

10   behind – / behind *1st, Grande Ronde Review, WI*
11   listening   smoking *1st, Grande Ronde Review*
12   taking notes? *1st, Grande Ronde Review, WI*
13–16 [omitted in *1st, Grande Ronde Review, WI*]

30   RHODES: in *ANTSM* 20–1.
2   or / nor *ANTSM*
6   nearby / near *ANTSM*
10   stay, / stay *ANTSM*
11   though / but *ANTSM*
17   stiff / stone *ANTSM*
18   figure of a man keeps watch
       on Turkey. *ANTSM*
21   from its tail and heads
       for cover. *ANTSM*
30   there's / I sense *ANTSM*
35–6 as my soul, like a cat, leaps into sleep. *ANTSM*

31   SPRING, 480 BC: *1st* in *Toyon* [Humboldt State Univ.] 9.1 (Spring 1963): 17; in
Western Humanities Review [Univ. of Utah] 17.3 (Summer 1963): 264, *NK* [27], *ANTSM*
15, *Poetry Now* [Eureka, Calif.] 15–18 [3.3–6] (1977): 19. In *Toyon* the poem is published
under the pseudonym John Vale.
9   that / the *1st, Western Humanities Review, NK,*
       ANTSM, Poetry Now
10   fetters, / fetters *1st, Western Humanities Review, NK,*
       ANTSM, Poetry Now

32   NEAR KLAMATH: in *NK* [1], *WI* 46, *Sou'wester Literary Quarterly* [Southern
Illinois Univ., Edwardsville] Winter 1972: 36.
3–4 [no stanza break in *NK, WI, Sou'wester Literary Quarterly*]
5   drink it / drink *NK, WI, Sou'wester Literary Quarterly*
6–7 [no stanza break in *NK, WI, Sou'wester Literary Quarterly*]
7   fishermen. And now / fishermen and *NK*
                       fishermen and now *WI, Sou'wester Literary*
                       Quarterly
8   on the snow and move upstream, slowly, *NK, WI*
       on the snow and move upstream, slowly *Sou'wester*
       Literary Quarterly
9   full of love, growing older with each step. *NK, WI, Sou'wester Literary*
       Quarterly

32   AUTUMN: in *NK* [15], *Quarry West* [Univ. of California, Santa Cruz] 6 (1976):
n.p., *ANTSM* 38.
1   yardful / yard full *NK*
7   [no indentation in *NK, Quarry West, ANTSM*]
10   logging gear / marine-gear *NK*
11–12 [stanza break between these lines in *NK, Quarry West,*
       ANTSM]
13   Slowly / And slowly *NK, Quarry West, ANTSM*
15   towards high water, the jack- *NK, Quarry West,*
       ANTSM
16   salmon and the sea-run cutthroat. *NK, ANTSM*
       salmon and sea-run cutthroat. *Quarry West*

33   WINTER INSOMNIA: in *WI* 23. The version in *WI* prints the four stanzas in an alternate sequence:

> The mind would like to get out of here
> Onto the snow. It would like to run
> With a pack of shaggy animals, all teeth,
>
> Under the moon, across the snow, leaving
> No prints or spoor, nothing behind.
> The mind is sick tonight.
>
> It wishes Chekov were here to minister
> Something – three drops of valerian, a glass
> Of rose water – anything, it wouldn't matter.
>
> The mind can't sleep, can only lie awake and
> Gorge, and listen to the snow gathering
> For the final assault.

33   PROSSER: *1st* in *Kayak* [Santa Cruz, Calif.] 28 (1972): 62; in *ANTSM* 12.
15   Ah, but everything is forgotten, almost everything, *1st*,
      ANTSM
24   hills / the hills *1st*
26   still: / still. *1st*

34   AT NIGHT THE SALMON MOVE: in *ANTSM* 14, *Poetry Now* [Eureka, Calif.] 15–18 [3.3–6] (1977): 19; separately published as a broadside (Santa Barbara, Calif.: Capra Press, 1983).
4   like Foster's, A&W, and Smiley's, *ANTSM, Poetry Now*
6   Wright Avenue / Wright *ANTSM, Poetry Now*

35   WITH A TELESCOPE ROD ON COWICHE CREEK: in *NK* [14], *WI* 18, *Prism International* [Univ. of British Columbia] 21.2 (Winter 1982): 26. All lines begin with capital letters in *NK* and *WI*.
2   direction / ambition *NK, WI*
7   pine / the *NK, WI*

35   POEM FOR DR PRATT, A LADY PATHOLOGIST: in *NK* [16–17], *WI* 45, *Carolina Quarterly* [Univ. of North Carolina, Chapel Hill] 23.3 (Fall 1971): 48. All lines begin with capital letters in *NK, WI,* and *Carolina Quarterly*.
Title: "Poem for a Lady Pathologist" *NK, WI, Carolina Quarterly*
5   McCormick / Cormac *NK, Carolina Quarterly*
8   And their disinfectant. They pretend I am not *NK, WI, Carolina Quarterly*
11–12 They embrace. Gradually,
      The room begins to fill with leaves.
      I am afraid. *NK, WI, Carolina Quarterly*
13   Sunlight. / Sunlight. I hear sprinklers. *NK, WI, Carolina Quarterly*
17–18 A green desk floats by the window.
      I begin to void. *NK, WI, Carolina Quarterly*
19   lies / sits *NK, WI, Carolina Quarterly*

20   Of affection, while her tiny *NK, WI, Carolina Quarterly*
21   Probing fingers rummage the endless strings *NK, WI*
        Fingers rummage the endless strings *Carolina Quarterly*
22   Of entrails. These considerations aside, *NK, WI, Carolina Quarterly*
24   hands / tiny hands *NK, WI*
25   I'm / I am *NK, WI, Carolina Quarterly*

36   WES HARDIN: FROM A PHOTOGRAPH: *1st* in *Western Humanities Review*
[Univ. of Utah] 19.3 (Summer 1965): 223; in *NK* [3–4], *WI* 21.
        3   outlaw, / outlaw *1st, NK, WI*
        29   [omitted in *1st, NK, WI*]
        30–1   but what makes me stare is this large
                        dark bullethole *1st, NK, WI*
        33   right hand. / lefthand. *1st, NK, WI*

37   MARRIAGE: in *Akros Review* [Univ. of Akron] 5 (Fall 1981): 74–5.
        29   children / children I fear *Akros Review*

38   THE OTHER LIFE: in *Missouri Review* [Univ. of Missouri, Columbia] 3.2
(Winter 1980): 16.
        3, 5   *scratch, scratch* / scratch, scratch *Missouri Review*

39   THE MAILMAN AS CANCER PATIENT: *1st* in *Levee* [Sacramento State Univ.]
2.2 (Jan. 1967): 6–7; in *NK* [9–10], *ANTSM* 41, *Tendril* [Green Harbor, Mass.] 11
(Summer 1981): 16. In *Levee* the poem is titled "Ca*", with a footnote expanding the
abbreviation: "*Cancer."
        4   they'll hold the job – / / they will hold the job, *1st, ANTSM*
                        they will hold the job *NK*
        5   and, besides,
                he needed a rest. *1st, NK*
        13   book / book, *1st, NK, ANTSM, Tendril*
        16   yet / and *1st*
                        but *NK, ANTSM, Tendril*
        16–17   [stanza break between these lines in *NK*]
        17   But sometimes / Yet sometimes *NK, ANTSM*
                        Sometimes *Tendril*
        18   bed / bed, *1st, NK*
        22   for / worst, for *1st*
                        worst for *NK*
        23   there's / there is *ANTSM, Tendril*
                there is nothing left
                of them, nothing
                whole to cling to; it is *1st, NK*
        24   he'd / he had *1st, NK, ANTSM, Tendril*
        25   anywhere, never done anything, *1st, NK*
                never met anybody; *1st*
                never met anybody: *NK*
        26   room / now *1st, NK*
        27–9   and he can only press
                his lips with his fingers
                and wait to go
                where the mad blood takes him. *1st*

    27   disappear / disappear again *ANTSM*
    29   light, / light *ANTSM*

41   TORTURE: *1st* in *Mississippi Review* [Univ. of Southern Mississippi] 21 [7.3] (Fall
1978): 116–17; in *Prism International* [Univ. of British Columbia] 21.2 (Winter 1982): 27.
    8–9   nice people don't talk about in classrooms.
             You want to be tied down and moan.
             You want to tell everything you know. *1st*
    14   and / again and *1st*
    31   wide / the wide *1st*

42   BOBBER: in *NK* [29], *Quarry West* [Univ. of California, Santa Cruz] 6 (1976): n.p.,
ANTSM 39, *Poetry Now* [Eureka, Calif.] 15–18 [3.3–6] (1977): 19. This poem exists in
two early versions. The first version appears in *NK*:

> On the Columbia River near Vantage
> Washington we fished for whitefish
> In the winter months of November,
> December, and January; my dad, Swede –
> Mr Lindgren – and I. They used belly-reels,
> Pencil-lead sinkers, red, yellow, or brown
> Whitefish flies baited with maggots.
> They wanted distance and they got out there,
> Clear out to the edge of the riffle.
> I fished in close with a quill bobber
> And a cane pole. It was always cold,
> Always early in the morning, and
> Sometimes the line froze to the guides
>   after each cast.
> My dad kept his maggots alive and warm
> Under his lower lip. Mr Lindgren didn't drink.
> I liked him better than my dad for a time.
> He let me steer his car, teased me
> About my name "Junior," and one day
> Said I would grow into a fine man,
> Remember all this, and fish with my own son.
> But my dad was right. He just kept silent,
> Stroked his chin, and went on
> Pissing an arc into the river.

The second version, printed in *Quarry West, ANTSM*, and *Poetry Now* (each with
variants), preserves many features of the *NK* text. At the same time, it more closely
resembles the version in *Fires*, from which it differs as follows:
    2   Washington, / Washington *ANTSM, Poetry Now*
    3–4   in the winter months of November,
             December, and January; my dad, Swede –
             Mr Lindgren – and I. They used belly-reels, *Quarry
             West, ANTSM, Poetry Now*
    7   went clear / they got *Quarry West, ANTSM, Poetry Now*
    8   to / clear to *Quarry West*
                  clear out to *ANTSM, Poetry Now*

14–16   about my name "Junior", and one day
said I would grow into a fine man,
remember all this, and fish with my own son. *Quarry*
West, *ANTSM*, *Poetry Now*

18–19   he kept silent, stroked his chin,
and went on pissing an arc into the river. *Quarry West*,
ANTSM, *Poetry Now*

42   HIGHWAY 99E FROM CHICO: in *NK* [8], *Midwest Quarterly* [Pittsburg (Kans.)
State Univ.] 11.1 (Oct. 1969): 49, *WI* 28. All lines begin with capital letters in *NK*,
Midwest Quarterly, and *WI*.

Title: "Highway 99E from Chico: November 1966" *NK*, *WI*
"Highway 99E from Chico: November 1967" *Midwest*
Quarterly

43   THE COUGAR: *1st* in *CutBank* [Univ. of Montana, Missoula] 1 (1973): 31;
in *ANTSM* 28–9. All lines begin with capital letters in *1st*.

Dedication: *For Keith Wilson and John Haines 1st*
for Keith Wilson and John Haines ANTSM

15   put it / put *ANTSM*

24   Southwest, / Southwest *1st*, *ANTSM*

25   poet / And all, poet *1st*
and all, poet *ANTSM*

27   writer / fiction writer *1st*

32   *me* / me *1st*, *ANTSM*

33   clear / clean *1st*

44   THE CURRENT: *1st* in *Levee* [Sacramento State Univ.] 2.2 (Jan. 1967): 4; in *NK*
[34], *WI* 54, *Sou'wester Literary Quarterly* [Southern Illinois Univ., Edwardsville] Winter
1972: 35, *ANTSM* 40. This is the only poem that appears in all three of RC's small-press
poetry books: *NK*, *WI*, and *ANTSM*. In *Levee* the entire poem is set in capital letters.

Title: "These Fish" *Levee*, *NK*, *WI*, *Sou'wester*, *ANTSM*

3   that scatter their roe and their milt *Levee*, *NK*, *WI*,
Sou'wester, *ANTSM*

5–6   But there is one that comes –
heavy, scarred,
sightless like the rest, *Levee*, *NK*, *WI*
silent like the rest, *Sou'wester*, *ANTSM*

6–7   [stanza break between these lines in *Levee*, *NK*, *WI*,
Sou'wester, *ANTSM*]

7–8   [no stanza break in *Levee*, *NK*, *WI*, *Sou'wester*, *ANTSM*]

8–10   opening and closing its dark mouth
against the current. *Levee*, *NK*, *WI*, *Sou'wester*, *ANTSM*

44   HUNTER: in *NK* [18]; in *Esquire* [New York, NY] 76.1 (July 1971): 14, *ANTSM*
27. All flush-left lines begin with capital letters in *NK* and *Esquire*.

Title: "The Hunter" *NK*

1   on top of / here at the very top of *NK*
on top *Esquire*, *ANTSM*

7   There's / There is *NK*, *Esquire*, *ANTSM*

8   can't / cannot *NK*, *Esquire*, *ANTSM*

9   underwear, / underwear *NK*, *Esquire*, *ANTSM*

10–11   [no stanza break in *NK*]
11   Suddenly,
        Her hand raises in alarm – *NK, Esquire*
        her hand rises in alarm – *ANTSM*
14–17   It is December, three o'clock of a Sunday afternoon. *NK*

45   TRYING TO SLEEP LATE ON A SATURDAY MORNING IN NOVEMBER:
1st in *Chelsea* [New York, NY] 22–3 (June 1968): 58; in *NK* [24], *ANTSM* 13.
All lines begin with capital letters in *1st* and *NK*.
3–4   We are approaching the
        Third and final phase, this *1st*
        third and final phase, this *ANTSM*
14   fishermen / fisherman *1st, NK, ANTSM*
20–2   My hair crawls.
        I begin to sweat under all the bedclothes. *1st, NK,
        ANTSM*

46   LOUISE: *1st* in *Ironwood* [Tucson, Ariz.] 19 [10.1] (Spring 1982): 133;
separately published with "The Baker" (see p. 9) in *Two Poems* (Salisbury, Md.:
Scarab Press, 1982).
25   back – / back. She *Two Poems*
25–6   and steps back from this near human shape. *1st*

46   POEM FOR KARL WALLENDA, AERIALIST SUPREME: *1st* in *Kayak*
[Santa Cruz, Calif.] 57 (1981): 27.
2–3   all over Magdeburg. In Vienna wind looked
        for you in first one courtyard then another. *1st*
8   the / those *1st*
27–32   on the first day of spring, that wind which has been
        everywhere and done everything with you,
        it comes in from the Caribbean
        to throw itself once and for all into your arms, like a young lover!
        Your hair crawls. You try to crouch, to reach for wire. *1st*

48   DESCHUTES RIVER: *1st* in *Western Humanities Review* [Univ. of Utah] 21.1
(Winter 1967): 56; in *NK* [5–6], *Esquire* [New York, NY] 76.2 (Aug. 1971): 76,
ANTSM 32.
4   so that / that *1st, NK, Esquire, ANTSM*
14   Later,
        eight mallard ducks fly over *1st, NK, Esquire, ANTSM*
16   Frank / Jack *1st, NK, Esquire, ANTSM*
23   away – / away, *1st, NK, Esquire, ANTSM*

48   FOREVER: *1st* in *Kayak* [Santa Cruz, Calif.] 16 (1968): 50; in *WI* 30.
Title: "The Wall" *1st, WI*
9   entire / whole *1st, WI*
12   tonight / tonight, *1st, WI*
24   down / down and wander *1st, WI*
25–6   back into the house. They are still
        there, God help them all, waiting, *1st, WI*
27   faces / faces now *1st, WI*

Where Water Comes Together with Other Water

First edition: New York, NY: Random House, 1985. Publication date: 1 May 1985.

First paperback edition: New York, NY: Vintage Books, 1986. Publication date: 24 Apr. 1986.

First selected and combined English edition: *In a Marine Light: Selected Poems*. London: Collins Harvill, 1987. Publication date: 1 June 1987.

Dedication: *for Tess Gallagher and Morris R. Bond*. Morris R. Bond is Tess Gallagher's brother, a writer, outdoorsman, and native of Port Angeles, Washington.

Copy-text: First edition, first printing, collated and corrected against later editions and printings overseen by R.C.

Small-press sources and separate publications: *My Crow* (Ewert, 1984), *For Tess* (Ewert, 1984), *TW* (Ewert, 1985), *Music* (Ewert, 1987), *Afghanistan* (Ewert, 1988), *In the Year 2020* (Okeanos, 1993).

53   WOOLWORTH'S, 1954: *1st* in *Paris Review* [Flushing, NY] 26.93 (Fall 1984): 42–4; in *TW* 11–13, *IAML* 18–20.

4–5	telling me he'd be here in a few minutes
	to go clamming *IAML*
5	go / take me *TW*
9	a stockboy like I was. He'd been *1st, TW*
10	there forever, and had worked his way *1st*
	there forever. Had worked his way *TW*
12	me / I was *1st, TW*
19	knew. He was / knew. Was AUP
21–2	Most important memory of that
	time: opening *1st*
	Most important memory of that whole
	time coming back to me now: opening *TW*
32	I got / got *1st, TW*
39	happened. / happened! *1st, TW*, AUP
45	skin. / skin! *1st, TW*
49	calves! / calves. *TW*
71	sister, / sister *IAML*
72	girls. / girls, *TW*, AUP
73	Grownup / grownup *TW*
74	I'll say it: dead. / I'll say it: Dead. *1st*
	Need I say it? Dead. *TW*

55   RADIO WAVES: *1st* in *Paris Review* [Flushing, NY] 26.93 (Fall 1984): 37–8; in *IAML* 152–3.

5	want to / want *1st*
12	the papers / newspapers *1st*
13	get away / absent myself *1st*

20   trustworthy / to be trusted *1st*

25   It didn't matter, it said, even if a man sang. *1st*

32   Then, Machado, the advent of your poetry in my life!*1st*

35   and / but *1st*

48   it / your book *1st*

57   MOVEMENT: *1st* in *Paris Review* [Flushing, NY] 26.93 (Fall 1984): 40.

11   slack. / slack! *1st*

12   for / For *1st*

58   HOMINY AND RAIN: *1st* in *Paris Review* [Flushing, NY] 26.93 (Fall 1984):
49–50; in *IAML* 150–1.

15   be true. That they smelled like that.
        Those blossoms. I can't say. *1st*

41   though that / though AUP

59   THE ROAD: *1st* in *Paris Review* [Flushing, NY] 26.93 (Fall 1984): 39.

8   glass / tiles in the courtyard *1st*

16   curtain / curtains *1st*

60   FEAR: *1st* in *Paris Review* [Flushing, NY] 26.93 (Fall 1984): 41; in *IAML* 155.

21   of waking / I'll wake *1st*

61   ROMANTICISM: *1st* in *Paris Review* [Flushing, NY] 26.93 (Fall 1984): 51; in
IAML 62.

        Dedication: (*For my friend Linda Gregg, after reading "Classicism"*) *1st*

61   THE ASHTRAY: *1st* in *Paris Review* [Flushing, NY] 26.93 (Fall 1984): 45–6.

2   apartment / flat *1st*

9   cigarettes and ashes during this painful conversation. *1st*

37   harm? / harm? he thinks. *1st*

63   STILL LOOKING OUT FOR NUMBER ONE: *1st* in *Paris Review* [Flushing, NY]
26.93 (Fall 1984): 48; in *IAML* 40.

17   I can't / can't *1st*, AUP

63   WHERE WATER COMES TOGETHER WITH OTHER WATER: *1st* in *Tendril*
[Green Harbor, Mass.] 19–20 (1985): 403; in *TW* 19, *IAML* 194–5.

10   join / meet *TW*

16   or / and *1st*, *TW*

22   45 / forty-five *1st*, *TW*, AUP

24, 25   35 / thirty-five *1st*, *TW*, AUP

65   HAPPINESS: *1st* in *Poetry* [Chicago, Ill.] 145.5 (Feb. 1985): 251; in *IAML* 15.

8   wear / have on *1st*

9   one / the one *1st*, AUP

18   pale / palely *1st*

20   love, / love *1st*

66   THE OLD DAYS: *1st* in *Pequod* [National Poetry Foundation, Univ. of Maine,
Orono] 18 (1985): 50–1; in *IAML* 179–80.

11   food / dinner *1st*

16–17   [no stanza break in *1st*]
18–19   as he was going upstairs with
         it and talked him down. *1st*
48   for trouble / to be used *1st*

67   OUR FIRST HOUSE IN SACRAMENTO: *1st* in *Pequod* [National Poetry
Foundation, Univ. of Maine, Orono] 18 (1985): 47; in *TW* 16, *IAML* 42–3.
27   firsthand / from first-hand *1st*, *TW*
                 from firsthand AUP
30   a / the *1st*, *TW*, AUP

68   NEXT YEAR: *1st* in *Grand Street* [New York, NY] 4.2 (Winter 1985): 88; in
IAML 54–5.
23   out of / out. Out of *1st*

70   TO MY DAUGHTER: in *IAML* 56–7.

71   ANATHEMA: *1st* in *Tendril* [Green Harbor, Mass.] 19–20 (1985): 427; in *IAML*
63–4.
24   in / by the *1st*, AUP
36   around would / would *IAML*

72   ENERGY: *1st* in *Crazyhorse* [Univ. of Arkansas, Little Rock] 27 (Fall 1984): 10; in
Tendril [Green Harbor, Mass.] 19–20 (1985): 428, *IAML* 50.
30   relentlessly / remorselessly *Tendril*

73   LOCKING YOURSELF OUT, THEN TRYING TO GET BACK IN: *1st* in *Pequod*
[National Poetry Foundation, Univ. of Maine, Orono] 18 (1985): 48–9; in *IAML* 177–8.
13   *friends / my dears 1st*
35   again / then *1st*

74   MEDICINE: *1st* in *New Letters* [Univ. of Missouri, Kansas City] 51.2 (Winter
1984–5): 14.

75   WENAS RIDGE: *1st* in *Tendril* [Green Harbor, Mass.] 19–20 (1985): 412–13; in
TW 14–15, *IAML* 88–9.
7   golden / gold *1st*, *TW*, AUP
11–12   To the top of Wenas Ridge.
         Where we walked out of pine trees and could see *1st*, *TW*
30–1   pushing into undergrowth. Shadows falling from trees now.
         But flat rocks that held the day's heat. And snakes. *1st*, *TW*
43   The / And *1st*, *TW*, AUP
49   I've / have *1st*, *TW*

77   READING: in *IAML* 138–9.

78   RAIN
9   Yes, if I had even half a chance. AUP

78   MONEY: *1st* in *Poetry* [Chicago, Ill.] 145.5 (Feb. 1985): 252–3; in *IAML* 24–5.
4   To go / Go *1st*
8   money / of it *1st*

27   love / love it, *1st*, AUP
28–9   who'd flip out to see him
        in his own boat, sails full, *1st*

81   AT LEAST
      19   the / that AUP

82   MY BOAT: *1st* in *Fiction Magazine* [London] 4.3 (June–July 1985): 17; in
IAML 106–7. Based on RC's revisions in the first and all subsequent printings of
the paperback edition of *WWCT* (1st pbk.), the following emendation has been
made to the copy-text (1st ed.):
      8   Annie, Jane 1st pbk. / Cindy, Jean 1st ed., *IAML*
Other variants:
      4   Hayden / Dan *1st*, AUP
      5   George, Harold, Don / George, Bob, Michael, Don *1st*,
              AUP
      8   And Kristina, Merry, Catherine, Diane, Sally, Annick, Pat, Judith, Susie.
              1st, AUP

84   WORK: first five lines quoted in the article "In the Works" by Tom Jenks in
Esquire 102.2 (Aug. 1984): 114. *1st* complete in *New Letters* 51.2 (Winter 1984–5):
16; in *Sunday Times* [London] 7 June 1987: 57, *IAML* 113.

84   IN THE YEAR 2020: separately published as a broadside "on the occasion
of an event honoring the life and work of RC" (Berkeley: Okeanos Press, 1993).
The event was a public reading held at Black Oak Books in Berkeley, Calif., on
9 Oct. 1993.

86   THE JUGGLER AT *HEAVEN'S GATE*: *1st* in *Tendril* [Green Harbor, Mass.]
19–20 (1985): 414.
      Title: "The Juggler" *1st*
      Subtitle: "(Or, The Scene to Remember from *Heaven's Gate*)" *1st*
      17   emigrants / landed emigrants *1st*
      24   Juggling / A juggler *1st*

88   THE FISHING POLE OF THE DROWNED MAN: *1st* in *Tendril* [Green
Harbor, Mass.] 19–20 (1985): 429; in *IAML* 105.
      Also published in this issue of *Tendril* is a version of "The Garden"
(see p. 180) that includes the following stanza:

                Redoubtable. There's a word!
                It suited him down to the ground.
                He'd fished with the rod that belonged to the deceased.
                It seemed like a good idea at the time.
                But later, he had his doubts. *Tendril* 411

The stanza is not preserved in the collected version of "The Garden".

89   MY DAD'S WALLET: *1st* in *New York Times Magazine* 24 June 1984: 38,
accompanying the article "Raymond Carver: A Chronicler of Blue-Collar Despair"
by Bruce Weber (36+); in *TW* 17–18, *IAML* 30–1.
      30   of / charges of *1st*

39–40   each of his cheeks as he looked
         up from his figures. The same poor light *1st*, AUP

92   ASK HIM: *1st* in *Tendril* [Green Harbor, Mass.] 19–20 (1985): 407–8; in
IAML 189–91. Based on RC's revision in the first and all subsequent printings
of the paperback edition of *WWCT* (1st pbk.), one emendation has been made
to the copy-text (1st ed.). A further revision, present only in *IAML*, is treated as
a variant:

24   untroubled 1st pbk. / ordered *1st*, AUP, 1st ed.
                            regulated *IAML*

Other variants:

2–3   through the iron gates of
        the cemetery in Montparnasse. *1st*, AUP
24   son and / son, or *1st*
                son or AUP
42   would / had *1st*, AUP

94   NEXT DOOR: *1st* in *Tendril* [Green Harbor, Mass.] 19–20 (1985): 421.
8   A / Is a *1st*

95   THE CAUCASUS: A ROMANCE: in *IAML* 171–3.
9   forests / forest AUP
44   Thursday / Thursdays AUP

97   A FORGE, AND A SCYTHE: in *IAML* 41.

98   THE PIPE: in *IAML* 124.
18   I'll / Instead, I'll AUP

98   LISTENING: *1st* in *New Letters* [Univ. of Missouri, Kansas City] 51.2
(Winter 1984–5): 17; in *IAML* 168.

99   IN SWITZERLAND: *1st* in *Tendril* [Green Harbor, Mass.] 19–20 (1985):
425–6; in *IAML* 186–8.

102   A SQUALL: *1st* in *New Letters* [Univ. of Missouri, Kansas City] 51.2
(Winter 1984–5), 14–15; in *IAML* 127.
24   in / of *1st*, AUP
      In the setting typescript of *WWCT* the poem includes a hand-canceled
final stanza:

            Now, there's the bell! That's all.
            Go home and write something
            before you die.

103   MY CROW: *1st* as a holiday greeting card (Concord, NH: William B. Ewert,
1984); in *Poetry* [Chicago, Ill.] 145.5 (Feb. 1985): 253, *IAML* 133.
8   there / here AUP

104   AFTER RAINY DAYS: *1st* in *New Letters* [Univ. of Missouri, Kansas City]
51.2 (Winter 1984–5): 18; in *IAML* 149.
11   breaking / and break *1st*

104   INTERVIEW: *1st* in *Tendril* [Green Harbor, Mass.] 19–20 (1985): 405.

  1–4   Talking about myself all day.
            It brought back
            something I thought over
            and done with. What I'd felt *1st*

105   BLOOD: *1st* in *Grand Street* [New York, NY] 4.2 (Winter 1985): 89; in *IAML* 90.

106   TOMORROW: *1st* in *Ohio Review* [Ohio Univ.] 34 (1985): 12; in *IAML* 72.

  13–14   Nevertheless,
            I wish for tomorrow. In all its finery. *1st*

106   GRIEF: *1st* in *Poetry* [Chicago, Ill.] 145.5 (Feb. 1985): 254; in *IAML* 134.

107   HARLEY'S SWANS: in *TW* 9–10, *IAML* 75–6.

  20   after / later *TW*

109   ELK CAMP: *1st* in *Tendril* [Green Harbor, Mass.] 19–20 (1985): 423–4; in *IAML* 101–2.

  3   ever were / ever *1st*
  8   coming. / coming! *1st*
  10   thrown up / put together *1st*
  39–42   behind the shoulder where the heart
            and lungs are located. "They might
            run, but they won't run far. Look
            at it this way," my friend said. *1st*

111   THE WINDOWS OF THE SUMMER VACATION HOUSES: *1st* in *New Letters* [Univ. of Missouri, Kansas City] 51.2 (Winter 1984–5): 12–13.

  5   when / where *1st*

113   MEMORY [1]: *1st* in *New Letters* [Univ. of Missouri, Kansas City] 51.2 (Winter 1984–5): 15. See "Memory" [2] in *U*, p. 150.

  13   A little / Little *1st*

113   AWAY: in *Ohio Review* [Ohio Univ.] 34 (1985): 11, *Tendril* [Green Harbor, Mass.] 19–20 (1985): 406.

  2   hillside / side of the hill *Ohio Review, Tendril,* AUP
  4   afterwards / then afterwards *Tendril*
  7–8   When I talked to you on the phone,
            I tried to joke. Don't worry *Ohio Review, Tendril*
            I talked to you on the phone,
            tried to joke. Don't worry AUP
  11   A week later / Been a week now *Ohio Review, Tendril*
  12   still haven't / haven't *Ohio Review, Tendril*

114   MUSIC: separately published as a holiday greeting card (Concord, NH: William B. Ewert, 1987).

115   ALL HER LIFE: in *IAML* 53.

  5   dreamt / dreamed *IAML*

116 THE HAT: *1st* in *Tendril* [Green Harbor, Mass.] 19–20 (1985): 418–19; in
IAML 116–18.
>   10   all the way / closed *1st*
>   11   and / but *1st*
>   17   a / which is a *1st*

118 LATE NIGHT WITH FOG AND HORSES: in *Ohio Review* [Ohio Univ.]
34 (1985): 6–7, *Tendril* [Green Harbor, Mass.] 19–20 (1985): 422, *IAML* 47–8.
>   4   another / it another *Tendril*
>   5–6   there was someone else. Tears were falling.
>   When a horse stepped out of the fog *Ohio Review, Tendril*
>   17   yard, where / yard. Where *Tendril*
>   28   ended, / ended. *Tendril*
>   29   something / Something *Tendril*
>   36   a / like a *Ohio Review, Tendril*

119 VENICE: *1st* in *Tendril* [Green Harbor, Mass.] 19–20 (1985): 415; in
IAML 86.
>   6   Sangallo / Rajione *1st*
>   9   total, or / total. Or *1st*
>   19   And history / History AUP

120 THE EVE OF BATTLE: *1st* in *Tendril* [Green Harbor, Mass.] 19–20 (1985):
416; in *IAML* 169–70.
>   24   anything. He's dressed in a morning coat and tails,
>   as if he's on his way to some important function. *1st*

121 EXTIRPATION: *1st* in *Tendril* [Green Harbor, Mass.] 19–20 (1985): 417.
>   9   each other / one another *1st*

121 THE CATCH: *1st* in *New Letters* [Univ. of Missouri, Kansas City] 51.2
(Winter 1984–5): 18.

122 MY DEATH: *1st* in *Ohio Review* [Ohio Univ.] 34 (1985): 13.
>   35   believe / oh believe *1st*
>   O believe AUP

123 TO BEGIN WITH: *1st* in *Ohio Review* [Ohio Univ.] 34 (1985): 8–10; in
IAML 32–4.
>   5   how every evening / every evening how *1st*, AUP
>   10   silent / sullen *IAML*

125 THE CRANES: *1st* in *New Letters* [Univ. of Missouri, Kansas City] 51.3
(Spring 1985): 63; in *IAML* 77.

127 A HAIRCUT: in *TW* 20–1, *IAML* 82–3.
>   7–8   as the library. There's a window
>   there that gives light. Snow's coming *TW*
>   23–4   Soon, light begins to pull away
>   from the window. He stares down, lost and *IAML*

128 HAPPINESS IN CORNWALL: in *IAML* 84–5.

129 AFGHANISTAN: *1st* in *Paris Review* [Flushing, NY] 26.93 (Fall 1984): 47; separately published as a broadside "to honor RC on his induction into the American Academy and Institute of Arts and Letters" on 18 May 1988 (Concord, NH: William B. Ewert, 1988).

130 IN A MARINE LIGHT NEAR SEQUIM, WASHINGTON: in *IAML* 28.

131 EAGLES: in *IAML* 100.

131 YESTERDAY, SNOW: *1st* in *Grand Street* [New York, NY] 4.2 (Winter 1985): 87; in *IAML* 192–3.
    9   sweating / I was sweating *1st*
    32   Goes on, Yes. *1st*

132 READING SOMETHING IN THE RESTAURANT
    9   going / thoughts going AUP

133 A POEM NOT AGAINST SONGBIRDS: *1st* in *New Letters* [Univ. of Missouri, Kansas City] 51.2 (Winter 1984–5): 16.
    11   friends / sweet darlings *1st*

134 LATE AFTERNOON, APRIL 8, 1984
    1   sport-fishing / sports fishing AUP

135 MY WORK: in *IAML* 129–30.

136 THE TRESTLE: in *TW* 7–8, *IAML* 73–4.
    Title: "Water" AUP
    6   woke / woke up *TW*, AUP
    24   I wish my own life, and death, could be so simple.
          I think it could, if I had any character.
          What I want is to perfect my life someway. *TW*, AUP
    25   on / up on *TW*, AUP
    36   once stood / stood once *TW*
    43   and phone calls, its stupid concerns – is unbecoming, *TW*

138 FOR TESS: *1st* as a broadside (Concord, NH: William B. Ewert, 1984); in *Poetry* [Chicago, Ill.] 145.5 (Feb. 1985): 252, *IAML* 81; reprinted in *Literary Cavalcade* [Scholastic Inc., New York, NY] 39.7 (Apr. 1987): 9, accompanied by RC's essay on the poem (*NHP* 120–2).
    3   out / out there *1st*, *Poetry*

Ultramarine

First edition: NewYork, NY: Random House, 1986. Publication date: 7 Nov. 1986.

First paperback edition: NewYork, NY: Vintage Books, 1987. Publication date: Oct. 1987.

First selected and combined English edition: *In a Marine Light: Selected Poems*. London: Collins Harvill, 1987. Publication date: 1 June 1987.

Dedication: *Tess Gallagher*

Epigraph: From "Mt Gabriel" by Derek Mahon, *Antarctica* (Dublin: Gallery Press, 1985) 18.

Copy-text: First edition, first printing, collated and corrected against later editions and printings overseen by RC.

Small-press sources and separate publications: *The Window* (Ewert, 1985), *EFTD* (Ewert, 1986), *The River* (Ewert, 1987), *The Best Time of the Day* (privately printed, 1988), *The Cobweb* (Jungle Garden, 1988), *Sweet Light* (Jungle Garden, 1990).

141   THIS MORNING: *1st* in *Ploughshares* [Emerson College] 11.4 (1985): 81; in *IAML* 35–6. Title listed in AUP table of contents but text omitted from proof.

6	walk – determined / walk. Determined *1st*
17–18	myself to see what I was seeing and
	nothing else. I had to tell myself *this* is what *1st*
19	mattered / matters *1st*
28	For a minute or two, though, I did forget *1st*
30–1	For when I turned back I didn't
	know where I was. Until some birds rose up *1st*

142   WHAT YOU NEED FOR PAINTING: in *IAML* 125.

143   AN AFTERNOON: *1st* in *Ploughshares* [Emerson College] 11.4 (1985): 79.

143   CIRCULATION: in *EFTD* 19–20, *IAML* 199–200.

1	pain / pain, *EFTD*
8	you were / it was *EFTD*
28	stinging / stinging pain *EFTD*
36	that you / you *EFTD*
40	climbed / got *EFTD*
54	far more / more *EFTD*

145   THE COBWEB: *1st* in *Caliban* [Ann Arbor, Mich.] 1 (1986): 102; separately published as a broadside (Fairfax, Calif.: Jungle Garden Press, 1988).

1–2	A few minutes ago, I stepped onto the deck of the house.
	From there I could see and hear the water, *1st*
11	Intricate / Intricate too *1st*

145   BALSA WOOD: *1st* in *Poetry* [Chicago, Ill.] 146.6 (Sept. 1985): 346; in *IAML* 21. Reproduction of revised typescript accompanies the essay "Raymond Carver" by William L. Stull in *Dictionary of Literary Biography Yearbook 1984* (Detroit: Gale Research, 1985): 236.

8	deeper / no deeper *1st*
16	mound / mound of stuff *1st*
19	to / and *1st*

146 THE PROJECTILE: *1st* in *Ohio Review* [Ohio Univ.] 37 (1986): 60–1; in *IAML* 16–17.

5	reoccurring / recurring *1st*
11	careening / careering *IAML*
17	going to / gonna *1st*
19	Only three / Three *1st*
46	got / get *1st*
52	down the stupid road, then turning the stupid corner *1st*

148 THE MAIL: *1st* in *TriQuarterly* [Northwestern Univ.] 66 (Spring–Summer 1986): 145; in *EFTD* 17, *IAML* 156–7.

18	for her a home of her own? *1st*, *EFTD*

149 THE AUTOPSY ROOM: *1st* in *Ontario Review* [Princeton, NJ] 24 (Spring–Summer 1986): 45; in *EFTD* 18, *IAML* 65–6.

4	was / had been *1st*, *EFTD*
5	or too late. / or late, *1st*
	or late. *EFTD*
6	for, so help me, they left things *1st*
12	running / still running *1st*, *EFTD*
26	strayed / strayed down *EFTD*, AUP

150 WHERE THEY'D LIVED: in *IAML* 69.

150 MEMORY [2]: see "Memory" [1] in *WWCT*, p. 113.

151 THE CAR: in *IAML* 44–5.

11	[omitted in *IAML*]
33	corroded / the corroded *IAML*
49	Car / The car *IAML*

152 STUPID: *1st* in *Poetry* [Chicago, Ill.] 147.3 (Dec. 1985): 129.

18	they're / how they're *1st*

153 UNION STREET: SAN FRANCISCO, SUMMER 1975: *1st* in *Ploughshares* [Emerson College] 11.4 (1985): 82–3; in *IAML* 60–1.

5	off in / in *1st*
14	company / company, as usual *1st*
20	*you* / you *1st*
22	how / what *1st*
29	little / little, *1st*
29–30	[no stanza break in *1st*]
33	you son / son *1st*
38	out from / from *1st*
42	afternoon / afternoon, *1st*

155 BONNARD'S NUDES: *1st* in *Crazyhorse* [Univ. of Arkansas, Little Rock] 27 (Fall 1984): 9; in *IAML* 126.

155   JEAN'S TV: in *IAML* 70–1.

"Margo": A version of this poem is printed between "Jean's TV" and "Mesopotamia" in AUP but does not appear in the finished book. See p. 274 and note.

157   MESOPOTAMIA: *1st* in *Poetry* [Chicago, Ill.] 147.3 (Dec. 1985): 128; in *IAML* 181–2.
    21   can see / know *1st*
    25–8   they're going better than ever because they're up
              early and talking about things of consequence
              such as death, and Mesopotamia. In any case, *1st*

159   HOPE: *1st* in *Paris Review* [Flushing, NY] 28.100 (Summer–Fall 1986): 58–9; in *IAML* 67–8.
    17–18   [no stanza break in *1st*]
    30   blasted / was blasted *1st*

160   THE HOUSE BEHIND THIS ONE: in *IAML* 137.

161   LIMITS: *1st* in *Northwest Review* [Univ. of Oregon, Eugene] 24.1 (1986): 59–60; in *EFTD* 7–8, *IAML* 91–2.
    24–5   with screen wire, rigged
              like a little cell inside. He'd broken *1st*, *EFTD*
    28   the barrel. / a barrel *1st*
                    the barrel *EFTD*
    29   because he'd had a brainstorm: *1st*, *EFTD*
    30   He'd / he'd *1st*, *EFTD*
    32   damnedest / damndest *1st*, *EFTD*

163   THE SENSITIVE GIRL: *1st* in *Poetry* [Chicago, Ill.] 146.6 (Sept. 1985): 344–7.
    3–4   on this pane of glass that's
              been around even longer. It doesn't *1st*
    13   alders / sorrels *1st*
    17   would've / would have *1st*
    26   to / who would *1st*
    28   fastened / broken *1st*
    44   Then closes the gate, and fastens it. *1st*
    46   that / there *1st*

165   EGRESS: *1st* in *Northwest Review* [Univ. of Oregon, Eugene] 24.1 (1986): 57–8; in *EFTD* 15–16, *IAML* 158–9.
    3   but / that *1st*, *EFTD*
    10   brother / brother, *1st*
    11   to me – the ear, nose, and throat man, fell dead *1st*
              to me – the ear-nose-and-throat man, fell dead *EFTD*
    14   his body / body *1st*, *EFTD*
    22   Dead / Was dead *1st*
    31   bracket / bracket than us *1st*, *EFTD*
    33   in / then in *1st*, *EFTD*
                    at the time in AUP
    39   brother / brother, *1st*, *EFTD*
    40   for the sake of / to allow egress to *1st*, *EFTD*
    41   hell! / hell? *1st*, *EFTD*

167   SPELL: in *IAML* 141–2.

168   FROM THE EAST, LIGHT: *1st* in *Northwest Review* [Univ. of Oregon,
Eugene] 24.1 (1986): 56; in *IAML* 58.
    16   litter / cover *1st*

169   A TALL ORDER: *1st* in *Poetry* [Chicago, Ill.] 148.3 (June 1986): 128.
    1–2   The old woman who kept house for them.
            She'd seen and heard the most amazing things. *1st*
    22   the rusty swing set and Jungle-Gym bars. *1st*

170   THE AUTHOR OF HER MISFORTUNE: in *IAML* 51.

171   POWDER-MONKEY: *1st* in *Northwest Review* [Univ. of Oregon, Eugene]
24.1 (1986): 55; in *EFTD* 14, *IAML* 120–1.
    11   and was destroyed
            by a logging truck. *1st*
    14   from his eyes / away *1st, EFTD*
    25   toward / towards *IAML*

172   EARWIGS: in *IAML* 103–4.
    54   alone / almost alone AUP

173   NYQUIL: in *IAML* 46.

174   THE POSSIBLE: in *IAML* 183–4.

175   SHIFTLESS: *1st* in *Poetry* [Chicago, Ill.] 146.6 (Sept. 1985): 344; in
IAML 22.

176   THE YOUNG FIRE EATERS OF MEXICO CITY: *1st* in *Crazyhorse*
[Univ. of Arkansas, Little Rock] 27 (Fall 1984): 11; in *Tendril* [Green Harbor, Mass.]
19–20 (1985): 404, *IAML* 119.
    2   and blow it out over a lit candle *1st, Tendril*
    9   in / within *1st, Tendril*
    10   scorched / parched *1st, Tendril*
    13   silent / poor *1st, Tendril*
    14–15   through the streets, silently,
            with a candle and a beercan filled with alcohol. *1st, Tendril*

176   WHERE THE GROCERIES WENT: *1st* in *Seneca Review* [Hobart and
William Smith Colleges] 15.2 (1986): 46–7.
    13   cupboards and / cupboards, and in *1st*
    24   jumped / may have jumped *1st*
    26   I wanted to tell you that machine is making *1st*
    32   doing / doing before I called *1st*

177   WHAT I CAN DO: *1st* in *Northwest Review* [Univ. of Oregon, Eugene]
24.1 (1986): 54; in *IAML* 49.
    3   so that my loved ones can't reach me to put the arm *1st*
    16   for the / the *1st*
    21   sunny / continued sunny *1st*

178   THE LITTLE ROOM: in *IAML* 53.

179   SWEET LIGHT: *1st* in *TriQuarterly* [Northwestern Univ.] 66 (Spring–Summer 1986): 144; in *IAML* 167; separately published as a broadside (Fairfax, Calif.: Jungle Garden Press, 1990).

180   THE GARDEN: *1st* in *Tendril* 19–20 (1985): 410–11; in *IAML* 131–2. All lines begin with capital letters in *1st*.
    4   that / *that 1st*
    11–15   Lines 13–15 immediately precede lines 11–12 in *1st*.
    21–30   Stanza six immediately precedes stanza five in *1st*.
    40–1   There is an additional stanza between these lines in *1st*. See note on "The Fishing Pole of the Drowned Man", (p.88).

181   SON: in *IAML* 23.

182   KAFKA'S WATCH: *1st* in *New Yorker* [New York, NY] 61.35 (21 Oct. 1985): 117; in *IAML* 128.
         Epigraph: [omitted in *1st*]
    6   Mohammedan / Muhammadan *1st*

183   THE LIGHTNING SPEED OF THE PAST: in *IAML* 87.

183   VIGIL: *1st* in *Ploughshares* [Emerson College] 11.4 (1985): 84.

184   IN THE LOBBY OF THE HOTEL DEL MAYO: *1st* in *Tendril* [Green Harbor, Mass.] 19–20 (1985): 420.
    10   looks / looks too *1st*
    19   Waving / Someone waving *1st*
    23   recall / be able to recall *1st*
    24   for the / the *1st*

185   BAHIA, BRAZIL: in *IAML* 135–6.

186   THE PHENOMENON: *1st* in *Scripsi* [Melbourne, Australia] 4.2 (Nov. 1986): 193; in *IAML* 154.
    1   wiped / whipped *1st*

188   MIGRATION: *1st* in *Ontario Review* [Princeton, NJ] 24 (Spring–Summer 1986): 48–9; in *EFTD* 9–10, *IAML* 161–2.
    5   You / Have you *1st*
    13   down / down, *1st, EFTD*
    16   might / might set me at ease and *1st, EFTD*
    29   My friend stood up, as I recall it, the whole time. *1st, EFTD*
    31   stay still, was / sit was *1st*
                        stay still was *EFTD*
    41–2   He kept moving
             until we reached the front door and stopped. *1st, EFTD*
    46   from / off *1st*
    51   He'll / He'd *1st*
    53   of him. Until he reached a place only he knew about. *1st*
    54   Arctic / arctic *1st*
    56   down, / down *1st*

357

190   SLEEPING: *1st* in *Paris Review* [Flushing, NY] 28.100 (Summer–Fall 1986): 60; in *IAML* 163.

> 14–15   In jail.
> Behind the wheel.
> On boats. *1st*
> 16   He slept in line shacks, and in a castle, once. *1st*
> 18–19   In blistering sun.
> On horseback he slept. *1st*

190   THE RIVER: *1st* in *Poetry* [Chicago, Ill.] 148.3 (June 1986): 127; separately published as a broadside (Concord, NH: William B. Ewert, 1986); in *IAML* 160.

> 5   grilse / grisle *1st, Ewert,* AUP
> 20   that other shore hung with heavy branches *1st, Ewert*
> 21   the dark mountain range behind *1st*
> dark lip of the mountain range behind *Ewert*

191   THE BEST TIME OF THE DAY: separately published as a broadside to honor RC upon his receiving an honorary Doctor of Letters degree from the Univ. of Hartford on 15 May 1988 (Lewisburg, Pa.: privately printed, 1988).

192   SCALE: *1st* in *Caliban* [Ann Arbor, Mich.] 1 (1986): 99–100, *Scripsi* [Melbourne, Australia] 4.2 (Nov. 1986): 190–1; in *IAML* 201–2.

> Dedication: [omitted in *Scripsi*]
> 5   rising / is rising *Caliban*
> 13   finishes / finished AUP
> 25   thirty / 30 *Caliban, Scripsi*
> 34   much / much, much *Caliban, Scripsi*
> 44   human / whole human *Caliban, Scripsi*

195   THE SCHOOLDESK: *1st* in *Scripsi* [Melbourne, Australia] 4.2 (Nov. 1986): 188–9; in *IAML* 143–5.

> 64   of / in *1st*

197   CUTLERY: *1st* in *New Yorker* [New York, NY] 62.5 (24 Mar. 1986): 38; in *IAML* 109–10.

> 1   twenty / 20 *1st*
> 16   inside; / inside, *1st*

198   THE PEN: *1st* in *Zyzzyva* [San Francisco, Calif.] 1.3 (Fall 1985): 121–2; in *IAML* 122–3.

199   THE PRIZE: *1st* in *Quarry West* [Univ. of California, Santa Cruz] 20 (1984): 50; in *Northwest Review* [Univ. of Oregon, Eugene] 23.1 (1985): 44.

> 7   What / But what *1st, Northwest Review*
> 10   As / Just as *1st, Northwest Review*
> 22   As / It was as *1st, Northwest Review*

200   AN ACCOUNT: in *IAML* 164–5.

202   THE MEADOW: *1st* in *Scripsi* [Melbourne, Australia] 4.2 (Nov. 1986): 194; in *EFTD* 21, *IAML* 26–7.

> 12   where he lived / he lived in, *1st, EFTD*

24   her / its *1st*
25   I will / I'll *1st, EFTD*

203   SINEW: *1st* in *Atlantic* [Boston, Mass.] 258.5 (Nov. 1986): 112; in *IAML* 98–9.
7   on / in *1st*
11   still and warm / still warm *1st*
12   cuckoo / cuckoo bird *1st*, AUP
23   all / is all *1st*
29   near. / near, *1st*
30   Holds / holds *1st*
31   smiles / smiles, *1st*

205   WAITING: in *IAML* 185.

206   ITS COURSE: *1st* in *Ontario Review* [Princeton, NJ] 24 (Spring–Summer 1986):
46–7; in *EFTD* 12–13, *IAML* 96–7.
9   *yonder*, where those houses are. *1st, EFTD*
       "*yonder*, where those houses are." AUP
14   It could wake you up from a deep sleep, he said. *1st, EFTD*
23   county / country *1st*
35   after / angling for *1st, EFTD*
37   after all. I remembered what he'd said *1st, EFTD*
       after all. I remembered what he's said AUP
38–9   about the young men who used to run
       at this hill with their motorcycles. *1st, EFTD*
41   else / else younger. *1st, EFTD*
42   my / My *1st, EFTD*

209   THE WHITE FIELD: *1st* in *Seneca Review* [Hobart and William Smith Colleges]
15.2 (1986): 48–9; in *IAML* 93–4.
6   him / that *1st*
42   back / went back *1st*

210   SHOOTING: *1st* in *Caliban* [Ann Arbor, Mich.] 1 (1986): 101; in *IAML* 108.
1   belly, / belly. *1st*
2   cradling / Cradling *1st*

211   THE WINDOW: *1st* as a holiday greeting card (Concord, NH: William B. Ewert,
1985); in *Scripsi* [Melbourne, Australia] 4.2 (Nov. 1986): 187, *IAML* 95.

211   HEELS: *1st* in *Scripsi* [Melbourne, Australia] 4.2 (Nov. 1986): 192–3.
7   dust / dust critters *1st*
21–2   that could stamp on things. Spiders,
       maybe, or garter snakes. Anything. *1st*
30   fumble / fumble and fumble *1st*

213   THE PHONE BOOTH: *1st* in *Northwest Review* [Univ. of Oregon, Eugene] 24.1
(1986): 52–3.
29   that close in there. The phone
       still warm to the touch *1st*
30   a / that *1st*
35   in coins / coins in *1st*

214 CADILLACS AND POETRY: *1st* in *Ploughshares* [Emerson College] 11.4 (1985): 80; in *IAML* 114–15.

    19   a / was a *1st*

    27   car / car again *1st*

215 SIMPLE: *1st* in *Ohio Review* [Ohio Univ.] 37 (1986): 59; in *IAML* 166.

216 MOTHER: *1st* in *Poetry* [Chicago, Ill.] 147.3 (Dec. 1985): 127; in *EFTD* 11, *IAML* 59.

    14   *goddamn / goddam 1st, EFTD*

218 THE FIELDS: in *IAML* 196–7.

    3   that'd / that's AUP

220 EVENING: *1st* in *Scripsi* [Melbourne, Australia] 4.2 (Nov. 1986): 187; in *IAML* 140.

    2   as darkness / into evening as it *1st*

220 THE REST: *1st* in *Poetry* [Chicago, Ill.] 146.6 (Sept. 1985): 347; in *IAML* 174.

    1–3   Clouds hang loosely over this mountain
              range behind my house. In a while
              the light will go and the wind come up *1st*

    18   high blue / dying *1st*

221 SLIPPERS: *1st* in *Raccoon* [Memphis, Tenn.] 24–5 (May 1987): 176; in *IAML* 198.

    6   told of / told *1st*

    21   Then called / Then AUP

    24–5   it has moment. Those lost slippers. And the discovery
              that brought a cry of delight. *1st*

222 ASIA: *1st* in *Ploughshares* [Emerson College] 11.4 (1985): 78–9; in *Northwest Review* [Univ. of Oregon, Eugene] 24.1 (1986): 61, *IAML* 203–4.

    27–8   [no stanza break in *1st*]

    30   rail, / rail *IAML*

    36   mind / minds *IAML*

    37–8   of the horses
              where it is always Asia. *1st, Northwest Review*

223 THE GIFT: *1st* in *Seneca Review* [Hobart and William Smith Colleges] 15.2 (1986): 50–1; in *IAML* 205–6.

    8   the airport / Galitea Airport *1st*

    9   left / left there *1st*

    15   even a / even *1st*

    21   onto the / onto *1st*

    27–8   sat in the bathroom close to the sink. If I shaved,
              as I did one morning, the pan of water bubbled *1st*

    30–1   I sat on the bed, dressed, clean-shaven, drinking
              coffee, putting off what I'd decided to do. Finally, *1st*

    36–8   this month. He didn't have it. "It's okay," I said.
              "I understand." And I did. We talked
              a little more, then hung up. He didn't have it. *1st*

    52   moves / moves me, *1st*

A New Path to the Waterfall

First edition: New York, NY: Atlantic Monthly Press, 1989. Introduction by Tess Gallagher. Publication date: 15 June 1989.

First signed, limited edition: "Of the first edition of *A New Path to the Waterfall* two hundred copies have been specially printed and bound. These books are signed by Tess Gallagher and numbered 1 to 200" (limitation leaf).

First paperback edition: New York, NY: Atlantic Monthly Press, 1989. Publication date: May 1990.

First English edition: London: Collins Harvill, 1989. Publication date: 21 Sept. 1989.

Dedication: *Tess. Tess. Tess. Tess*

Epigraph: "Gift" by Czeslaw Milosz, *The Collected Poems 1931–1987* (New York, NY: Ecco Press, 1988) 251.

Copy-text: First edition, first printing, collated and corrected against later editions and printings.

Small-press sources and separate publications: *NK, WI, ANTSM, F, TD, His Bathrobe Pockets Stuffed with Notes* (Raven, 1988), *Looking for Work/Downstream* (n.p., 1988), *The Painter and the Fish* (Ewert, 1988), *The Toes* (Ewert, 1988).

229   WET PICTURE (JAROSLAV SEIFERT): *The Selected Poetry of Jaroslav Seifert* (New York, NY: Macmillan, 1986) 37.

230   TWO WORLDS: *1st* in *Midwest Quarterly* [Pittsburg (Kans.) State Univ.] 14.1 (Oct. 1972): 63; in *TD* 15.

231   SMOKE AND DECEPTION (CHEKHOV): from "The Privy Councillor", *The Wife and Other Stories*, vol. 5 of *The Tales of Chekhov*, trans. Constance Garnett (1918; New York, NY: Ecco Press, 1985) 237.

231   IN A GREEK ORTHODOX CHURCH NEAR DAPHNE: *1st* in *South Dakota Review* [Univ. of South Dakota] 10.4 (Winter 1972–3): 88; in *TD* 16. All lines begin with capital letters in *1st* and *TD*.
       7–8   Ruined walls.
               Wind rises to meet the evening. *1st, TD*

233   TRANSFORMATION: in *WI* 38–9.
       Title: "The Transformation" *WI*
       19–23   Later we play the entire film
               again and again.
               I see the woman keep
               falling and getting up, falling
               and getting up, Arabs
               evil-eyeing the camera.
               I see myself striking *WI*
       27   Holy Land / Holyland *WI*
       32   with / like *WI*
       37–8   My grin turns to salt. *WI*

234　THREAT: in *WI* 33. All lines begin with capital letters in *WI*.
　2　　　　it / it, *WI*

234　CONSPIRATORS: in *WI* 11. All lines begin with capital letters in *WI*.
　2　　　　woods, / woods *WI*
　8　　　　three / 3 *WI*

235　THIS WORD LOVE: *1st* in *Poet and Critic* [Iowa State Univ.] 7.1 (1972): 2; in
ANTSM 44. In *1st* RC's assigned critics are Simon Perchik and Christine
Zawadiwsky.
　　　　　Title: "This Word *Love*" *1st, ANTSM*
　2　　　　*I love you* / I love you *1st, ANTSM*
　10　　　　my arm throws no shadow even, *1st, ANTSM*
　11　　　　it too is consumed
　　　　　　with light *1st*
　14　　　　heavy and shakes itself, *1st*
　　　　　　heavy and shakes itself *ANTSM*
　15–16　　and begins to eat
　　　　　　through this paper.
　　　　　　Listen. *1st, ANTSM*
　17–21　　[omitted in *1st, ANTSM*]

235　DON'T RUN (CHEKHOV): from "A Visit to Friends", *The Unknown Chekhov*,
vol. 14 of *The Tales of Chekhov*, trans. Avrahm Yarmolinsky (1954; New York, NY:
Ecco Press, 1987) 223.

236　WOMAN BATHING: *1st* in *West Coast Review* [Simon Fraser Univ.] 2.1 (Spring
1967): 9; in *NK* [19]. All lines begin with capital letters in *1st* and *NK*. In *1st* and *NK*
there is an additional line after line 7:

　　　　　A few minutes only?

In *1st* and *NK* a stanza break follows this line. The two resulting eight-line stanzas are
printed side by side.
　10　　　　*Time is a mountain lion.* *1st, NK*

237　THE NAME (TOMAS TRANSTRÖMER): *Selected Poems 1954–1986* (New York,
NY: Ecco Press, 1987) 93.

237　LOOKING FOR WORK [2]: in *WI* 16; see "Looking for Work" [1] in *F*, p. 13;
separately published with "Downstream" (p. 279) as a broadside (n.p.: 1988). The *ANP*
version is identical with that in *WI*. The broadside, which otherwise agrees with *WI*
and *ANP*, lacks the comma ending line 6 (likely a typographical error).
　1　　　　I have / I've *F*
　13　　　　door, / door. *F*
　14　　　　gleaming. / They are gleaming. *F*

238　THE WORLD BOOK SALESMAN: *1st* in *Levee* [Sacramento State Univ.] 2.2
(Jan. 1967): 5; in *Prairie Schooner* [Univ. of Nebraska] 17.2 (Summer 1968): 122–3, *NK*
[28], *WI* 42. Lexically, all four versions agree. Punctuation and spelling differ slightly in
each text, as does lineation in *1st*. Illustrations:
　3　　　　turns he / turns, he *1st, Prairie Schooner, NK, WI*

12	itself / himself *1st*
13	to large, freshwater rivers, *1st, TD*
14	100 / a 100 AUP
	and takes a 100 years getting around
	to its first mating. *1st, TD*
14–15	[no stanza break in *1st, TD*]
17	that weighed / weighed *1st, TD*
34	of the Yukon River
	in Alaska *1st, TD*
39	that went / went *1st, TD*
40	at Celilo Falls
	on the Columbia River. *1st, TD*
42	a story then
	about 3 men he knew long ago in Oregon *1st, TD*
52–5	even then –
	just my father there beside me
	leaning on his arms over the railing,
	staring,
	the two of us staring up
	at that great dead fish,
	and that marvelous story of his, *1st, TD*
56	surfacing, / all surfacing *1st, TD*
	surfacing AUP

254   NIGHT DAMPNESS (CHEKHOV): from "Across Siberia", *The Unknown Chekhov*, vol. 14 of *The Tales of Chekhov*, trans. Avrahm Yarmolinsky (1954; New York, NY: Ecco Press, 1987) 270.

255   ANOTHER MYSTERY: *1st* in *Poetry* [Chicago, Ill.] 154.1 (Apr. 1989): 3. Lineation varies considerably in *1st*:

2–6	What'd I know then about Death? Dad comes out carrying a black suit in a plastic bag. Hangs it up behind the back seat of the old coupe and says, "This is the suit your grandpa is going to leave the world in." What on earth could he be talking about? I wondered.
8–9	that was going away, along with my grandpa. Those days it was just another mystery.
10–13	Then there was a long interval, a time in which relatives departed this way and that, left and right. Then it was my dad's turn. I sat and watched him rise up in his own smoke. He didn't own a suit. So they dressed him gruesomely
25–7	from the dry cleaners and hung it carefully behind the back seat. I drove it home, opened the car door and lifted it out into the sunlight. I stood there a minute

256   RETURN TO KRAKÓW IN 1880 (CZESLAW MILOSZ): *The Collected Poems 1931–1987* (New York, NY: Ecco Press, 1988) 416.

257   SUNDAY NIGHT: *1st* in *December* [Highland Park, Ill.] 9.2–3 (1967): 64; in *TD* 13.

257   THE PAINTER & THE FISH: separately published in a limited edition (Concord, NH: William B. Ewert, 1988).

259   AT NOON (CHEKHOV): from "Across Siberia", *The Unknown Chekhov*, vol. 14 of *The Tales of Chekhov*, trans. Avrahm Yarmolinsky (1954; New York, NY: Ecco Press, 1987) 281.

259   ARTAUD: *1st* in *Discourse* [Concordia College (Moorhead, Minn.)] 9.2 (Spring 1966): 183; in *NK* [25]. All lines begin with capital letters in *1st* and *NK*. In AUP the sequence of this poem and the following one is reversed.

      Title: "Antonin Artaud: From a Photograph" *1st*

                "Antonin Artaud" *NK*

      5–7   One at the desk, the one with the cigarette and no teeth

                To speak of, is prone to boldness, to a certain excess *1st, NK*

      8   in speech, in gesture / In his speech, his gesture *1st, NK*

      9   even. But / even, but *1st, NK*

      10–11 At certain moments, hints broadly of his existence. *1st, NK*

      12   masterpieces. / masterpieces, *1st, NK*

      13   hands / hand *1st*

      14–15 And behind every arras there was a rustling. *1st, NK*

260   CAUTION: In AUP the sequence of this poem and the preceding one is reversed.

260   ONE MORE: *1st* in *Hayden's Ferry Review* [Arizona State Univ.] 4 (Spring 1989): 135–7.

      36–7   it occurred to him, he was sick of all business, but he went on in this fashion, finishing one last letter that should have been *1st*, AUP

262   AT THE BIRD MARKET (CHEKHOV): from "The Bird Market", *The Cook's Wedding and Other Stories*, vol. 12 of *The Tales of Chekhov*, trans. Constance Garnett (1920; New York, NY: Ecco Press, 1986) 236.

262   HIS BATHROBE POCKETS STUFFED WITH NOTES: *1st* in *Caliban* [Ann Arbor, Mich.] 1 (1986): 96–8; separately published in a limited edition "on the occasion of RC's receiving an honorary Doctor of Humane Letters degree from the Univ. of Hartford" on 15 May 1988 (Elmwood, Conn.: Raven Editions, 1988).

      6   sixteenth-century / 16th century *1st, Raven*

      29   in – / in, *1st, Raven*

      30   words – / words, *1st, Raven*

      31   Three / 3 *1st, Raven*

      37   hook / receiver *1st, Raven*, AUP

265   SOME PROSE ON *POETRY*: *1st* in *Poetry* [Chicago, Ill.] 151.1–2 (Oct.–Nov. 1987): 204–7. Seventy-fifth anniversary issue of *Poetry*. Untitled in *1st*.

269   LETTER: *1st* in *Michigan Quarterly Review* [Univ. of Michigan] 28.1 (Winter 1988): 73–4.

      7   our doctor friend, Ruth, / our friend, Dr R.– *1st*

      9   the doctor's / Dr R.'s *1st*

      10   that her / her *1st*

      45–6   stays longest – the hands." And the woman's hands. I made a note at the time, as if I could see them anchored on her *1st*

270   THE YOUNG GIRLS: *1st* in *Tendril* [Green Harbor, Mass.] 19–20 (1985): 409.

271   from EPILOGUE (ROBERT LOWELL): *Day by Day* (New York, NY: Farrar
Straus Giroux, 1977) 127.

274   SORREL (CHEKHOV): from "An Unpleasantness", *The Unknown Chekhov*,
vol. 14 of *The Tales of Chekhov*, trans. Avrahm Yarmolinsky (1954; New York, NY: Ecco
Press, 1987) 142–3.

274   MARGO: *1st* in *Poetry* [Chicago, Ill.] 151.5 (Feb. 1988): 416. A version of "Margo"
appears in the AUP of *U* but does not appear in the finished book. See note p. 355.
    6   Commanding / A commanding *U*, AUP
    10   places / those places *U*, AUP

277   FIVE O'CLOCK IN THE MORNING (CHEKHOV): from "Difficult People",
The Wife and Other Stories, vol. 5 of *The Tales of Chekhov*, trans. Constance Garnett (1918;
New York, NY: Ecco Press, 1985) 84–5.

278   HUMMINGBIRD: *1st* in *Poetry* [Chicago, Ill.] 154.1 (Apr. 1989): 4.

278   OUT: Lineation differs in AUP.
    19–20   about logging for Mormons on Prince of Wales Island (no booze, no
             swearing, no women. Just *no*, except for work
    23–5   All morning you'd wanted to tell me something and now you began
             to tell me; how your wife wants you out of her life, wants

279   DOWNSTREAM (CHEKHOV): from "Across Siberia", *The Unknown Chekhov*,
vol. 14 of *The Tales of Chekhov*, trans. Avrahm Yarmolinsky (1954; New York, NY: Ecco
Press, 1987) 289–90; separately published with "Looking for Work" [2] (p. 237) as a
broadside (n.p.: 1988).

280   THE NET: *1st* in *Quarry West* [Univ. of California, Santa Cruz] 20 (1984): 49;
in *Poetry* [Chicago, Ill.] 151.1–2 (Oct.–Nov. 1987): 28.
    The texts in *Poetry* and *ANP* agree. The following is the *Quarry West* version in full:

> Toward evening, the wind changes. What boats
> are left on the bay
> head for shore. A man with one arm
> sits on the keel of a rotting-away boat,
> working on a glimmering net.
>
> He raises his eyes. Pulls something to
> with his teeth, and bites hard.
> I go past without a word.
>
> Reduced to confusion
> by the variableness of this weather,
> the importunities of my heart.
>
> Then turn back to look.

283   FOREBODING (CHEKHOV): from "Perpetuum Mobile", *The Unknown Chekhov*,
vol. 14 of *The Tales of Chekhov*, trans. Avrahm Yarmolinsky (1954; New York, NY: Ecco
Press, 1987) 40. Title omitted in AUP.

283   SPARROW NIGHTS (CHEKHOV): from "A Dreary Story", *The Wife and Other Stories*, vol. 5 of *The Tales of Chekhov*, trans. Constance Garnett (1918; New York, NY: Ecco Press, 1985) 203–4, 205.

284   LEMONADE: *1st* in *Esquire* [New York, NY] 112.1 (July 1989): 78–9. A comment by Tess Gallagher accompanies the poem in *Esquire*: "This is a fictionalized account based on the death of a workman's child who fell into a river and drowned. It was written in the last months of Ray's life and is, in that proximity, elegiac of the life he knew he was losing. Read this poem aloud and something else takes hold – Ray's genius for transmitting subtle inflections of emotion, including humor at the saddest moments. For when a sorrow is too relentlessly pursued, we can't help ourselves – we laugh, refreshing ourselves for the hardest truths. The poem's meditation forces reason as far as it will go until it erodes into unreason, and we're thrown back upon the human voice, calming its pain. Story and prose elements are so strong that the boundary between fiction and poetry gives way. Poetry? Fiction? Who cares. It's the haunting that matters" (78).

287   SUCH DIAMONDS (CHEKHOV): from "A Nightmare", *The Bishop and Other Stories*, vol. 7 of *The Tales of Chekhov*, trans. Constance Garnett (1919; New York, NY: Ecco Press, 1985) 72.

287   WAKE UP: *1st* in *Michigan Quarterly Review* [Univ. of Michigan] 28.1 (Winter 1988): 71–2; in *Poetry* [Chicago, Ill.] 154.1 (Apr. 1989): 1–2.

1	Kyborg / Kyburg *Poetry*
22	And / and, *1st*
23	knows – / knows? *1st*
26	*Jesu Christo* / *Jesu Christe Poetry*
	Jesus Christo AUP

289   WHAT THE DOCTOR SAID: *1st* in *Granta* [London] 25 (Autumn 1988): 162.

290   LET'S ROAR, YOUR HONOR (CHEKHOV): from "Across Siberia", *The Unknown Chekhov*, vol. 14 of *The Tales of Chekhov*, trans. Avrahm Yarmolinsky (1954; New York, NY: Ecco Press, 1987) 270.

290   PROPOSAL: *1st* in *Harper's* [New York, NY] 278.1666 (Mar. 1989): 32.

13	oh lethal / Oh lethal *1st*
39–40	In Reno, I told her, it's
	marriages and remarriages twenty-four hours a day seven days a week. No *1st*

292   CHERISH: *1st* in *Hayden's Ferry Review* [Arizona State Univ.] 4 (Spring 1989): 134.

13–14	of promise, of treasure. My hand on her wrist to bring her close, her
	eyes green as river-moss. Saying it then, against *1st*

292   GRAVY: *1st* in *New Yorker* [New York, NY] 64.28 (29 Aug. 1988): 28.

293   NO NEED: *1st* in *Poetry* [Chicago, Ill.] 154.1 (Apr. 1989): 4.

293   AFTERGLOW: *1st* in *New Yorker* [New York, NY] 65.10 (24 Apr. 1989): 36; in the *Sunday Times* [London] 27 Aug. 1989: G4. Title spelled "After-glow" in copy-text.

294   LATE FRAGMENT: *1st* in *Granta* [London] 25 (Autumn 1988): 167. Accompanied by Tess Gallagher's essay "Raymond Carver 1938 to 1988".

Uncollected Poems: *No Heroics, Please*

First edition: London: Harvill, 1991. Foreword by Tess Gallagher.
Publication date: Nov. 1991.

First American edition: New York, NY: Vintage
Contemporaries, 1992. Publication date: 24 June 1992.

Dedication: *For Georgia Morris Bond*. Georgia Morris Bond is Tess
Gallagher's mother, a longtime resident of Port Angeles, Washington.

Epigraph: From an interview with Raymond Carver, "The Art of Fiction
LXXVI", by Mona Simpson, *Paris Review* [Flushing, NY] 25.88 (Summer
1983): 214.

Copy-text: First edition, first printing, collated and corrected against later
editions and printings.

Sequence: Chronological order by first publication.

Small-press sources and separate publications: *NK, WI, ANTSM, TD, Two
Poems* (Ewert, 1986).

297   THE BRASS RING: in *Targets* [Sandia Park, N.Mex.] 11 (Sept. 1962): 35, *NK*
[33], *NHP* 75. "The Brass Ring" is RC's first published poem.

297   BEGINNINGS: *1st* in *Grande Ronde Review* [Folsom, Calif.] 1.4–5 (n.d.
[1965–6]): n. pag. [18]; in *NK* [12], *ANTSM* 17, *NHP* 76.
       8   Rainier / Ranier *NK*

298   ON THE PAMPAS TONIGHT: *1st* in *Levee* [Sacramento State Univ.] 2.2
(Jan. 1967): n. pag. [8]; in *TD* 4, *NHP* 94.

298   THOSE DAYS: *1st* in *Poet and Critic* [Iowa State Univ.] 2.3 (Spring 1966): 6; in
TD 3, *NHP* 93. The dedicatee ("C.M.") has not been identified. In *1st* RC's assigned
critics are Paul Baker Newman and S. L. Friedman.

299   THE SUNBATHER, TO HERSELF: *1st* in *West Coast Review* [Simon Fraser Univ.]
2.1 (Spring 1967): 23; in *TD* 8, *NHP* 98.

300   NO HEROICS, PLEASE: *1st* in *December* [Highland Park, Ill.] 9.2–3 (1967):
64; in *TD* 12, *NHP* 99.

300   ADULTERY: *1st* in *December* [Highland Park, Ill.] 9.2–3 (1967): 65; *WI* 52–3,
NHP 80–1.

302   POEM ON MY BIRTHDAY, JULY 2: *1st* in *Grande Ronde Review* [Folsom,
Calif.] 7 [2.1] (n.d. [1967]): 7–8; in *TD* 5–6, *NHP* 95–6.

303   RETURN: *1st* in *Grande Ronde Review* [Folsom, Calif.] 7 [2.1] (n.d. [1967]): 9; in
TD 7, *NHP* 97.

303   FOR THE EGYPTIAN COIN TODAY, ARDEN, THANK YOU: *1st* in *Kayak*
[Santa Cruz, Calif.] 16 (1968): 51; in *WI* 37, *NHP* 82.

303   IN THE TRENCHES WITH ROBERT GRAVES: in *NK* [30], *ANTSM* 26, *NHP* 77.

Subtitle: "[After reading *Goodbye to All That*]" *ANTSM*

304   THE MAN OUTSIDE: in *NK* [31–2], *NHP* 78–9.

305   SEEDS: *1st* in *University of Portland Review* [Portland, Oreg.] 22.1 (Spring 1970): 38; in *WI* 47, *NHP* 83. The dedicatee is RC's daughter, Christine LaRae Carver.

305   BETRAYAL: in *WI* 12, *NHP* 84.

306   THE CONTACT: in *WI* 22, *NHP* 85.

306   SOMETHING IS HAPPENING: in *WI* 48, *NHP* 86–7.

307   A SUMMER IN SACRAMENTO: in *ANTSM* 42–3, *NHP* 88–90.

309   REACHING: separately published with "Soda Crackers" (below) as *Two Poems*, a holiday greeting card (Concord, NH: William B. Ewert, 1986); in *NHP* 91.

310   SODA CRACKERS: separately published with "Reaching" (above) as *Two Poems*, a holiday greeting card (Concord, NH: William B. Ewert, 1986); in *NHP* 92.

Appendix 6

Chronology

1938   Raymond Clevie Carver, Jr., born in Clatskanie, Oregon, on 25 May, first child of Clevie Raymond ("C.R.") Carver (b. 17 September 1913 in Leola, Arkansas) and Ella Beatrice Casey (b. 11 July 1913 in Malvern, Arkansas).

1941   The Carvers move to Yakima, Washington. C.R. works for the Boise Cascade Lumber Company.

1943   RC's only sibling, James Carver, born in Yakima on 5 August.

1956   RC graduates from Yakima High School in June. He and his mother then follow C.R. to Chester, California, where RC and his father both work in a sawmill. In November, RC returns alone to Yakima.

1957   In February, C.R. suffers a mental and physical breakdown that keeps him unemployed until 1964. On 7 June RC marries sixteen-year-old Maryann Burk in Yakima, where he works as a pharmacy deliveryman. Their daughter Christine LaRae born on 2 December. RC takes classes at Yakima Community College during 1957–8 academic year.

1958   In August, RC moves his wife, daughter, and in-laws to Paradise, California, where he enters nearby Chico State College as a part-time student. His son, Vance Lindsay, born on 19 October.

1959   In June, the Carvers move to Chico, California. In the fall, RC takes Creative Writing 101, taught by John Gardner.

1960   During the spring semester, RC founds and edits the first issue of the Chico State literary magazine, *Selection*. In June, the Carvers move to Eureka, California, where RC works in the Georgia-Pacific sawmill. In the fall, he transfers to Humboldt State College in nearby Arcata and begins taking classes taught by Richard Cortez Day.

1961   RC's first published story, "The Furious Seasons", appears in *Selection* 2 (Winter 1960–1). A second story, "The Father", appears in the spring issue of the Humboldt State literary magazine, *Toyon*. In June, the Carvers move to Arcata, California.

1962   RC's first play, *Carnations*, is performed at Humboldt State College on 11 May. His first published poem, "The Brass Ring", appears in the September issue of *Targets*.

1963   In February, RC receives his A.B. degree from Humboldt State. During the spring, he edits *Toyon*. RC receives a $500 fellowship for a year's graduate study at the Iowa Writers' Workshop. After spending the summer in Berkeley, where RC works in the University of California library, the Carvers move to Iowa City, Iowa.

1964–6 In June 1964, the Carvers return to California and settle in Sacramento, where RC is hired as a day custodian at Mercy Hospital. After one year, he transfers to the night shift. In the fall of 1966, RC joins a poetry workshop led by Dennis Schmitz at Sacramento State College.

1967   The Carvers file for bankruptcy in the spring. Clevie Raymond Carver dies on 17 June. On 31 July RC is hired as a textbook editor at Science Research Associates (SRA). In August, the Carvers move to Palo Alto, California, where RC meets the editor and writer Gordon Lish. RC's story "Will You Please Be Quiet, Please?" is included in *The Best American Short Stories 1967*.

1968–9 In the spring of 1968, RC's first book, *Near Klamath* (poems), is published by the English Club of Sacramento State College. Maryann Carver receives a one-year scholarship to Tel-Aviv University, and RC takes a year's leave of absence from SRA. The Carvers move to Israel in June but return to California in October. From November 1968 until February 1969 they live with relatives in Hollywood, where RC sells movie theater programs. In February, he is rehired by SRA as "advertising director", and the Carvers move to San Jose, California. RC's period of increasingly heavy drinking begins.

1970   RC receives a National Endowment for the Arts Discovery Award for poetry. In June, the Carvers move to Sunnyvale, California. RC's story "Sixty Acres" is included in *The Best Little Magazine Fiction, 1970*, and his first regularly published book, *Winter Insomnia* (poems), is issued by Kayak Books. On 25 September, RC's job at SRA is terminated. Severance pay and unemployment benefits allow him to write full-time for nearly a year.

1971   Gordon Lish, now fiction editor of *Esquire*, publishes RC's story "Neighbors" in the magazine's June issue. RC is appointed visiting lecturer in creative writing at the University of California, Santa Cruz, for 1971–2, and in August the Carvers move to Ben Lomond, California. RC's story "Fat" appears in the September issue of *Harper's Bazaar*.

1972   RC receives a Wallace E. Stegner Fellowship at Stanford University for
        1972–3 and a concurrent appointment as visiting lecturer in fiction
        writing at UC Berkeley. In July, the Carvers buy a house in Cupertino,
        California.

1973   RC is appointed a visiting lecturer at the Iowa Writers' Workshop for
        1973–4. His story "What Is It?" is included in the O. Henry Awards
        annual, *Prize Stories 1973*, and five of his poems are reprinted in *New
        Voices in American Poetry*.

1974   RC is appointed visiting lecturer at UC Santa Barbara for 1974–5.
        Alcoholism and family problems force him to resign in December,
        and the Carvers subsequently file for their second bankruptcy.
        Unemployed, RC returns to Cupertino, California. He remains there
        with his family for the next two years, during which he does little writing.

1976   *At Night the Salmon Move*, RC's third book of poetry, is published by
        Capra Press in February. In March, his first major-press book, the short-
        story collection *Will You Please Be Quiet, Please?* is published by
        McGraw-Hill under its Gordon Lish imprint. Between October 1976
        and January 1977, RC undergoes four hospitalizations for acute
        alcoholism. The Carvers' house in Cupertino is sold in October, and
        RC and his wife live apart.

1977   *Will You Please Be Quiet, Please?* receives a National Book Award
        nomination. RC moves alone to McKinleyville, California, and on
        2 June he stops drinking. Reunited with his wife, he continues living
        in McKinleyville through the year. In November, *Furious Seasons
        and Other Stories* is published by Capra Press. That month, at a writers'
        conference in Dallas, Texas, RC meets the poet Tess Gallagher.

1978   RC receives a John Simon Guggenheim Fellowship, and from March
        through June, he and his wife live together on a trial basis in Iowa City.
        They separate in July, with RC leaving for the University of Texas, El
        Paso, where he has been appointed visiting distinguished writer in resi-
        dence for 1978–9. In August, he meets Tess Gallagher for the second
        time, and the two writers begin their close association. RC's book
        reviews begin appearing in the *Chicago Tribune*, *Texas Monthly*, and the
        San Francisco Review of Books.

1979   On 1 January, RC and Tess Gallagher begin living together in El Paso.
        They spend the summer in Chimacum, Washington, on the Olympic
        Peninsula, near Gallagher's home town of Port Angeles. In September,
        RC and Gallagher move to Tucson, where she teaches at the University
        of Arizona. RC is appointed Professor of English at Syracuse University
        in Syracuse, New York. He defers the appointment for one year in order
        to draw on his Guggenheim Fellowship and write.

1980   RC receives a National Endowment for the Arts Fellowship for fiction. Because of an unexpected retirement at Syracuse, he begins teaching in January, one semester earlier than planned. From May through August, RC and Gallagher live in a borrowed cabin near Port Angeles. In September, the two move to Syracuse, where Gallagher joins the University as Coordinator of the Creative Writing Program. RC and Gallagher jointly purchase a house in Syracuse.

1981   RC and Gallagher continue their routine of teaching in Syracuse from September to May and summering near Port Angeles. RC's second major-press story collection, *What We Talk about When We Talk about Love*, edited by Gordon Lish, is published by Knopf on 20 April. RC makes his first appearance in the *New Yorker* with the story "Chef's House", published on 30 November. Thereafter, he becomes a frequent contributor to the magazine.

1982   During the summer, Gallagher is invited to teach at the University of Zürich, and RC accompanies her to Switzerland. Guest editor John Gardner includes "Cathedral" in *The Best American Short Stories 1982*. (Gardner dies in a motorcycle accident on 14 September.) RC and his wife, separated since July 1978, are legally divorced on 18 October.

1983   Capra Press publishes *Fires: Essays, Poems, Stories* on 14 April. On 18 May, the American Academy and Institute of Arts and Letters awards RC and Cynthia Ozick its first Mildred and Harold Strauss Livings: renewable five-year fellowships that carry annual tax-free stipends of $35,000. (Recipients are chosen by a jury of writers who are members of the Academy: Donald Barthelme, Irving Howe, Philip Roth, and Elizabeth Hardwick.) As a condition of the award, RC resigns his professorship at Syracuse. RC's third major book of stories, *Cathedral*, is published by Knopf on 15 September. On 12 December, it receives a National Book Critics Circle Award nomination.

1984   In January, to escape East Coast publicity, RC flies to Port Angeles. Living alone in Sky House, he writes poetry during the day and occasional nonfiction during the evening. In the summer, he and Gallagher make a reading tour of Brazil and Argentina for the US Information Service. In the fall, they return to Syracuse, where Gallagher arranges to teach only one semester each year. *Cathedral* receives a Pulitzer Prize nomination.

1985   Five of RC's poems appear in the February issue of *Poetry* (Chicago). Thereafter, he becomes a frequent contributor. Random House publishes RC's poetry collection *Where Water Comes Together with Other Water* on 1 May. RC and Gallagher travel to England, where *Fires* and *The Stories of Raymond Carver* are published on 16 May, and to the Irish

Republic and Northern Ireland, where he meets many poets. In November, RC receives *Poetry* magazine's Levinson Prize.

1986   RC serves as guest editor of *The Best American Short Stories 1986*. Random House publishes his poetry collection *Ultramarine* on 7 November. In the winter he travels to Australia.

1987   "Errand", RC's last published story, appears in the *New Yorker* on 1 June. From April to July, RC and Gallagher travel in England, Scotland, and continental Europe, visiting Paris, Wiesbaden, Zürich, Rome, and Milan. In London, Collins Harvill publishes *In a Marine Light*, a selection of poems from *Where Water Comes Together with Other Water* and *Ultramarine*, on 1 June. In September, RC experiences pulmonary hemorrhages, and on 1 October doctors in Syracuse remove two-thirds of his cancerous left lung.

1988   In March, RC's cancer reappears. During April and May, he undergoes a seven-week course of full-brain radiation treatments in Seattle. *Where I'm Calling From*, a major collection of his new and selected stories, is published in May by Atlantic Monthly Press. On 18 May, he is inducted into the American Academy and Institute of Arts and Letters. Shortly afterward, cancer reappears in RC's lungs. He and Gallagher marry in Reno, Nevada, on 17 June. Working together, they assemble *A New Path to the Waterfall*, and in July they make a fishing trip to Alaska. After a brief stay in Virginia Mason Hospital in Seattle, RC dies at his new house in Port Angeles on 2 August at 6:20 a.m.

Appendix 7

Posthumous Publications

1988   *Elephant and Other Stories* published in London by Harvill on 4 August.

1989   *A New Path to the Waterfall* published by Atlantic Monthly Press on 15 June and by Harvill in September.

1990   *Conversations with Raymond Carver*, a collection of interviews, published by University Press of Mississippi on 31 October. *Carver Country: The World of Raymond Carver*, with photographs by Bob Adelman and introduction by Tess Gallagher, published by Scribner's on 14 November.

1991   *No Heroics, Please: Uncollected Writings* published in London by Harvill in November.

1992   *No Heroics, Please* published in the US by Vintage Contemporaries on 24 June. *Carnations: A Play in One Act* published by Engdahl Typography in September.

1993   *Where I'm Calling From: The Selected Stories* published in London by Harvill in September. *Short Cuts: Selected Stories* published by Vintage Contemporaries in September and by Harvill in November.

1996   *All of Us: The Collected Poems* published in London by The Harvill Press in September.

Index of Titles

Index of First Lines